18 Holes of Green

Timothy McHugh

18 Holes of Green

Copyright © 2017 Timothy McHugh
All rights reserved.

ISBN: 0-9994059-1-8
ISBN-13: 978-0-9994059-1-8

Brunswick Publishing
www.brunswickpublishing.com

18 Holes of Green is a work of fiction. Names, characters, places and incidents are the product of the author's imagination. Any resemblance to actual persons, living or dead, locations or events is entirely coincidental.

Thank you to my loving wife Amy, who inspired me to finish this book.

Thank you to my parents. To James Neil McHugh, for taking me to get my first job at the golf course. And to Mary Clare McHugh, for always correcting my grammar.

A special thanks to PGA Master Professional Greg Sanders, who gave me my first job and taught me so much.

Thanks to all the PGA of America professionals with whom I worked and played. You were so good to me over the years…and even tried in vain to fix my ugly swing.

Thanks to the "old gang" for all the memories.

Original cover art by Gannon McHugh

Baseball Caps and Bad Golf

      The sun was about to rise over the hills as the dew withdrew from the first tee. The dark sky was ready to fade away, leaving us with a beautiful spring day. All hell was about to break loose. This was my favorite part of the day, the moments just before dawn. It was my last chance for peace before the rising sun would bring the morning's first golfers. Unfortunately, I had to get to work just four hours after the bars closed to enjoy much of it. I didn't always make it to work that early, but it was well worth it when I did.
      The golf course had healed slightly from the previous day's beating. The dew glistened in the morning's first light. The chirping of a few early risers could be heard and the fading gray moon had not yet retreated. I was sitting on the last golf cart that I had driven out of the barn and parked in a line outside the clubhouse. I leaned back with my left leg casually sticking out of the cart and my foot on the ground. I faced away from the clubhouse gazing out onto the course. With my right hand resting on the steering wheel, I held a bottle of Mountain Dew in my left hand.
      John, one of our assistant golf professionals was inside getting the pro shop ready. I had the carts and the starter's table set-up and ready to go. After a few moments of tranquility, I heard the door of the clubhouse open. I turned to my right spotting John coming through the door. Then, I noticed cars turning into the golf course driveway. The headlights were getting closer and closer. My beautiful, quiet, empty golf course was about to be invaded. The wonderful

public. The public who park their carts six inches from our greens. The public who fail to replace their divots in our fairways or repair their ball marks on our greens. The ritual unleashing of the animals was about to begin.

John was approaching me with a big grin on his face. I was afraid that he might have bad news. Maybe, Mark, our other assistant pro who was supposed to be the morning starter had called in sick. Then, I would have to deal with the tee.

I pulled myself out of the cart and sipped my version of coffee. John was still smiling when he arrived. John was tall and intimidating. He stood about six feet three inches. He had wavy brown hair and a young-looking face. He was one of the strongest players in town, but he was a country boy at heart.

"Guess who's going to be late?" he asked me.

"Well, I hope he's bringing us breakfast," I replied acknowledging that I knew he was indeed referring to Mark.

"Yeah, he said he'd hit the McDonald's drive-thru for us," John replied.

"I'm just glad he's coming in," I commented. "I don't want to be stuck out here all day."

We both turned toward the parking lot as we heard the first cars parking. The sound of doors and trunks opening and closing accompanied the image of modern day soldiers preparing for battle. They scurried about, putting on their golf shoes and arranging clubs in their bags.

"Brian, it looks like we have some hungry golfers today," said John.

"Yeah, you'd think we were giving away something," I replied.

"We're giving away freedom," said John. "It's the frustration we charge for."

18 Holes of Green

"Sounds reasonable," I responded.

"Give me a hand with the phone, while I ring up the first groups," he suggested. "They won't be out to the tee for a while."

I followed John inside. As soon as I made it in the door I could hear the phone already ringing. We walked behind the counter of the pro shop to start our Saturday morning. I began answering the opening barrage of phone calls.

"White Lake Golf Course, Brian speaking, can I help you?"

"What's it looks like down there?" an old man's voice asked.

"Well, it looks pretty nice. The grass is green and the sky is blue." I answered.

"No! I mean are they playing?" "Is who playing?" I asked.

"Are you open? Damn it!" the old man demanded.

"Sir, it's 73 degrees and the sun is rising. Yes, we are open," I said sincerely.

He slammed his phone down.

I couldn't help but get frustrated by some of the stupid questions. I met a lot of people at the golf course. Most of them were very nice and friendly, but some were just clueless. Golf has a way of bringing out the best in some people and the worst in others. As Shivas Irons says in Michael Murphy's *Golf in the Kingdom*, golf is a microcosm of the soul.

White Lake was such a large facility in the heart of town that it drew all kinds of people. In addition to the 18-hole golf course, the facility included a driving range with
80 tees, practice greens and a nine-hole par three course.

Timothy McHugh

On weekday mornings, the course would swarm with senior citizens. Then, there would be a nice break from just before noon until around 4:30 when the "factory pros" came out. That's what we called our after-work rush and evening leagues. When the factories let out, they headed to White Lake. On weekends such as this particular Saturday, we would be booked solid with tee times through 3:00 PM.

Although the lake itself had been dry since shortly after the golf course opened in 1949, the county never bothered to change the name White Lake. The large lake that once separated the land that is the front and back nines was said to appear white when the sun hit it. Before the golf course was built, it was a very popular fishing spot. In 1944, the county closed it down when a fisherman was apparently attacked by an alligator. The story goes that a plane carrying snakes, alligators and other wild animals for a show crashed on approach to nearby Williams field. Only two out of the four alligators on board were found in the wreckage.

Some hunters were hired to capture the gator, which was eventually taken to the zoo. However, many people believed that there was either a mate or offspring left behind. Rumors of occasional sightings were enough to keep the fishermen away, so eventually the fishing hole was closed. In the era of great public works projects, the lake was drained and the county built the golf course. The project coincided with the expansion of nearby Williams Field, a small municipal airport.

Now, trees, shrubs and a small creek fill that gully known as "the jungle." During the construction of the golf course in 1947, workers reported seeing a 12-foot alligator several times. In order to ensure the land was free of alligators before the course opened, the area was searched

18 Holes of Green

by the 1940s versions of The Crocodile Hunter, but nothing was found.

Since then, there have been numerous sightings that the county has tried to keep quiet. After all, White Lake was a strong source of revenue. However, many of us who worked there certainly believed in Vader the gator, as he had been named after Darth Vader in Star Wars. We all used extra caution when retrieving balls from the jungle.

People new to the course would come in and ask me, "Where's the lake at?"

I would tell them, "It dried up as the result of a dangling preposition." Most would walk away confused, but some would inquire further until they got the condensed story out of me.

We actually had one old guy come in and ask us, "What a beautiful lake you folks have here, are there any fish in it?" John and I had to ride out there just to make sure we weren't crazy. Maybe the old guy was.

It was still early, but the clubhouse was coming alive. It was a large, old, English Tudor building that seemed lifeless without people in it. It had high ceilings like a ski lodge and was divided into two sections.

The pro shop, where John and I were, was filled with golf equipment and clothing. There was dark green carpet with stonewalls. We had a small section of top of the line equipment, but most of our sales came from our large stock of cheap clubs, shoes and used balls.

The grill was filled with tables and chairs. There was a concession stand at one end and a large TV at the other. A fireplace was on the rear wall and four ceiling fans hung from the rafters. From sunrise to sundown, there was usually a group of old men huddled together playing cards and lying about their rounds. The concession stand wasn't much, but it had the essentials. Beer was the hot item and it flowed all day long.

There were people browsing through the merchandise and others eating breakfast. I continued answering the phone and giving out tee times, while John sold greens fees.

Once the first groups were making their way outside, I abandoned the phone and headed outside to play starter until Mark showed up. I didn't mind being starter first thing in the morning. It was easy when you were running on time and there weren't any walk-ons yet begging to be squeezed in. I got the first four or five groups off with relative ease. I even got a few "nine holers" off on number ten. It was actually kind of fun to stand on the tee, shoot the shit and watch everyone tee off. It sure beat answering that damned phone. I could see through the window that John had drafted Paul, one of our senior citizen volunteers, to help answer the phone.

After the sixth group got off the first tee, I saw Mark heading toward me from the parking lot with a McDonald's bag and a cup of coffee in his hands.

"Well at least you came bearing gifts," I said as he approached.

"But of course," he replied.

Mark was about five-foot-ten and pretty stocky. He had straight brown hair and always had a smile on his face. He had a red staff shirt on with khaki pants and brown and black saddle shoes.

"Did Ashley make you clean up the house before you left this morning?" I asked.

"Funny," he replied.

I showed him where we were on the tee sheet as he pulled his Egg McMuffin and hash brown out of the bag. I took what remained in the bag inside with me and relieved Paul from phone duty. John and I each ate with one hand and

18 Holes of Green

worked with the other for a while. The morning began to fly by as groups of golfers continued to pour in. After a while, I peered out the window to see how much of a mess was out there.

Mark had them lined up on the first tee like an amusement park ride. We could have probably used some turnstiles. He was standing by the starter's table talking to Paul. Paul was a retired cop who spent more time gabbing at the clubhouse than he did watching the pace of play on the course. He was actually pretty helpful though when you were in a pinch.

"I hope that you left Mark some starter times," said John.

"Oh, but of course. We have the Marley foursome. The Garcia group, and oh yes, the Allman foursome."

"Very nice," said John.

Giving the starter some bogus tee times gave him a way to either catch up or work in some walk ups that made it worth his while. I doubt that the county would approve, but we did what we had to.

As I hung up the phone I heard a woman in her twenties ask John if she and her friend could start on number ten since they were only playing nine holes.

"No ma'am, you can't start on the back nine because I have people making the turn," he explained.

She turned and walked outside to Mark with a confused look on her face. I learned long ago that sometimes you have to just smile and laugh with people.

John was only 28 years old but he had this way about him that demanded respect. I think it was because he was such a great player. John more or less became a golf professional by accident. He grew up in Virginia and learned how to play working at a country club. After high school, John and a buddy hit the road for California. A year later he had only made it to Cincinnati. He ended up at White Lake hustling people by day and tending bar at night. When the head pro, Andy Pader, found out how good John was, he offered him a job teaching. Andy was overwhelmed with people who wanted lessons and needed some relief from handling it himself.

The phone rang again and I could see from the caller ID that it was Ashley, Mark's fiancée, who had the endearing habit of calling for him about every 30-90 minutes. She had always called for him a lot in the past; but since they had been planning the wedding, she had gotten out of control.

"Guess who?" I said sarcastically.

"Isn't it too early for her to be lost in her car already," replied John.

One day earlier, she had gotten lost on the way to look for wedding dresses and Mark had to talk her back to the interstate.

"White Lake Golf Course, Brian speaking, can I help you?"

"Hey Brian, is my Mark standing nearby."

I hated the way she said, "My Mark." At least she was very up front about being overly possessive.

"No, I'm sorry Ashley, but there was another alligator sighting so he headed out to the jungle with a garbage can and some rope," I answered.

John started laughing as he made change for a customer.

"I'm going to kill him," she replied. "He has new pants on. Have him call me on my cell, will you?"

I assured her that I would and said goodbye knowing I had momentarily gotten her all worked up. It felt great.

18 Holes of Green

The morning went by quickly because we were so busy. It was about 1:30 in the afternoon and I was getting anxious to play. Mark had already spoken to Ashley several times and had eventually convinced her that he hadn't gone out after Vader the gator. I had my clubs out and was swinging them behind the counter. I was a little upset because I played poorly the day before.

John had just finished helping a customer with a pair of shoes and came over to the counter. He was wearing a white golf shirt and a pair of olive colored pants. Black spikeless shoes and a Ping hat made him look like a typical club pro. That was until he spoke with his southern twang. He watched me take a few swings brushing the green carpet of the pro shop.

"Not bad Bri, playing today?" he asked.

"Yeah, as soon as I get off," I answered. "Mark said he might play with me. Help me a little."

"It will be crowded as hell out there at 2:00. You'll have to skip around a little."

"That's OK, I'm not worried as much about playing as I am practicing," I replied.

"All the time you spend out there, you're gonna be good soon," John commented.

I laughed, "I don't know about that. Seems like the harder I try, the harder it gets."

"Yeah, that's the way it is. That's why all these people are screwed up. The more they practice, the worse they get. It's an evil game. Hasn't Mark been giving you lessons?" he asked.

"Yeah, he says my head is screwed up," I answered.

"I could have told you that."

Timothy McHugh

"Screw you," I replied and turned to look out the window at the first tee, as John greeted a group of college guys.

I had seen a lot of faces that morning. It had been a typical Saturday morning for White Lake, busy as hell. The Saturday morning skins game had just come in off the course. I could hear them carrying on over in the grill. It had been sunny and clear all morning, but now I could see darker clouds moving in. It looked like it might rain. That actually made me feel better. It meant that the course would be less crowded. Though I had been working continuously, there was only one thing on my mind. I wanted to be out on the golf course.

My fingers felt dry from handling all the morning's cash as I turned and grabbed my sand wedge that had been leaning against the wall. I stood behind John and began to take a few swings toward the back of the counter area. I dropped some range balls onto the carpet and hit a few short lobs. After five near misses, I landed three balls in a row in the garbage can.

Working at the golf course was a good job for a 22-year-old college student. I got to play golf for free, got my balls cheap, and made enough money to support my interests. I sold greens fees, merchandise, answered the phone and found enough excuses to ride out onto the course a few times a day. The job was fun. I liked the people that I worked with and the people who hung out there. I was usually busy enough that my shift went by quickly.

"You guys might get lucky," John said. "Things have been slowing down now that the clouds are rolling in."

Indeed, things were slowing down. Afternoons were always less crowded, but the threat of rain had kept a few more would-be golfers at home. By 2:00, Hank, one of our retiree cashiers, had arrived. We had a lot of retired guys working at the course. Sometimes it felt like I worked at a rest home. I considered it my community service.

Actually, I did feel a bond with some of the old guys. They had more experiences to share, more to teach me than people my own age. Some of them worked very hard, some were just in it for the free golf, but they were all characters.

Anyway, with my relief on duty, I headed to the grill to have some lunch. I walked behind the counter, poured myself a beer and grabbed a burger. Lisa, the snack bar manager was selling old Charlie Pendyke a beer. Charlie was one of our regulars, a 74-year-old retired realtor. He liked to talk as if he owned half of the town. He was about five feet six inches, bald and plump as Santa Claus. I think it was more like three apartment buildings that he owned.

"What's up Charlie?" I asked.

"Haven't made a par in six months, Brian," he said with a frown and walked back to his table.

"How's it going, Brian?" asked Lisa as she started to take down the candy and snacks from the counter.

"I'm good. You're not doing away with the chips and candy, are you?" I asked

"No. Cunningham's wife called and said to clear off some counter space. Something about a water bottle display."

Hugh Cunningham was the director of golf for the county. His wife was the governor's daughter and also worked for the distributor that supplied the county owned golf courses with all their food and drinks. Most people would consider that a conflict of interests, but somehow, they got away with it.

"Water bottle display, don't you have some bottled water back in the fridge with the bottled sodas?" I asked.

Timothy McHugh

"Yeah, we sure do," answered Lisa. "I don't bother asking her questions. I just go with the flow."

"That's probably a good decision. Got any good horses for me today?"

Lisa had given me a couple of great tips over the years for the nearby horse track. Not too many, but when she did; boy, were they worth it.

"No, nothing today, but I hear there's a poker game tonight if you're looking to lose some money."

"That's OK," I replied as I dropped a couple dollars in her tip jar. "See ya later."

"Bye Brian," she said in her sweet voice as I walked away. Lisa had a sweet voice and a nasty voice. She was sweet most of the time, but she sure could cut into you if you upset her.

The guys around White Lake, who played cards, were about as honest at it as they were their golf. There is something about golf that easily lends itself to gambling. I guess that's why golfers love to play cards and go to the track.

"Get in the hole damn it!" shouted old Charlie. He and the rest of the guys from the skins game were watching the tournament on TV. I walked over and had a seat with them while I ate my burger. Jim Furyk was back in contention after another long absence and that had most of the boys excited and drinking even more than usual.

"You know what the problem with Furyk is?" Charlie asked. "He wears a damn baseball cap. No good player wears a cap. Mickleson wears a visor, Vijay wears a visor, and Nicklaus wore a visor. None of these guys wearing caps are worth a damn."

Charlie had a theory on everything.

18 Holes of Green

"You're full of shit, Charlie!" yelled Al Harper. "Tiger wore a cap."

"Yeah and where the hell is he now?" replied Charlie with a grumble.

Al and Charlie always found a way to get an argument going. Before I knew it, the whole table was arguing over baseball caps versus visors. Even news junkie Fred looked up from his morning paper and weighed in.

"Villains throughout history have always had a piece of signature headwear," he said. "Look at Castro, Osama Bin Laden and Saddam."

Fred was married to Alice who was the regular cashier at the driving range. He didn't play golf anymore. He was sitting in front of the TV here at the clubhouse on September 11, 2011 and he has virtually stayed there ever since. He was addicted to cable news. Each day he still came to the golf course; but instead of going out to play with the rest of the guys, he just sat in front of the TV. We'd have to fight with him just to put a golf tournament on the TV once in a while. On weekends, Fred generally read his paper and insisted on frequent news checks during commercial breaks in the golf tournaments. He stayed on top of the news and insisted on keeping us all informed.

"Hitler was rarely pictured wearing a hat," commented Al Harper.

"There's always the exception," replied Fred.

It was just one of the many deep philosophical debates that went on within the confines of the White Lake clubhouse. I didn't want to get caught in this one so I swallowed the last of my burger, got up and walked back toward the pro shop with my beer.

"And another thing," I could hear Charlie say. "What's with these collarless shirts some guys are wearing? They look like they should be mowing the fairways."

I was happy to be missing this debate.

When I got back to the pro shop, I realized Mark was stuck on the phone with the wedding warrior herself. I couldn't keep my food down and listen to him talk to Ashley so I walked into the office behind the counter. I sat down at the desk and watched John chip balls into a short, narrow, metal garbage can. He had made five in a row that I saw.

Mort, one of our part time starters, had taken over for Mark, so as soon as he could shake Ashley, we'd be on the course. John bounced his sixth chip shot off the front edge of the garbage can with a loud bang. The ball bounced backward and rolled toward John.

"Fore," shouted Hank from the counter.

"Caught it a little thin," I commented.

"Yeah, I think I've worn down this spot on the carpet," he replied.

Unfortunately, I could still hear Mark. He spent a few moments trying to convince Ashley that he loved her more than golf. It was starting to make me sick by the time he was off the phone with her.

After hanging up the phone, Mark stepped back into the office.

"You are the sorriest piece of crap," said John.

"Yeah, it's really painful to listen to you talk to her," I agreed as I sipped my beer.

"Then don't listen," Mark answered defensively. "Let's go. There's hardly anybody on the back nine. I told everyone we had to keep the back open for a shotgun outing."

18 Holes of Green

"Shotgun outing," said John sardonically. "You come up with more shit. If someone calls downtown, it will be your ass."

"No, it will be the starter's ass," said Mark. "I'm the assistant pro."

"Yeah, Mort is retired anyway," I said.

"Exactly," said Mark as he dragged his staff bag out of the closet and began pulling out a few clubs.

I picked up my clubs and headed outside. I knew better than to grab a cart. Mark believed that walking was the only way to play the game. He tried to walk at least nine holes every day. He claimed to be a traditionalist, but we all knew he was trying to stay thin. Ashley would kick his ass if he got any more of a beer belly before the wedding. I would have rather ridden in a cart since I could do it for free, but I wasn't about to upset Mark.

As I stepped onto the first tee, the sun disappeared behind the clouds. It was a perfect day to play. It was cloudy enough to keep all the fair-weather golfers at home, but it still wasn't raining. I took some practice swings with my eight-degree Ping driver. I was ready to play and forget about everything else in the world.

Mark arrived at the tee carrying his old MacGregor persimmon three wood, a five iron, a wedge, and an old wooden shafted putter in one hand. He had two bottles of Budweiser in his other hand.

"Where's your bag," I asked.

"This is all I need," he replied as he handed me a beer.

I had played the par-three course with just a few clubs before, but never the regulation course. I couldn't imagine him playing too well with only four clubs. I had fourteen and I still had trouble.

Timothy McHugh

After taking a drink of my beer I teed up a ball. I had been waiting so long to play today, that I had a lot of built up energy. I wanted to kill the ball. I wanted to hit it straighter and farther than I ever had.

I took a big swing and struck the ball with everything I had. The ball flew straight up and landed about 160 yards out.

"Shit. I popped it up," I moaned to myself as I walked off the tee. I waited for Mark to tell me what I did wrong, but he said nothing. He stepped forward and teed up his ball without saying a word. He lined up, addressed the ball and knocked it straight down the fairway with his three-wood. I was too pissed off to say anything, so I hurried along to my ball. I had a double strap on my bag which made it easier to carry a beer as I walked. Mark followed along still not saying a word. I wasn't going to let one bad shot get to me. The thing about walking is that you have more time to think between your shots. Sometimes that was a good thing and sometimes it wasn't.

By the time I reached my ball, I had 20 different swing thoughts in my mind. Determined to reach the green on this 380 yard par four, I hurriedly addressed my ball and waggled my three-wood a couple of times. I successfully cleared those thoughts from my mind and without thinking about the shot; I swung and ripped one onto the back fringe.

"Cool," I muttered as I saw where my shot landed. Mark birdied the hole with a tap in after landing his approach shot one foot from the pin. I was happy with my par after my bad day yesterday and today's terrible drive to start this round.

On the next hole, my drive was better, but I struggled to make bogey. I just wasn't hitting the ball solidly. Mark made

18 Holes of Green

birdie again with ease. We moved on to the third hole and Mark still hadn't said anything about my swing.

I took out my driver and addressed the ball. Gathering myself together, I remained calm and thought about just making contact. I tried to focus on an image of the drive that I wanted, but as I started my back swing, the thought of my ball heading right and into the trees popped into my head. I swung at the ball. It made an ugly ascent into the air then sliced right and down hard rolling under a pine tree. It was damn near a shank.

"Shit," I said with a whine of exasperation.

"What did you want to do that for?" Mark asked.

I couldn't believe him. I wanted to scream at him for saying that, but all I could mutter was, "I dunno?"

Then, he hit another tee shot down the middle and I hurried off to my ball. I was hoping that it had rolled through the trees. If it did, I would still have a chance to make par.

However, I wasn't that lucky. My ball had made it past the trunk, but there was still a limb impeding my swing. I studied the shot. I can make this, I thought. A half swing three-iron should roll far enough to get to the green if it fades a little. If it didn't fade, it should still be close to the green.

I took a few practice swings to see how far I could go back without hitting the limb. Adjusting my stance, I got ready to swing. I tried to imagine my perfect shot rolling onto the front of the green, but I couldn't. The only image that entered my mind was that tree limb.

As I swung, my club went too far back and hit the limb. That threw my timing off and I couldn't get the club back to the ball. My club hit the ground first, then skipped into the ball making it trickle about 20 yards into the fairway.

I could feel my blood pumping. My head began to get hot. My hands tightened on the grip of my three-iron. My arms began shaking. First, I looked at the tree limb, then my club head. I raised the club with my trembling arms. I wanted to hit that limb. I squeezed the club tighter. I thought of my ball laying 20 yards ahead of me. I wanted to break the damn limb and my three-iron. But with some ounce of self-control left in me, I turned away from the tree. I raised my club over my head and threw it as hard as I could. It landed about 30 yards down the fairway. It was farther than my ball had gone.

"Nice throw," Mark said casually.

I walked to the ball, dropped my bag on the ground, and addressed the ball without lining up the shot. Not caring what the hell happened, I took a swing with my seven-iron. The ball just floated in the air, hung there for a while, and then landed softly on the green.

"Nice shot," Mark said as he walked to his ball.

I could only mutter a breath type grunt noise in reply. I was still in awe of my shot. Mark landed his second shot on the green and made par. I two putted for a bogie.

We played the rest of the front nine rather quickly. Mark was very quiet for someone who normally talked so much inside. It was amazing how well he was playing with only four clubs. I spent the time playing poorly and bitching about my swing and a few other things I thought of during the course of the round. By the time we walked off the ninth green I could see dark clouds rolling in. It was definitely going to rain.

I was pissed off by then. I was blaming everyone and everything for my terrible round. I followed Mark into the clubhouse. He walked up to the snack bar and I dropped my clubs behind the counter of the pro-shop. Hank was on the phone giving someone a weather report.

"You want a beer," Mark yelled back to me.

18 Holes of Green

"Yeah, sure," I said as I sat down in a chair looking out at the first tee. I was about as depressed as I could get. Having worked at a golf course for the past five years, you'd think I would have learned how to play. I was physically and emotionally exhausted.

Mark returned and handed me my beer.

"You want to play another nine?" he asked as though he hadn't seen my pitiful performance on the front nine. I couldn't believe him.

"I thought you were gonna help me," I lashed out at him. "You didn't say one damn word to me out there. What the hell is the matter with you?"

"Brian. I was watching you out there," he replied. "You analyze every inch of your swing from start to finish. I can see the gears turning inside your head while you address the ball. I know you. You think about five things each time you swing. One is dangerous."

"Well how am I supposed to get better?" I replied.

"By analyzing your swing on the practice range with a purpose in mind. You don't even pick a target before you swing. You only think about the swing itself. If you don't line yourself up and concentrate on where you want that ball to go, the best swing in the world isn't worth a damn. What did Harvey Penick say? Take dead aim."

"You are kind of right," I confessed.

"Go back to the basics. Pick a spot in front of the ball that is in line with your target and line up with that. Think about where you want the ball to land. A specific spot, not just a general area. We can fine tune your swing little by little on the range."

"Ok, I'll play some more, but it looks like rain," I said.

"We'll take a cart," he replied.

Timothy McHugh

"That means a cooler," I said and walked towards the grill.

18 Holes of Green

Lessons, Weather Vanes, and Hustlers

Mark had said to meet him outside and he'd grab a cart. I got a six pack and a cooler of ice from Lisa. She gave it to me and I tipped her five dollars.

I met Mark just outside the clubhouse. The clouds were getting darker and the temperature had dropped a little. I enjoyed that familiar feeling of a rainstorm approaching. It was soothing for some reason.

The front nine still had quite a few golfers so we would have to play the back again. There were two married couples standing on the tenth tee trying to decide whether to risk playing on. Unwilling to wait, Mark and I drove around the tenth tee and down a maintenance road farther out onto the back nine.

We spotted a group of men in their thirties playing very slowly around the thirteenth green. I say around the thirteenth green because they were still chipping and apparently they had never heard of "ready golf." You can stereotype older people and women, but these guys were obscenely slow. They appeared to be arguing over who was away and should chip first. Instead of whoever was ready chipping onto the green first, they went around in a very precise order.

Timothy McHugh

Mark and I took advantage of the situation. While I'd hate to be behind that group of slow sons of bitches, I'd love to be in front of them. We rode to the fourteenth tee and parked. If the group behind you is slower than the group in front of you, there's time to practice and relax without being pushed.

We stepped out of the cart, grabbed our clubs and slowly walked onto the tee. Number fourteen is a 435-yard par four with a slight dogleg right. There were trees to the right; but if you cut the dogleg, it made the hole a lot shorter.

Mark teed up his ball and stepped behind it. After taking his line, he addressed the ball and waggled his three-wood. Then he took one of the smoothest swings I had ever seen. It was Ben Hogan pure. It sailed down the right side of the fairway and then curved to follow the dogleg as if he were steering it. I lost it behind the trees, but it had to be great.

I stepped onto the tee and smiled at Mark. "Nice shot," I said as I teed up my ball.

"Now, you hit a good one," he said.

"We'll see," I replied.

"We'll see?" he repeated the words to me as though they were the most ludicrous two words he had ever heard strung together.

"I'll try," I offered as an alternative.

"How about a little confidence," Mark replied.

I teed up my ball and stood behind it to find my line.

"You know that you can hit the ball," he added. "Pick an exact spot in the fairway as a target. Don't just point in the general direction."

I tried to follow his instructions as I picked a spot on the right side of the fairway to cut off some of the dogleg.

"Hit the ball with some confidence," he said. "Save the swing analysis for the range."

18 Holes of Green

Once I had my line, I addressed the ball and only thought of hitting the ball at my target. I fought to keep any swing thoughts out of my mind.

The wind was picking up quite a bit as the trees rustled and leaves blew by my ball. As I concentrated on that spot on the right side of the fairway, I swung with almost an automatic motion. The ball flew low, but directly at the corner of the fairway at which I had aimed.

I could feel that I struck the ball a little thin as evidenced by its low trajectory. Despite my shot's imperfection, it was solid and dead at the edge of the dogleg. My ball landed a few feet inside the rough at the bend and rolled straight into the center of the fairway. I was pleased with the result if not the sting of the way I struck the ball.

"Wow, great play," exclaimed Mark. "That's the way to take the wind out of it."

"Thanks," I responded with relief. "Better lucky than good."

I was within 150 yards of the green for sure. I might have been as close as 120 yards.

We hopped back into the cart and headed out the path. As I took a drink of my beer, I enjoyed the all too rare feeling of satisfaction. As we left the path and crossed into the fairway, I could see my ball in the center and a little short of the red stake. Mark's ball appeared to be 30—50 yards from the green. An impressive shot with a three wood.

We reached my ball. I was 128 yards out. Wanting a little extra club in the wind, I grabbed my eight-iron. I thought about taking a three-quarter swing and aiming right at the pin. I didn't have many shots in my repertoire so rather than hitting a low knock-down shot into the wind, I had to hit my normal shot with more club.

Timothy McHugh

Again, I concentrated on the pin rather than a swing thought and hit a nice high shot that was dead on. It landed pin high, about a foot to the right and skipped toward the back of the green.

"Great shot," said Mark.

"Thanks." I answered as I wiped off my eight-iron and returned it to my bag. It felt good to be hitting the ball well. I actually felt like I was playing golf.

The clouds were getting darker as we rode back into the right side rough and progressed towards Mark's ball. As we curved back into the fairway, it became clear that his ball was inside of the 50-yard marker. We pulled up next to it and saw a sprinkler cap five feet ahead of his ball marked 29 yards to the center of the green. Harley, our eccentric maintenance worker, had ensured that every sprinkler head had the yardage marked on it. It was one instance of Harley's attention to detail that we all appreciated.

Mark pulled out his sand wedge and took a few practice swings. He went through his usual methodical routine. As he addressed his ball and prepared to swing, another ball bounced in the rough and rolled directly in front of Mark about 15 feet away. The ball appeared to have come from number 11. An ill-timed errant approach shot from another group. Mark was unflinching in his concentration. As he started his swing, I couldn't help but be impressed by his focus.

However, just as he reached the top of his backswing, the delayed cry, "Fore!" came bellowing from behind the trees that separate the two holes. I cringed in anticipation of the havoc this would cause Mark.

He seemed to hold his swing together quite well. He finished strong and the ball flew high and toward the green. However, it did seem to fade a little rather than Mark's usual

18 Holes of Green

draw. The pin was on the left side of the green, but the ball landed on the far-right side. Mark was on the green, but clearly it was not the shot he had hoped for.

"Damn good considering that moron," I commented.

"Yeah, he rivals old Paul in timing," Mark replied.

Besides being a volunteer ranger and jack of all trades, Paul was our resident storyteller and Bob Hope caddy who had a knack for talking just as you swung. He was completely oblivious to the habit though. Most gabbers are.

As Mark sat down in the cart with me, a guy in his 20s popped out though the trees holding a club.

"Sorry. My bad," he said. "Hope my ball didn't bother your swing."

"No, your ball didn't bother me," answered Mark emphasizing the word "ball."

"That's good," the guy replied.

We rode toward the green and left the hacker to his ignorance. Mark didn't let things like that bother him. He was very easy going. I could use some of his patience.

When we arrived at the green, I could see that my ball had rolled off the green. Mark had a long put himself. Probably 30 feet.

My ball was sitting up and I wasted no time addressing it. I chipped on and right at the hole using a low risk bump and run. The ball died about five feet short of the hole. I could live with that considering how I had played the first nine.

Mark had at least 30 feet to the hole. There was a slight drop in the green halfway between his ball and the hole. It wasn't an easy put. He took his usual graceful practice swings and then rolled the ball to within one foot.

"Great speed," I commented.

Timothy McHugh

He tapped in his par putt as I lined up my five-footer. I tried to take a nice easy swing and the balled rolled straight for the hole. I got eager for a moment, but the ball stopped just two inches short.

"Bogie isn't bad there," said Mark.

"Yeah, I'm not complaining." I had no reason to complain. I was playing golf. It had never felt so good to be disappointed in a bogie.

It was looking more and more like rain, but that seemed to help us both concentrate. There was something calming about the cooler temperature and rustling of the wind through the trees. We played the next two holes extremely well for each of us. Mark birdied 15 and parred 16. I was ecstatic to par them both.

We each opened another beer as we parked at the 17th tee.

"Feeling better?" asked Mark.

"Hell yeah," I replied.

At that point we heard a cart getting closer from the next fairway. I thought perhaps it might be another lost soul searching for his ball, but then John came barreling through the tree line on a ranger cart. He had his clubs strapped on the back of the cart and was wearing his golf shoes. It was obvious he had been playing. He pulled up next to our cart.

"I guess Andy went home, huh?" Mark asked.

"Yeah, I told Hank that I had to go out to ranger," answered John.

"He knows better than that," replied Mark. "Rangering with your clubs on the cart."

"Relax, he's cool," John replied. "He can handle it."

Hank was one of the better old guys to work with. He did a good job and never bothered anyone. He often doubled as a starter and cashier. He was a nice guy who was

18 Holes of Green

always willing to cover for us. He did spend a lot of time in the restroom though. I know a lot of the older guys do that, but he really spent a lot of time in there occasionally. We would joke to each other that he must fall asleep on the toilet.

"It's awesome," I said. "There's no one out here."

"That's because we're really going to get it in a few minutes," John said as he pointed to the southwest.

We could see a hazy line of rain moving closer to us from the front nine across the jungle. The rain always seemed to come from the valley toward the old lakebed.

"I think it's time to play it in boys," suggested John.

"Let's cut over the barn," suggested Mark as he pointed toward the maintenance barn. "Tee off here at seventeen and play in to the practice green in front of the clubhouse."

John and I agreed to this imaginary hole. It was the most direct route to the clubhouse.

"How's five bucks?" Mark asked. "That's fine," I said.

"We'll give you a stroke on this hole, Bri," John said.

" Well, yeah," I replied.

John grabbed his Titleist driver and stepped onto the tee. This was not an easy hole by any means. I would venture to say that it rivaled any tournament hole considering we were going at it completely blind. From seventeen's tee, we had to go over the 16th fairway and carry the maintenance barn. From the other side of the barn, somewhere in the fifteenth fairway, we would have about 100 yards over a tall tree line to a small practice green about 20 feet from the clubhouse. The green was half the size of a normal one. Both the tee shot and approach shot would have to be based on our best guesses. No yardage and no line of sight.

There was a fierce wind coming straight at us. John teed his ball up high, took a big swing and launched his ball over the sixteenth fairway. The ball was still rising as it sailed over the maintenance barn.

"Wow," was all I could bring myself to say.

"A little off the toe," John said as he walked off the tee.

"Yeah. Off the toe my ass," replied Mark, as he took the head cover off his old Macgregor persimmon three wood. "You're too long for your own good."

"I'll have a shot at the green," John replied. "You won't make it over the barn with that antique in this wind."

"We'll see," said Mark as he addressed the ball.

He took a slow, easy swing and hit a low-ball dead straight. The ball barely made it over the maintenance barn and then dropped out of sight.

"That low ball is gonna get you in trouble one of these days," said John.

"Not in this wind," Mark replied. "Brian, get up there and let's see what happens."

"Yeah, let's see what kind of bullshit Mark's been teaching you," said John.

"Hit it right over that weather vane," said Mark.

I looked at my Callaway three-wood but opted for my Ping Driver and slowly stepped onto the tee. John and Mark were talking to each other, but I was successfully blocking out what they were saying. Once on the tee, I didn't look back. I teed up my ball and stepped behind it.

I lined up my with the weather vane on the roof of the maintenance barn. I walked around and addressed the ball. I looked up one last time and focused on the top of the weather vane. Then, I looked down at the ball and thought of making a smooth swing. That was it. No other thoughts were in my head.

18 Holes of Green

I took a nice easy swing concentrating on the Titleist logo. I never felt the club strike the ball. When I looked up, I saw the ball flying right at the roof. I felt relieved, like I had made the best swing I could possibly make.

The ball continued on line right at the weather vane. Would it make it over? Yes, it looked as if it would. I pictured having the best lie out of the three balls. I couldn't have hit it any better. It was pure. Too pure.

My ball struck the weather vane making a loud and sharp bang as the ball bounced off the rod iron and rolled down the roof into the gutter with a clang.

I waited to hear if it dropped further. There was nothing. It was stuck in the gutter.

Then, I heard a creaking sound as the weather vane wobbled a little in the strong wind. It swayed first to right and then back to the left almost crying in pain. It lingered in a feeble attempt to stand and then fell off its perch on the near side of the peak. It slid down the side of the roof skipping over the gutter and crashed onto a pile of rocks with a loud crash.

"Holy shit," John said slowly with a laugh.

"Nice swing, Bri," Mark added also laughing.

I couldn't help but laugh myself. "I guess you can't complain when you hit it where you aim," I said. I really wasn't upset. I was laughing too hard to be upset. I hit the ball well. I hit the ball perfectly. Like a hole in one.

"We better get going," said John as he sat down in his cart and drove off.

The first few rain drops had begun to fall. Mark and I hopped into our cart and followed John.

When we got to the other side of the barn, Mark's ball was sitting up in the middle of 15 fairway. John was at the far rough looking for his ball.

Timothy McHugh

"Nice shot, Mark," I said as I hopped out of the cart and headed over to help John look for his ball. John and I walked up and down the tree line looking for his ball.

"I know I crushed it, but this is ridiculous," he said.

I started to walk in the opposite direction from him when I saw a ball next to a tree.

"Is this your flying lady?" I asked.

"Go to hell," John replied.

"It's over here," Mark yelled from the other side of the fairway.

"There's no way," John yelled. "Callaway 3?" Mark asked.

"Shit," John muttered as he got into the cart and drove back to his ball.

"Let me know when you want to learn how to hit that low ball," Mark said with a laugh as John stopped his cart.

John walked behind his ball and surveyed the shot. He probably had about 115 yards to the green. The tree line made it impossible to see the green.

The only thing showing was the roof of the clubhouse and the satellite dish.

"You think it's about 35 feet to the left of the satellite dish," John asked.

"Yeah, about 35 to 40," Mark replied.

"This is a practice green we are going to. Which hole are we playing to?" asked John.

"Let's say whichever is closest to the clubhouse," Mark said.

John agreed.

The wind was still strong in our faces. John wasn't taking any chances this time. With a nine iron in his hands he addressed the ball. John took about a three-quarter swing

18 Holes of Green

and launched the ball right on line with where we thought the green should be.

"Well, no noise," said John.

"That's a good sign," I replied.

Mark was about 25 yards closer than John. He took out a pitching wedge and lined up his shot. He made a nice, easy swing and the ball flew high and straight over the tree line toward the clubhouse. A few moments later we heard a loud crash and the sound of glass breaking.

"Oh, my god, you're probably inside the clubhouse," I said.

John burst into laughter and I couldn't help but chuckle myself.

Mark was not as amused as we were. "There's no way I hit the window," he said.

"Andy is going to be pissed if he has to tell Cunningham," I said.

"Yeah, it's hard to explain how one of your golf professionals hit a ball through the clubhouse window," John added.

"We can say that Vader the gator broke the window," I suggested.

"Too many witnesses," commented John.

"There is no gator and I couldn't have hit the clubhouse," replied Mark.

"There's only one way to find out," John replied.

We hopped in the carts as the rain began to get harder and headed around the trees and in toward the clubhouse. Mark was a bright guy, but I wasn't convinced that Vader wasn't out there somewhere.

As we approached the clubhouse, there was a crowd of about 10 to 12 standing on the patio. The windows of the clubhouse didn't appear to be broken; but judging by the crowd, something must have happened.

When we pulled up, I saw John's ball on the practice green about five feet from the pin. The guys from the skins game who were gathered on the patio to watch us come in were laughing hysterically. Al Harper, old Charlie and Paul were at the front of the pack. Mark and I walked up to the patio where a broken beer pitcher was shattered on the concrete in a foamy puddle.

"You owe me a pitcher of Budweiser, Brian," said Charlie.

"It wasn't me. It was Mark," I said.

"You mean Mark hit that bad a shot that he almost killed us?" said Al Harper.

"Hey, it was a tough shot," Mark replied.

"Hell, it's not even a real hole you boys are playing," replied Paul.

"Either way, I'm on the green," John commented.

"You think that was a tough shot Mark, look where your ball ended up," said Charlie as he pointed at the bushes at the edge of the patio.

Mark's ball was lying underneath the two-foot-tall hedge that lined the edges of the patio. The ball was about 15 feet from the green. It was lying at the edge of the bush so there was nothing between it and the green. However, Mark would have to swing through the bush to get to the ball.

"Hey, where's your ball Brian," asked Paul.

Paul was one of the old guys whom I liked the best, but I really didn't feel like explaining that my ball was in the gutter of the maintenance barn in front of everyone.

"Oh, I decided to sit this hole out."

"What the hell was that noise we heard out there?" asked Charlie.

18 Holes of Green

"I don't know, must have been the weather," John said as he tried to keep from cracking up.

I could see that Mark was also attempting to hold in his laughter as he addressed the bush. He had his putter in his hands. He was working it down into the bush so he could just knock his ball out. Everyone stopped talking. Mark flicked his wrists back and then through. He struck the ball after breaking a few thin branches.

The ball rolled onto the green past the hole and stopped at the back fringe.

John sank his putt for birdie. Mark rolled his ball right on line, but it stopped two inches short of the cup.

"Did your putter get caught on your skirt Marky?" asked John.

"Yeah, I wussed it," said Mark as he tapped his ball in for a bogie on this made-up hole.

"That was a good hole," I said.

"Yeah, any hole that I take money from Mark on is a good hole," said John.

"Enjoy," replied Mark as he handed John a five-dollar bill and walked into the clubhouse.

"You're off the hook, Brian," said John. "I don't want your money."

"You're not off the hook, Mr. Golf Pro," Charlie said to Mark following him inside. "You still owe me a pitcher of beer."

"Yeah, alright, but you you're going to have to share it," I could hear Mark reply.

It was then that Hank sounded the lightening siren to clear the course. The rain was really coming down hard and thunder started to rumble, so everyone started heading inside.

"Who won all the money in the skins game?" I asked Paul as he walked toward the door.

"I think Charlie's team won. Al got a skin, but I don't think the teams were fair," he replied as he walked inside.

As everyone else went inside, I remained on the patio.

"Aren't you coming in, Bri?" asked John as held the door open.

"I'll be in, in a minute. I just want to watch nature kick up her heels for a few minutes."

"Alright," he replied with a confused look. Then, he walked inside.

John wasn't the type of person who would understand my need to sit and contemplate a round of golf. He lived for the moment and never gave his game much thought. It just came naturally to him. I sat down in one of the steel patio chairs and began picking the grass out of my spikes with a tee. The wind was now blowing the rain sideways and the remaining golfers on the course were all converging on the clubhouse from different directions. The mad dash was an amusing spectacle.

I think I learned something from Mark that day. I never realized exactly what until much later. I found it hard to be satisfied after hitting a ball on the roof of the maintenance barn. That was the part of the game that I was not willing to accept.

I didn't know which was better; hitting poor shots that wind up in good places, or perfect shots that wind up in bad places. I had never heard the cliché, "It's a frustrating game," ring more true than on that day. The worst part was that I should have known better than to get upset. I spent day after day watching people get angry with themselves. I saw how foolish they acted because of a bad round of golf. I had seen

18 Holes of Green

people destroy themselves as they tried to get better at the game.

    I pulled myself together with the reassurance that I would play better tomorrow. My shoes were now as clean as they were going to get. I stood up and walked inside. Everyone was sitting around the big screen. John was at a table by himself. Mark was at the bar with Paul and Charlie buying beer and gabbing. I sat down next to John and glanced at the television. Al Harper and News Junkie Fred were sitting at the table next to us.

    "Hey Charlie, Sergio is taking fashion tips from you." I said as he and Mark approached each with a pitcher of beer.

    "How's that," asked Mark.

    "He's wearing a white belt," I replied.

    Mark and John both laughed. Mark sat down next to me while Charlie sat down between Al and Fred.

    "Yeah, those Europeans do dress a little funny," added John.

    "That's style," countered Charlie. "What's wrong with it? It's not Labor Day yet."

    "It is a classy look," added Al Harper. "You young guys with your brown belts and khaki pants don't know how to dress."

    "Reminds me of Herb Tarlek on WKRP," said John.

    Mark and I laughed with John as we drank our beers.

    "But you can still wear a white belt after Labor Day," continued Al. "You just can't wear white pants or shirt."

    "You cannot wear a white belt after Labor Day," responded Charlie.

    "I don't think you should ever wear a white belt," said John.

    Charlie and Al didn't hear him though. They began arguing again. News Junkie Fred tried to interrupt to declare that the terrorists were making people sick on cruise ships, but nobody seemed to pay him any attention.

"You know what, Brian," said John. "I think if you stop wearing that damn baseball cap you'd be OK."

"Go to hell. I like my hat."

"Don't tell me you two are having this discussion too," said Paul as he sat down with us.

"It's better than European fashion and white belts," said John.

"Those Europeans do dress nicely," commented Paul. "They aren't afraid of some color."

That was enough for me. I wanted out. I could hear some shouting coming from the pro shop.

"I'm gonna go over and see if Hank needs a hand with rain checks," I told John and Mark. As I got up from the table, I could hear that Fred was still talking about biological warfare and hoping for someone to listen. He had flipped the TV to CNN, but the natives were growing restless and calling for the golf tournament.

When I got to the pro shop, I saw that Hank already had a line of 5 people. As I walked behind the counter, I noticed that Hank was in an argument with a customer.

"I'm sorry sir, if you've reached the sixth hole, you don't get a rain check," Hank said to the irate man, who appeared to be in his late thirties.

"Buddy, I'm telling you we only made it to the fourth green before we decided to come in," said the guy. His face was red with emotion.

I walked over to the counter and looked at the man's greens fee receipt.

"Sir, according to your receipt you teed off at 3:00. It is now 5:30. You should be finished by now or at least on number eight or nine." I said to the customer.

18 Holes of Green

"Hey, we're beginners. We play slow," he said.

"How come that group that just left reached number five? They teed off an hour after you did?" asked Hank.

"We let them play through."

"And the five groups that were in between too, I suppose," Hank said sarcastically.

"Nice try," I added.

The man's fierce determination withered away leaving his face pale. He turned and walked away without admitting he was wrong. Some people will try anything. Rain checks are the invention that keeps you from having to give money back. Many will go unused which was one of the dirty little ways a golf course makes money. I answered the phone a few times to free up Hank. It was easy to field calls when it was raining.

"Yes, it is raining steadily down here," I would repeat to callers.

Hank was giving out rain checks left and right. Whenever it rained, it seemed that everyone was on number five. After about 30 minutes, Hank seemed to have everything under control so I walked back over to the grill. Things had quieted down there since I had left. Most of the guys were gone and Furyk was leading the tournament.

John, Mark, and Paul were sitting at a table finishing off the last of a pitcher. I sat down with them and pored myself a cup. Paul was telling them a story about how he played nine holes with Bob Hope back during World War II.

"I was a private, who was assigned to caddie for Mr. Hope's partner. He was some Colonel who never showed up. So, Mr. Hope asked me if I could play and that's how it happened."

As Paul continued telling us how he straightened out Bob's hook, I began thinking about chicken wings and beer.

Timothy McHugh

I had heard Paul's Bob Hope story a dozen times. He told it every time that he got a few beers in him.

At the conclusion of his story, Mark, John and I instinctively stood up. It was obvious that we had all had enough of White Lake for that rainy day.

As Paul stood, he looked at Mark and said, "son you ought to think real hard about getting married to that girl. You have 18 holes of green here, why would you want to ruin it?"

We all laughed at Paul saying what we all thought, in his unique way.

Paul said his good byes and we left the table.

"See ya Hank," I shouted as Mark and I headed out the back door near the grill. We said goodbye to Lisa as she scoured the grill and John headed to the pro shop to check on Hank before leaving. After all, John had technically been working this entire time.

I was meeting John and Mark down the road at The Hangar. It was a local bar and grill that Mark's uncle owned at William's Field, a small airport a few blocks away. It was a nice local spot and knowing the owner had its advantages.

Mark and I each threw our clubs in our cars and changed our shoes.

"I got to call Ashley," Mark said. "I'll see you there."

"Yeah see you in an hour I guess," I replied.

"Screw you," he answered.

I got in my Jeep and pulled out of the parking lot. I could see him already glued to his cell phone. The poor guy. It wasn't such a bad thing that he was whipped. It was just too bad that he was whipped by such a bitch.

I arrived at The Hangar first. When I walked in, I saw Willie Boylan holding court at the bar. His brother Nate was a shady young attorney who hung out at White Lake and volunteered as a starter on Fridays. Willie needed a good

18 Holes of Green

attorney. He had a few DUIs in his day. He was one of the biggest bull-shitters around. He dressed like Tiger, but he talked like Daly. His face was very brightly tanned. He ran a landscaping service, but I don't think that's where most of his income came from.

Willie was entertaining some golf enthusiasts with a story about how he beat local PGA champ John Anderson from White Lake. He hadn't seen me yet and I listened intently has he spun a web of lies. It was going to be interesting when John arrived from around the corner.

I could tell that Heather, the barmaid knew better, and was fighting the urge to shoot holes through Willie's story. Moments later, I saw Mark enter the door. He walked up behind me as I hovered in a corner eavesdropping on Willie.

"What the hell are you doing," he asked.

"Slick Willie is telling some folks about how he beat John the week after the chapter PGA championship. "How he beat John?" asked Mark.

"You heard me," I replied.

"Didn't John have Willie Beat by the 15th hole that day?" asked Mark.

"Yes, that sounds right to me," I replied.

"Oh, this is going to be good," answered Mark. "Let's set him up."

Willie was facing away from the entrance toward his audience, while leaning on a barstool. Mark and I walked to the corner of the bar behind him and sat down. Heather set us up with a couple of Bud Lights on the house.

Willie continued to ramble about his prowess on the golf course and his domination of White Lake. In fact, he began telling these two unsuspecting young couples that he gave lessons with group discounts.

Timothy McHugh

It was well known that he would drag gullible wannabe golfers to the Farm Crest Driving Range a few miles away from White Lake. It was an old cow pasture that a local farmer ran as a practice range to help offset his struggles with soybeans.

Mark and I drank our beers and discussed how best to pull the rug out from under Willie and his tall tale. I suggested that I ask Willie about the story once John arrives and let nature run its course. Mark preferred a more subtle, but complex scheme where we would convince the two couples that Farm Crest Driving Range was no place for them. We called John on his cell phone to tell him what the deal was. Mark told him to sit at the bar when he arrived opposite of Willie and to follow our lead.

Willie went on with his bullshit trying to impress the unsuspecting couples. He was in the middle of expounding on his theory that success was relative to the golfer.

"What looks like failure to others could be success for you," he said.

That was Willie's way of preparing them for the inevitable lack of improvement in their swings that would come from taking lessons from him.

It was then that John walked in the door. He walked to the bar and sat on the other side of Willie and his eager students. As soon as Willie saw John, he lost track of his sales pitch and was noticeably uneasy. He likely was worrying that somehow John would undo his story.

John played it cool and simply ordered a beer. He sat and watched Sports Center on the TV without even acknowledging Willie.

Visibly shaken, Willie had to get some air. He said he was going to the restroom and promised his prey that he'd be right back.

18 Holes of Green

As soon as he left the bar, Mark turned to me and said loudly, "I wish they'd spray some pesticides on that driving range."

"Yeah, it really is a public health hazard," I replied. John leaned forward on the bar stool to see us around the two couples and asked, "What driving range is that?" "Farm Crest driving range," Mark replied.

"Really, what's the matter there?" asked John.

The two couples sitting in between us had no choice but to listen. They were noticeably interested.

"Why, they've got the biggest mosquitoes around," I answered.

"Yeah, they'll eat you alive," added Mark.

"Really, they're that bad?" asked John with a great show of concern.

"Oh yeah, they had two cases of West Nile last summer," Mark said.

"Are you serious," John played it up.

"Yeah, the CDC shut the whole place down for a month," I said.

"The poor lady who died had just taken up the game and was in group lessons," added Mark.

"She died?" exclaimed John.

"Yeah, but only after spending a few weeks struggling for life in the hospital," I answered.

With that, the two couples had heard enough. They quickly paid their tabs and headed for the door to avoid Willie before he came back.

Just as they walked out the front door, Willie was returning from the rear entrance.

"Nice work, boys," said John.

"We had to defend your reputation," I said. "I appreciate it," John replied.

Willie was stunned when he returned.

"What the hell did you bastards do to my students?" he asked.

"Students?" I laughed.

"We told them about your bug problem," said Mark.

"My bug problem?" he asked with a puzzled look.

"You're such a fucking liar," said John.

"About what?" asked Willie.

"About you beating John," I suggested.

"I never claimed to beat the All City PGA champ John Anderson," said Willie.

"We heard you," said Mark.

"You heard a hypothetical event based on the relative set of circumstances," replied Willie.

"The event was your round of golf with John on Tuesday July 31," I answered.

"The circumstances were that you lost," added John.

"Well, the facts aren't the important thing," weaseled Willie.

We sat around bullshitting for a few minutes, each poking fun at Willie and then receiving his barrage of return insults. It was stimulating. Even though we enjoyed giving Willie a hard time, he was always entertaining. Much like his brother Nate, he never let things get dull. He would try to coerce you into betting on anything.

We gambled on what type of plane would land or take off next. Heather was an expert and our rules official since her father and brothers were all pilots. A mixture of Pipers, Cessnas, Leers and Gulfstreams kept us busy for a while. After about an hour, the airport traffic had slowed and it was too dark for us pick out the different makes.

Heather set us up with another round as we transitioned to the Golden Tee Golf Game against the wall. I

18 Holes of Green

might not be able to beat these guys on the golf course, but I had a knack for Golden Tee. As far as I was concerned, Peter Jacobson was the man.

Timothy McHugh

The Great Golf Shoe Heist

     I had just banged a wedge off the side of the caged jeep about 90 yards out. Harley, the range ball picker, let out a bellowing howl. We waved to each other, and he drove on. It was about 9:00 the next morning after my interesting lesson from Mark. I was hitting balls, trying to straighten out my swing. Mark's lesson had made sense to me the day before. If I was going to give into the temptation to analyze my swing and find a mechanical solution, I needed to do it at the driving range and not on the course. I was certain that I was getting the clubface open at the top. I was making a conscience effort to keep the clubface perpendicular to my target as I reached the top of my swing. While I was finding moderate success with this new idea in my head, it still didn't feel completely right.

     I spent the first 15 minutes just working on my wedges and short irons. That helped me get into a rhythm. I could never understand it when I would see someone come in with just a driver and buy a large basket of balls. They were making it awfully tough on themselves.

     I enjoyed aiming at the ball picker. It was good for my short game and it felt good deep down inside. After all the hours, I had spent as a moving target picking balls when I was younger, it felt good to be on the other end of it now.

18 Holes of Green

     Harley soon had the baskets on the ball picker full and drove behind the protective fence on the left side of the range. He began unloading the large baskets of balls into his maintenance cart. I stopped aiming at him and kept on with my practice. After I was in a groove with my short irons, I began to hit my five-iron. Maybe it was because I no longer had Harley as a target, but I began to struggle with my swing. He had stopped picking balls. I had lost my touch. I was topping the ball on one swing and chunking it on the next.

     I tried to go back to the basics. I shortened my swing a little and just tried to hit the ball straight. After hitting about 15 balls with my five-iron and a three-quarter swing, I started to make better contact. I guess it just takes time. I could hear the sound of a cart behind me as I took my next swing. The sound of an approaching golf cart is one that is recognizable, yet easy to blame for a poor swing. It is probably one of the most common sounds and equally common excuses. The sound of the cart stopped, and I continued to hit balls. I tried so hard to block out the sound of the cart that I never thought about who it was.

     "You'd be all right if you would get your belly button through before you hit the ball," said Harley from behind me. He was standing beside his maintenance cart watching me swing. Standing confidently in his mud-stained overalls, the sleeves and collar of his yellow golf shirt poked out in contrast. He wore a faded blue PING baseball cap. It only left his head when he wiped the sweat from his brow.

     Harley was as eccentric as he was intelligent. He was in his late forties and had retired early from a nuclear plant in Arizona. He supposedly had some sort of mental breakdown. He apparently made a fair amount of money because he got by on next to nothing working as a greens keeper and range picker. He was actually a pretty decent golfer.

"My belly button?" I asked.

"Yeah, imagine that there is a bungee cord connecting the end of your club to your belly button. That way, the club face is bungee jumping from your belly," he replied.

"OK, thanks Harley." I wanted to humor him, but I really didn't need any more advice.

"Well, Alice needs more balls," he said, as he turned and walked toward his cart loaded with baskets of range balls.

Alice ran the driving range and kept Harley on his toes. She was like a grandmother. She looked out for everyone, but she was also sharp as a tack. You couldn't fool Alice. Harley drove off in his cart to wash the balls. He really had some strange ideas about the golf swing. His swing was flat and long. He usually scored in the low 70s though, so there must have been something to it. Perhaps it was simply his confidence. He was never one to display any self-doubt, and confidence goes a long way on the golf course. I was just the opposite, obsessed with self-analysis and doubts.

John had just finished drooling over a lesson about 30 yards down from me on the large grass tee. Sometimes I think that the only reason he gave lessons was to get dates. He had an understanding with Alice that she would push the men who wanted lessons to Mark or Andy. Since she answered the phone at the range most often, she did virtually all of the scheduling of lessons. This arrangement kept John with almost entirely female students. Most of them were cute, too. As John accepted the lady's $40 and her phone number, he waved goodbye and walked over to me.

"She wasn't bad looking," I said.

18 Holes of Green

"Not bad? She was great," he said. "Did you see that ass?"

"No, I missed it."

"Oh, it was awesome," he replied.

John grabbed some of the balls out of my basket and dropped them a few yards to my left. He began hitting little pitch shots to a sewer lid with his sand wedge.

"Did you hear Harley's new thought for the day?" I asked him.

"No, what is it today?"

"Something about the club being tied to your belly button with a bungee cord," I said.

"Shit, he's a strange one," said John.

"Yeah, and you said Mark has a funny teaching style," I replied.

"No, Mark's OK. He straightened me out a while ago with this drill when I wasn't turning all the way," said John. "I'll show you. Hand me your driver and a towel."

He teed a ball up as high as he could and then dropped my towel on the ground. He bent down and knelt on the towel as he waggled the driver. From his kneeling position, he addressed the ball. Then, he swung back and then around, knocking the ball 240 yards straight out. It was amazing.

"If I can do that with just my upper body, think how little you need to use your lower body," he said as he stood up."

As if I didn't have enough thoughts in my head already. Mark's lesson yesterday, my analysis today, Harley's bungee jumping idea, and now this.

"Yeah, that makes sense," I said, trying to be nice and hoping John would drop it.

"Here, you give it a try," said John as he teed-up a ball an backed away from the towel.

"I'm not sure that would be a good idea," I replied.

"Do it, you wimp," he said firmly. "It can't hurt you."

"Gee thanks," I answered as I stepped toward him. Reluctantly, I carefully knelt down on my towel. I addressed the ball and made a couple of slow practice swings. It felt really awkward. Finally, I swung.

My club hit the ground about a foot behind ball and then skipped over it. I couldn't help but to laugh at myself.

"Try it again, and concentrate on the ball," John said. With the ball still teed, I took a shorter swing. The club head flew under the ball popping it straight up about thirty feet. It landed 20 yards in front of us.

"Fore!" said Paul who was now standing behind us.

"I think I'll stick to standing on my feet for now," I said in complete embarrassment.

"You guys are always up to something," said Paul.

"Yeah, so are you old man," I said as I put my driver away.

John and I started hitting balls normally now. Paul was watching John's swing and asking him about it. I enjoyed the lack of attention for the moment and continued with my practice. After a few minutes of quiet practice, Paul broke the silence.

"Since you guys can hit the ball from your knees, I got a good bet for you today," said Paul.

"What is it?" asked John, who never passed on a golf wager.

Paul walked in front of where John was hitting and dropped a quarter on the ground.

18 Holes of Green

"I bet you guys each a dollar that you can't make a full swing and hit the quarter with the butt of the grip during the down swing," said Paul.

John and I thought for a few seconds. Each of us was trying to decide if it was possible. Finally, John said, "That's impossible. We can't win."

"No, it's definitely possible," said Paul. "To prove it, I'll do it after you guys try. And I don't win unless I do it. You're not afraid of an old man are you?"

"Sounds fair," I said.

"Yeah, you're on," said John.

I stepped up and addressed the quarter, holding my five-iron upside down. I was gripping the shaft just below the club head with the grip touching the ground. I waggled the club a couple of times, concentrating on the quarter. I looked at Paul to see if I was on the right track.

"You didn't say how we had to hold the club," I said looking for assurance.

"Hold it any way you want," Paul replied.

Then I went ahead and swung. The grip of the club went flying about five inches over the quarter.

"You whiffed," said John.

"Yeah, I noticed," I replied in disgust.

"One down. One to go," said Paul.

John then walked over and addressed the quarter.

"I got this figured out boys," said John.

He focused on the quarter with a regular grip. Then he took the club back fast. As he brought the club down, he bent down very low and swung the butt of the grip towards the quarter on the ground. The grip hit the ground about six inches past the quarter. As John tried to follow through and let the club head swing around and up, he fell forward and rolled over, landing on his back.

"He's an acrobat as well as a golf professional," said Paul.

"I give it an 8.5," I said.

"All right Paul, let's see you do it," said John with a bitter tone, climbing back to his feet.

"OK," said Paul as he addressed the quarter. "You had the right idea, John. You were just a little quick."

Paul then took the club back the way he normally would, but then he started his down swing in extreme slow motion. He slowly bent down and pressed the butt of the grip against the quarter. Then, he stood up and made a normal follow through.

"That will be a dollar each," he said.

"That's not fair," I said.

"Sure it is," answered Paul. "I said a full swing. I didn't say what it had to look like or how fast it had to be."

"That's a cheap one, Paul," said John.

Admitting defeat, we each handed over our dollar. It wasn't often that John lost a bet on his golf swing. He began hitting balls again to reassure himself of his ability. I took a break from hitting balls and joined Paul as we watched John make his graceful swings. There was something rewarding about watching an excellent golfer swing.

Paul began telling me one of his stories about an old friend from the Birdie Hunters who was a jokester. I wasn't paying complete attention to him. Sometimes his stories would run together in my mind. As he talked to me, I could hear the garage door to the back of the driving range open. A few moments later, Harley came riding up the cart path again and stopped behind us.

"I'm going to grab a bite to eat. Anyone want anything?" Harley asked.

18 Holes of Green

We all told him that we were fine. Then, I saw Harley reach into the back of the cart and reach for something. There was some loud rattling, which caused John to stop hitting balls, and we all looked to see what he was doing. The noise stopped and Harley raised his arms out of the cart. He was holding up the weather vane that I had knocked off its perch the evening before. I got a little nervous, thinking that my secret would now come out.

"Look fellas. The damn storm blew down the weather vane last night. Isn't nature wild?" said Harley.

"Yeah, that is something," said Paul.

"I'm going to take it back up to the clubhouse. I might be able to get it back up on the barn," he said.

"I wouldn't go climbing around on the roof of the barn," said Paul.

John and I both cracked smiles, trying to refrain from laughing.

"Maybe a golf ball hit it," suggested John. I could feel my face turning red.

"No way a golf ball hit it," said Paul. "Had to be that storm."

"Nature is awesome, man," said Harley as if mystified. He placed the weather vane back in his cart and headed towards the clubhouse.

"He's a strange one," said John.

Harley was one of a kind, but he really was a good guy. John made me squirm a little, but he was letting me get away with my secret. His generosity would no doubt require a payback.

As I stood next to Paul, I noticed that there was a woman in her fifties struggling with her swing further down in the grass. Paul was a widower and enjoyed talking to women around the course. He also could never resist giving out his advice to unsuspecting victims. He would never admit that, but we all knew it about him. I watched the woman roll her fifth consecutive ball along the ground.

"Hey Paul, that lady is having a hard time. Why don't you give her a hand," I said.

"No, I don't give lessons. I don't believe in giving advice to people who don't ask for it," he replied.

John looked up at me as he addressed a ball and rolled his eyes. We both knew better. John had nearly finished off my basket of balls when he decided to quit. I decided to work on my bunker shots for a while so grabbed the remaining balls and said goodbye to John and Paul. I walked down to the practice bunker and began hitting a few shots. After about 15 or 20 minutes, I was satisfied. If I wanted to get a round in before work, I needed to head towards the clubhouse now. As I walked by the practice tee, I noticed Paul had just approached the woman. She was still rolling the ball.

"I couldn't help but notice you were having a little trouble," he said to her.

She seemed eager to listen to someone who thought they knew what they were talking about. Paul began lecturing her on the need for her head to remain still. It was good for him. Paul was at his best when he was walking the range, helping people who were struggling. It made him feel needed. I waved to him and began walking up the cart path.

The clubhouse was about 200 yards from the practice range. As I walked up the path, I began surveying the course. I was curious to know how busy it was. I hated playing when it was crowded. It didn't look too bad yet. White Lake wasn't exactly known for speedy play. Not that everybody who played there was slow, but all it took was a couple of groups to screw up the pace of play.

18 Holes of Green

When I arrived at the clubhouse, there were two groups waiting on the first tee. I waved to Hank the starter, and he motioned to me to come over. I acknowledged him and started walking in his direction. I thought he might need me to cover while he went to the men's room, but instead he wanted to show me something. He put his hand on my back and faced me toward the back nine. He raised his hand and pointed to the 15th tee.

"Cunningham has the water works on his pet project out there," said Hank.

There were two bright yellow water works trucks and a backhoe parked behind the tee. Hugh Cunningham did not have many fans at White Lake. He lived to drop names and point out the fact that he had an MBA. He always checked the thermostat as soon as he arrived at the clubhouse to make sure it was set at 77 degrees. Any lower, and we'd be wasting money according to him.

He had wasted a sizable amount of money on a study to calculate the best temperature to which the clubhouse should be cooled. Engineers came down and measured the doors and windows. They counted the number of times the doors were opened and closed, and they brought in light meters and thermometers. It was quite an ordeal. Apparently, his brother-in-law worked for the contractor that did the study.

"What are they doing out there?" I asked.

"He's got them tearing up the whole damn course checking for lead pipes," answered Hank. "He says the drinking fountains might not be safe."

It was then that Oscar, our other weekend starter, pulled up in a cart. Weekends were generally busy enough that we needed two starters for a while. Especially since Leo, our weekend ranger, was usually asleep out there. Oscar had been working as a starter for 12 years. He was friendly, but he had no tolerance for bullshit and had no problem letting people know it.

"That boy from downtown sure has torn the place up good," said Oscar.

"Is Cunningham himself out there?" I asked.

"Not anymore," Answered Hank. "He took a cart out to supervise for a while, but he came in and left in a hurry about 30 minutes ago."

"Probably going to try some bullshit at one of the other courses," said Oscar.

I agreed with Oscar and walked inside the clubhouse. Mark was in the pro shop straightening the displays and dusting them. He wasn't just being diligent in his job, cleaning was a habit for him. Ashley had him well trained. We all called him the maid.

"So, we've got lead in our water?" I asked him jokingly.

"Cunningham has lead in his head," replied Mark.

"So, are they going to replace all the pipes?" I asked.

"No, that would cost too much," answered Mark. "If they turn out to be unsafe, he's going to just rip out the water fountains and cap off the pipes with concrete."

"No water fountains?" I asked with alarm.

"No water fountains," replied Mark.

No water fountains on White Lake golf course would change everything. While most of the newer courses outside of the city had water jugs and cup dispensers in nicely built wooden stands; this was White Lake, a municipal golf course. It should have drinking fountains just like a park.

"I'm not going to get stuck filling up all those water jugs," I said to Mark.

18 Holes of Green

"I don't think Cunningham plans on putting out any water jugs," he responded.

"What do you mean?" I asked.

"Well, when I asked him about it, he said that the concession stand would soon be stocking more sizes of bottled water," Mark answered. "And you know who sells them the bottled water."

"Nicole Cunningham," I answered. "Lisa said something about needing counter space for a bottled water display."

As the governor's daughter and first lady of the county golf courses, she treated them like her own private country clubs. She would bring her gaggle of friends to the courses to play with her for free.

"Sounds like a good deal all around for the Cunninghams," said Mark.

"It's illegal," I responded. "Nobody cares," said Mark.

"The Times might be interested," I answered.

"Yeah, you go ahead and tell the paper," responded Mark with a laugh. You'd be on the nightly news but out of a job."

"Someone will catch him eventually," I commented. "He almost caught me turning the air conditioning down this morning," said Mark.

"What happened?" I asked.

"As usual when it gets too hot in the clubhouse, I popped open the lock box on the thermostat with a screwdriver and turned the temperature down to 72 degrees. Just as I got back into the pro shop he walked in and of course checked it. I had no idea he would show up today."

"What did he do?" I asked with a grin.

"Well, he accused me of changing it of course, but I told him that I didn't have a key to the thermostat and didn't know how it was changed. He went out to check on the water project for a while. He apparently called the county building maintenance from his cell phone because one of their guys showed up just as he came back in. Cunningham walked over to the thermostat with the maintenance guy and rather than using a key, the guy popped it open with a screwdriver."

"Oh great," I said.

"Yeah, Cunningham walked back over to the pro shop and said to me, 'You don't need a key, do you?' He told me that he would be having a more secure lock put in place."

"What did you say?" I asked.

"I just played dumb," responded Mark.

"Shouldn't have been too hard," I replied.

"Funny. You gonna play?" asked Mark.

"Yeah, I thought that I would try to squeeze in nine before work," I said.

"It's not too bad out there. Shouldn't take you too long," he said.

Mark was straightening the shoe display in the pro shop, and I leaned up against the counter. As we were talking, Harley walked in from the back door wearing his dirty overalls and carrying his golf bag.

"Are you going to play, Harley?" I asked.

"Yeah. What about you?"

"Sure. Let's do it," I said.

"Yeah, uh…OK. But I'll have to clean my golf ball first," said Harley.

"OK. Go tell Hank and I'll meet you on the tee," I said as he walked out the door to the patio where there was a ball washer.

I knew it would take Harley a few minutes to clean his ball. That's singular. He had one ball. He carried one ball in his pocket and he kept it very clean. The ball had only one

18 Holes of Green

small scuff on the cover. Harley could tell you when and which tree it was that "hurt" the ball. It was really quite amazing. I had known him for two years, and he had been playing with the same Titleist the entire time. He kept a sleeve of new balls in his bag for emergencies, but they had never been touched.

Harley could really piss me off sometimes with the amount of time he would spend searching for his ball, but he always found it. After all, there was no water on White Lake. I, on the other hand, wouldn't spend more than a minute looking for a ball. I went through new balls like they grew on trees. Mark, John and Andy got so many balls from the sales reps that they always gave me their extras.

"What the hell are these?" asked Mark in a confused tone as he looked inside a shoebox.

"What's the matter?" I asked.

Mark was holding a Foot Joy box in his hand and had a blank look on his face.

"This box has a pair of dirty old shoes in it," he said. "They're not even Foot Joys."

"What do you mean? They're used?" I asked.

"Yeah. These are somebody's shoes," he said as he stood up and quickly looked around. "There was some guy over here looking at shoes about 15 minutes ago."

Mark quickly walked around the corner of the display and scanned the grill area looking for anyone who might be trying on shoes. I walked into the men's restroom to check, but it was empty.

"He's nowhere," said Mark.

"Shit. He's probably long gone by now with his new pair of Foot Joys," I said.

"Yeah. I imagine so. God-damned thief," said Mark.

Timothy McHugh

"Well, I don't want to be around when Andy finds out you let someone walk out with a pair of shoes."

"Thanks Bri," he replied.

I walked over to the Grill to grab a hotdog and a Mountain Dew. The guys from the skins game were gathered around a few tables playing cards and Fred was in his spot right in front of the TV. I thanked Lisa and threw a buck in her tip jar.

As I was walking back through the tables, Fred turned and shouted, "Hey, Bill Clinton fell down and broke his leg at Greg Norman's house in Florida."

He turned up the sound on the TV as everyone turned to listen. As I was listening, Oscar walked inside and stopped next to me to hear the update. When it was over, I turned to Oscar and asked him how things were this morning.

"Guy comes here with his wife and says she don't play," began Oscar. "Just wants to watch. Wants to know what we can do. Leave her ass at home, that's what you can do. Let her do some cleaning. Women all over the place now. They're on the golf course, they're on TV. Every time you turn on the TV, there's a woman telling you what the news is for the day. I wake up at five in the morning and turn the TV on, there she is talking away. I want to know how she gets up that early. I go to bed at night and there's a different one telling me the same damn news. Didn't used to be that women were all over the TV talking. Doesn't matter what it is, you can pick anything and there's a woman on some channel talkin' about it on the TV. They make news out of everything. Telling us if the president pisses and whether it's straight or not."

Me and few others in earshot couldn't help but laugh at Oscar's commentary. He certainly had some strong opinions.

18 Holes of Green

"Clinton falls down the steps at Norman's house and they're in his bedroom telling us this and that," Oscar continued. "The doctor says this. Here's his X-ray. It's all women just talking about bullshit. I wake up at two in the morning and there's a lady selling pots and pans on the TV. I turn that shit off. They're selling the hell out of stuff on TV and women are buying it right up."

I got a chuckle out of Oscar, but I still didn't know how crowded the course was. I walked back over to the pro-shop and Mark was still looking for those missing Dry-Joys. I wished him luck and walked outside. Once on the patio, I picked up my clubs from the rack and headed toward the tee. Harley had a cart and was waiting in line at the tee. He was warming up and talking to Hank. He had three clubs in his hands and was swinging them from side to side like a baseball player. He went through the same routine every time he got ready to play. There was just a threesome ahead of us.

"Doesn't look like it will be too bad out there," I said as I strapped my bag on the cart.

"No, looks like you guys will get right around," said Hank.

"Good. Alice is going to need balls at the range again later," said Harley.

Just then, I noticed that one of the guys in the threesome ahead of us was wearing what looked like a brand new pair of shoes. I couldn't believe my eyes. No one would be stupid enough to stick around wearing the shoes they just stole.

"Guys, I think that guy just stole a pair of shoes from the pro shop."

"How do you know?" Hank asked.

"Because Mark found a pair of used shoes stuffed in a box and the new shoes were missing."

"Ooh, stealing is bad," said Harley.

"Now, I've heard everything," said Hank.

I walked up next to the threesome and began using the ball washer by the tee to get a better look. It was obvious the guy was wearing a new pair of Foot Joys. He looked like he was about fifty years old. He had some K-Mart golf bag and a set of generic clubs. I was pretty certain that this was the guy. I ran inside to tell Mark. By this time, Andy was in the pro shop with Mark giving him a hard time.

"I bet you were so busy on the phone with Ashley that you weren't paying any attention," said Andy.

"No, I wasn't" Mark tried to explain, but Andy cut him off.

"I'm surprised we didn't lose the whole shop the way you talk to her."

"Guys, I found our man," I interrupted.

"Where?" asked Andy.

"He's out there about to tee off," I said.

"Are you sure?" asked Mark.

"Yeah, this guy doesn't look like he would buy Foot Joys," I replied. "Especially, not Dry-Joys. He has K-Mart written all over him."

"Mark, you call the police. Brian, show me where this guy is," said Andy.

As Mark turned to the phone it rang before he could pick it up. I could tell by the way he stopped his greeting short that it was Ashley.

"Sweetie, I can't talk now," I could hear him say. "I have to call the police...No I'm fine, I'll explain later."

18 Holes of Green

Obviously, Ashley was just more alarmed by that statement. He would just never learn to not say things like that to her.

"I'll call you back in a moment. Well, just go with whichever one you like the best," he said in as he hung up the phone.

"The pre-wedding bliss," commented Andy as we hustled out the door.

Andy and I made our way toward the tee. The threesome was still waiting for the group in front of them to hit their second shots. I pointed out the guy I suspected to Andy and we approached him. He was standing on the side of the tee box watching his friend make practice swings and providing analysis. It was obvious that he was wearing new shoes. Andy walked right up and confronted him.

"Excuse me sir, but we seem to have a little confusion here. I think you left your golf shoes inside," said Andy.

"What are you talking about?" said the man. "Are those size 11?" asked Andy.

"Yeah, they are. So what?" he asked.

"So you took them from my pro-shop," answered Andy.

"I don't know what the hell you're talking about, but you're getting on my nerves," said the guy.

"OK," replied Andy.

I couldn't believe he was going to let that joker get away with stealing a pair of shoes.

"What are you doing? Those are the same style. They have to be the shoes," I said.

"They are. But I'm gonna wait until the police get here," he replied. "He had his chance to come clean."

Andy and I walked back inside the clubhouse and told Mark what happened.

"Well, the cops ought to be here soon," said Mark. "I called 911."

"We gotta nail these guys. They're serious chops," I said.

"I know. Look at this guy's swing," said Mark looking out the window.

The first golfer had teed up his ball and was making fast and furious practice swings. It was quite a sight.

We all were staring out the window. Harley and Hank kept glancing back at us to see what Andy was going to do. We watched the first golfer top his ball and roll it about 30 yards. Then he stood there and started making very slow swings apparently trying figure out what he did wrong.

"You jumped out of your shoes!" shouted Mark. The door was closed so the golfers could not hear him.

The golfer finally walked off of the tee and allowed the second guy to give it a try.

"Look at this guy's stance," said Andy.

The guy had a terrible stance. He bent his knees so much that it looked like he was sitting on a toilet.

If that wasn't bad enough, he was too far away from the ball. His arms were completely straight. They were also at such an angle that they were in line with the shaft.

"Looks like he's ready to chop down a tree," said Mark. "He'll be lucky to make contact," added Andy.

"If he does, it will go high and right," said Mark.

Sure enough, the guy made wild baseball swing, and the ball went flying high and way right. Swinging so much around his body, he practically fell on his face.

"Good call," I said.

18 Holes of Green

At that point, the jerk with the stolen shoes was ready to hit. He had a similarly awful looking stance. As he began to address the ball, a police car pulled into the parking lot. A lot of the precinct's cops played at White Lake, and we took good care of them. That ensured prompt service each time we had to call them.

"It's big Jack. We got him now," said Andy.

He picked up the box with the old shoes and walked toward the front door facing the parking lot. Jack was one of the officers who played White Lake the most. We always let him play for free, so he was definitely willing to help. He was also big enough to intimidate anyone. Andy met him outside the clubhouse and they began walking around back together.

The thief on the tee finally took a swing and sliced the ball toward the third tee.

"Must have been the shoes," I said to Mark.

"Maybe it was the guilty conscience," he replied.

He naturally teed up another ball. By this time, Andy and big Jack were approaching the tee. He hit his second ball high and to the right.

As the guy walked back to his cart, Jack stopped him. It was obvious he was playing dumb, but Jack was pretty persistent. Before I knew it, he had the guy sitting on a bench taking off the shoes and trying on the old ones. I was reminded of O.J. Simpson trying on the gloves. However, in this case the shoes fit. I decided to walk outside to hear what was going on. As I approached the tee, it was obvious to everyone that the guy stole the shoes.

"Mr. Long, there is no doubt in my mind that you took these shoes out of the pro shop," said Jack. "That's shoplifing."

"Honest, I wasn't trying to cheat you," the guy said to Andy in a sudden change of attitude.

I leaned toward Hank and whispered that the guy must have just wanted to try them out.

"You stole 'em damn it!" yelled Andy.

"Mr. Pader, would you like to press charges?" asked Jack.

"Well, that's up to Mr. Long here," said Andy.

"What do you mean?" the guy asked.

"Well, I might be inclined not to if you bought the shoes and a few dozen balls," said Andy.

"What! That's extortion," said the guy.

"It sounds fair to me," said Jack.

Once the guy realized that it was his only way out, he began quite a shopping spree. I think he really just wanted to save himself from any further embarrassment. He ended up buying the shoes, two-dozen balls, and a towel, all for about $210. I guess it was better than going to jail.

18 Holes of Green

Playing Through

Since the golf shoe ordeal seemed to be resolved and no one appeared to be making the turn, Harley and I headed over to the tenth tee in our cart. We didn't want to be anywhere near those three guys.

I got out my Ping Driver and began taking a few practice swings. Harley went through his traditional warm-up routine all over again.

"What are we playing for?" I asked.

Harley, who loved to gamble, began thinking.

"How about I give you two strokes at a dollar a hole. Double for birdies. Best dancer gets a beer," said Harley.

"Yeah, OK," I agreed.

Best dancer meant least putts. I liked playing something for the least putts, because it gives you some incentive to stay together if your drives are off that day.

"Alright, Brian my boy, watch my belly button knock the ball out there," said Harley.

He addressed the ball, made a few waggles, and swung. It was a real loopy baseball type swing. The ball went flying straight down the middle of the par five. It was weird. His bellybutton really was pointing toward the target before the club made impact. It hurt my back just thinking about it.

"Not bad," I said.

"Yeah. I was just being physical."

Harley was always talking about the difference between being physical and being social. It was an amusing contradiction, because he talked so much about not being social.

I stepped onto the tee and addressed the ball. I tried to focus on what Mark had told me the day before. I picked a spot in the fairway and imagined my ball landing there. I took a swing with that thought in my head. I struck the ball pretty well, but it had a bit of a hook on it. The ball landed in the left rough.

"That will play well enough," said Harley.

"Yeah. I've been in a lot worse places on this hole," I answered.

We started driving down the fairway toward our balls. I really did prefer walking, but it was too tempting to ride being able to do it for free. I guess that I was spoiled. I hated walking at White Lake when we were crowded. If I got stuck behind a slow group, I wanted to be able to skip over to an open hole or come in to the clubhouse. I know that's not what golf is all about, but neither is the way we would cram people onto the course like a factory.

Harley and I played out the hole with relative ease. We both made par. As we walked off the green, Harley stopped and looked in toward the clubhouse. I could tell that he was thinking deeply about something.

"Brian, that stealing is screwed up. I bet that guy wasn't very physical as a kid. I bet he didn't play many sports. He probably sat around drinking beer and smoking dope as a kid."

"I don't know, Harley. It's always the real quiet clean-cut guy that kills everyone," I said.

18 Holes of Green

"Yeah. I bet he was a real social person. Yak, yak, yak," he continued. Harley was in his own little world. Anything bad was the result of being social. As we parked near the eleventh tee, Harley continued talking about why people should talk less. The irony was really quite amusing.

When we stepped onto the tee, I noticed that it was in pretty bad shape. There were scars and divots all over the tee. I could see about ten fresh divots, but only one that was repaired. It was a shame, but many of the people who played White Lake didn't know how to treat a golf course. Even though White Lake wasn't a spectacular course, it still deserved the same respect given to any golf course.

Andy had this unwritten rule for his employees that whenever we played, we left the course in better shape than we found it.

"It blows me away that people can treat a golf course like this, Harley," I said as I grabbed a scoop of divot patch from the wood box beside the tee.

"It's a failure to act physically, Brian, my boy. People get so caught up jabber jawing that they don't even think about the damage they imposed on the golf course. That's what being social will get you."

I gave Harley a slight laugh, even though there really was some truth to what he had said. As I filled the numerous divots with mixture of sand, seed and fertilizer, Harley again began to swing his driver back and forth like a batter warming up.

"Yep, my old back has tightened up already," he said.

After repairing the divots, I grabbed my driver and teed up a ball. As I addressed the ball, I started to think that I might be standing to close to it. Once this thought had entered my mind, I couldn't help but think the grip was too close to my body. I then began considering the effect of this position on my swing. I started to think about how I should adjust my swing. I had only been standing there a few seconds, but my mind was going a mile a minute. As I looked down the fairway to check my alignment, I suddenly lost confidence in where I was aiming. Now, I was not only tense, but I doubted my stance and alignment.

Although I knew that the smart thing to do would be to back off and start over, I couldn't. Something really stupid and stubborn inside of me would not let me back off. I was intent on hitting the ball no matter how uncomfortable I was. So, I took the club back consciously attempting to guide it. My thoughts turned to directing the club head in order to compensate for my poor stance. By the time my club hit the ball, I knew the result would not be pretty. I didn't even have to watch the flight of the ball. It sliced way right and headed toward the jungle.

"Whoa...Nelly," shouted Harley.

"Sit damn it!" I shouted.

Luckily, the ball held up before entering the brush and weeds of the jungle. It was ugly, but not as bad as a lost ball.

"That'll play, Bri," said Harley as he stepped onto the tee. He addressed the ball, made a few waggles, and swung.

Again, he made a real loopy baseball type swing and again, his ball sailed an average distance down the middle of the fairway.

"Nice shot, Harley," I said.

"Thanks, my boy," he replied with his usual sense of camaraderie.

We got in the cart and headed down the path. Harley stopped even with my ball. My ball was in some thick rough, but it was sitting up. I had about 185 yards to the center of

18 Holes of Green

the green. Allowing for the rough, I grabbed my three-iron. Harley sat in the cart and lit up a cigarette.

I was only four feet from the start of the dense brush. As I surveyed the situation, I heard some loud rustling just inside the jungle. The sounds of movement definitely indicated some type of animal.

"Did you hear that?" I asked.

"Yep. Sounds like Vader lurking back there," replied Harley.

"Great," I said as I lined up my shot.

I didn't really think that an alligator was crawling through the brush, but I didn't have an urge to find out. I addressed the ball quickly. Without thinking, I swung my three-iron and struck the ball well. My ball flew toward the green. It bounced in front and then rolled onto the front left side of the green.

"Good out," commented Harley.

"Let's get out of here," I replied.

I quickly jumped into the cart while still holding my 3 iron. We then drove on to Harley's ball and he quickly hit it to the back of the green. We rode up the path and parked even with the green.

As I approached my ball, I could see a foursome of men standing on and around 14 green down the hill to my left. I wasn't paying much attention to them until I heard them start to shout. I looked down at them to see what was going on and I noticed that there were five balls on the green. I watched them for a minute to try to figure out what they were shouting about and another ball landed on the green. I looked down to 14 fairway to see where it came from. There was a foursome of guys hitting onto the green from about 120 yards out.

Timothy McHugh

The foursome on the green was shouting and flipping them off. This was so bizarre that I just stood there watching them. Harley's ball had apparently rolled onto the fringe, so he went ahead and putted it with the pin in while I was looking away. I turned when I heard him putt and saw him walking toward his ball, which was now just a few feet from the hole.

"Harley," I said. "Come check this out."

Harley came closer and I turned back to check out the action. The foursome from the fairway had hit three balls onto the green and one over. They were now walking onto the green screaming at the other foursome. Harley was now standing next to me.

"What the hell are they yelling about down there?" asked Harley.

"I think the one group just hit into the group on the green and they're both pretty pissed at each other."

After a raised putter and barrage of curses, I witnessed the strangest thing I had ever seen on a golf course. An all-out fistfight ensued. These guys actually brawled on the 14th green in the middle of the day. All eight of them were swinging away. They weren't just pushing each other around; they were really going at it.

Harley and I just stood there speechless. As we watched them fight, it looked as though the foursome that had been putting was moving in slow motion. It became obvious after a few moments that these guys were really drunk.

The other foursome that had hit onto the green kept backing off. They were trying to get out of the confrontation, but the drunkards kept coming after them. After several minutes of scuffling, three of the four guys in the drunken foursome were lying on their backs. The other was leaning

18 Holes of Green

against a cart still swearing at the sober foursome who was just standing around laughing.

It was then that Andy and Mark pulled up to the scene in the ranger cart. They got out and talked to the eight guys for a few minutes. After a brief exchange, the foursome that was standing began to putt out.

Andy and Mark got back in their cart and headed back towards the clubhouse. The golfers continued onto the next hole like nothing had happened. The four drunkards started to get up and staggered to their respective balls.

"Look at those goofs," said Harley. "They're drunk, and it's not even noon yet."

"Yeah, only at White Lake," I said.

The incident was the most extreme case of hitting into a group that I had ever witnessed. However, it wasn't the most outrageous case I had ever heard of. Willie's brother, Nate Boylan, hit into a group of old guys once and then proceeded to get in a shouting match with them on the green. No punches were thrown, but one of the old guys was so worked up that when he reached the parking lot, he had a heart attack and died. It was awful.

Slow play was probably the biggest drawback to White Lake. You couldn't pay me to play a round there on a weekend between 10:00 a.m. and 4:00 p.m. People get so worked up about golf sometimes; I'm surprised more altercations didn't occur.

Harley and I finished our nine holes without any further incidents. I think that we were both shaken by the experience because we each bogied the rest of the holes on the backside.

As I pulled my bag off the cart, I could see Mark coming through the clubhouse doors. He walked out and met me on the patio with a big grin on his face.

Timothy McHugh

"Did you guys see that out there," he asked.

"Yeah, what the hell happened?" I asked.

"We had all kinds of complaints about slow play coming into the clubhouse," Mark said. At least five different people called from their cell phones, so Andy and I decided to go check on it since Leo was nowhere to be found."

"Naturally," I responded as Harley joined us.

"It turned out that those guys were too drunk to hit the ball," he continued. "They were playing so slowly that there were four open holes in front of them. The group behind them had been trying to play through for three holes. Apparently, they just got so pissed off that they finally decided to hit into them. I can't say that I blame them."

"They beat the shit out of those guys," I said. "What did Andy say to them?"

"Well, we pulled up and asked the only guys standing what happened," Mark replied. "Once they told us the story, Andy just walked up to the drunken foursome as they lay on the ground and said, 'Fellas, you have to let this foursome and any others play through.'"

After playing with Harley, it was time to start work. I always started a little early so I could milk some hours. I walked into the grill to grab something to eat. The food wasn't great, but it was free. Old Paul was sitting at the table closest to the snack bar. He was flirting with Lisa when I walked up to the counter.

"What's up, old man?" I said.

"Nothing at my age," he replied. "How'd you do out there?"

"Oh, besides seeing a brawl on the backside, it was OK."

"Yeah, Mark was telling me about that. Too bad Al Harper couldn't have been involved in it," he said.

18 Holes of Green

"Al could probably have kept up with them beer for beer," I said.

I noticed Lisa was busy unloading bottles of water from large boxes. The fancy new refrigerated display had been sitting empty for days. Nicole Cunningham showed up at the clubhouse the day before to inspect the set-up. She insisted that Lisa move the display two inches closer to the cash register. I realize that she had an MBA as well, but we weren't running a Target. I grabbed one of the bottles and looked at the label.

"Filtered water?" I read aloud. "It's not even spring water."

"Exactly," responded Lisa.

"We might as well drink tap water," I said.

"Or from a drinking fountain," chimed Paul.

Lisa laughed as she finished unloading the box. She quickly punched through the bottom of the box, collapsed it, and tossed it on top of a stack of others.

"What do you want for lunch today, Bri?" asked Lisa.

"I think I'll go healthy today. How about a tossed salad and a ham and turkey on rye?"

"No problem," she answered as she slid a salad in a plastic container across the counter.

"Thanks," I replied as I reached over the counter to pour myself a Mountain Dew. Lisa started working on my sandwich, and I sat down next to Paul and ate my boxed salad. Paul was always good for conversation. Each of the guys was like a separate podcast and I learned what to expect from each.

"You know what I don't understand, Brian?" asked Paul. "How could a group hold up another group for three holes, with four open holes in front of them, without the ranger seeing it?"

Timothy McHugh

"That's because Leo was too busy looking for lost balls next to number six," I said.

"That figures," replied Paul. "He isn't worth a shit. He just rides around in a cart for a couple hours a week, finding some balls and getting his free golf."

"I've come to the conclusion that the only thing anyone really wants out of life is free golf," I said.

Paul started laughing at my claim. The truth is, though, I was serious. After working at a public golf course for seven years, I had formed my own theory about golfers. I have divided golfers into two categories: those who play golf for free, and those who want to.

It's not about how good you are. It is a simple distinction. It doesn't matter what you do. You could be a golf pro, a greens keeper, a fireman, a pilot, or a caddie. If you have ever played golf for free, you might know what I'm talking about. It seems to me, that if you paid money to play or had to wait in line for 30 minutes to tee off, you probably missed some of the enjoyment.

"I can't blame people for wanting to play," I said. "But I can't imagine a round of golf meaning so much that if you play poorly, you freak out. It's not that I don't think a round of golf is worth $50 or more, but the freedom of having an entire golf course at your disposal is priceless."

"We do get spoiled," said Paul. "We have 18 holes of green."

"Yes we do," I agreed.

On that note, I stood up and grabbed my sandwich from Lisa. I thanked her and headed over to the pro shop to start taking people's money. The irony was amusing, but I didn't feel guilty, just lucky.

18 Holes of Green

As I walked behind the counter, I could tell Mark had something to tell me. He would get a funny look on his face whenever he had something to say. He was like a little kid.

"Well, Mort Stew called in sick. Oscar left already and Hank can't stay. So, it looks like you're gonna be starter today."

"He's sick?" I asked.

"He can't find his teeth or something."

"I thought it was his glasses that he can never find."

"I think he can't find his glasses to find his teeth," said Mark.

"Sounds like Mort. That's okay. It's a nice day to be outside."

I flipped my sunglasses on and headed outside to relieve old Hank. It was obvious that Hank had had enough. He dropped his clipboard on the table and took his nametag off as soon as he saw me. It gets kind of hectic at the starter's station. It was tough on me, so I know that it was tough on the old guys.

I could see that there were two groups waiting on the first tee as well as a steady flow of 18 holers making the turn to the back. Not a bad time to make the switch.

"You ready to call it quits yet, Hank?" I asked.

"Yes, I will happily hand it over to you Brian," he replied.

Hank showed me where we were on the tee sheet. We weren't too far behind considering the slow-play incident. There was just one group of walk-ins waiting for a spot. I was prepared for the worst, however. Normally, we got a rush of walk-ins around 3:00. Since we were also booked solid with tee times, it wasn't easy getting the walk-ins out. Although they'd have to wait longer than they'd like, I usually managed to cram everyone out there.

Timothy McHugh

Just then, a foursome checked in with me. I punched their receipts and put them in line behind the walk-ins.

"What time does the group in front of us have?" asked one of the guys in the foursome.

"Well, what time do you have again?" I asked.

"2:12"

"Well, they have the 2:04 time," I said.

I loved being in control of the tee. I could tell people anything. Besides, it would be slow as hell, whether they went off in front of the walk-ins or not. People think they can play faster if they can get in front of even one group, but it just doesn't work that way. Slow is slow. That was White Lake on a Sunday afternoon.

With a group leaving the first tee, I now had just two foursomes waiting. It was turning into a beautiful day. The sun was out, and the temperature was nearing 85 degrees. A twosome was walking over from the ninth green to make the turn. I checked their receipts and told them that if I got another twosome they might be paired up later. They said they understood and made their way over toward the tenth tee.

A few moments later, two older men came walking out of the clubhouse dragging pull carts. As they approached me, I greeted them the usual way.

"Hello, do you have a tee time?"

"No, we're just a twosome looking to play nine holes," one of them replied.

"Okay, I've got a twosome over on ten that you can go off with."

"Oh! That's a bunch of horse shit!" said the other old guy.

"Yeah. The hell with that!" the first one said.

18 Holes of Green

They caught me so off guard that I didn't know what to say.

"Excuse me?" I replied.

"We come down here for a relaxing round of golf, and you starters always ruin it by pairing us with someone else," the second one said.

"Sir, I can't promise you that you will enjoy playing with that other twosome, but I can promise you that it will be about two hours before you get off by yourselves," I replied, keeping my cool.

"Well, that's a load of crap! What the hell do we pay taxes for if we can't play," yelled the first old guy.

"I didn't say you couldn't play…"

"I don't want to hear it," the second one shouted.

By this time, a crowd had begun to watch the exchange. Leo and Joe, one of our other volunteer rangers, came over to see if they could help. They tried to explain the situation, but these two didn't want to listen. They stormed back into the clubhouse shouting, "We're gonna take this to the county commissioners." Once they were inside, we smiled at each other and couldn't resist laughing.

"They won't get their money back will they?" asked Joe.

"No, the county won't let us. We can only give rain checks," I replied. "That should piss them off even more."

"Shit. It's not like you asked them to play with women or something," said Leo.

"Careful, Leo," I said. "We don't need 60 Minutes down here doing a story on that subject."

"Yeah. You can't pair people up or talk about women these days. It will get your ass fired," added Joe.

Timothy McHugh

Meanwhile, I attempted to restore order to the tee. "Now does anybody else have a problem?" I asked sarcastically.

The group on the tee and the foursome waiting began to laugh. Things eventually calmed down. I got caught up on my tee times, and the two old farts left the clubhouse. I had only been working for 45 minutes, and I already had my blood pumping. I never claimed to be a saint, but I was fair with people. I was just a golfer. I was not about to attempt to pacify two people who were so blatantly rude to me right off the bat.

I headed inside to find out what happened. To my surprise, Andy had returned. My stomach tightened a little when I saw him because he always worked hard for good customer relations. I hoped I hadn't upset him. After all, though, I was just doing my job.

When I walked in, Andy just smiled at me and said, "You just don't get along with old guys, do you Bri?"

"I think they just don't get along with me," I said. I wasn't sure if he was kidding or not.

"That's OK. They would have held up half the course anyway," he replied.

"That is a good way to weed out the assholes. If they won't pair up, screw 'em," said Mark.

That was pretty much the rule of thumb at White Lake. We just didn't have any choice. It was ironic, though, because I wouldn't want to be paired up if I were playing. Then again, I know better than to expect to go off by myself in the middle of a Sunday afternoon. There's only so much daylight.

I walked over to the grill and grabbed a Mountain Dew. I sucked it down and walked back outside to face the golfers. The tee times were running pretty much on time. I

18 Holes of Green

was just sitting at the starter's table taking it easy, when I saw old Wes heading toward me. It was like watching something in slow motion. First, he would put his walker out in front of him. The he would shuffle forward to meet it and repeat the process. He was moving so slowly that I wondered if I still had time to leave the table and avoid him, but I was too comfortable. I sat and watched him inch toward me.

Old Wes was a founding member of the Birdie Hunters. That was our men's senior league; the oldest in the state and boy were they quick to remind you of that. He was the only founder still living. He hadn't played in years, but his wife would drop him off from time to time to be around his friends. He was in his late 80s. He always had something to say, but I could rarely follow him. I was enjoying the peace, but Wes had a good heart and was always good for a laugh. He sat down at the table next to me but never said hello or any other greeting. He just started talking as if he had been sitting with me all day.

"You know what I want to know?" he asked with his low and hoarse voice.

"What's that?" I answered.

"What's with these touring pros that can't putt? Why don't they practice?"

"I don't know. Maybe it never occurred to them."

"Well, I just think it's crazy," he said. "Look at those basketball players. That seven foot tall one is making 20 million dollars and the damn union still isn't happy."

"Yes sir."

"It's crazy," he repeated.

"Yes sir."

"And the football players aren't any better. They've been playing on artificial turf since 1970. Now, all of a sudden, they keep getting hurt. I don't think that they're in shape. I think they need to exercise more."

"I'll tell them you said so."

"Take that McGuire. His batting average is way down, and he keeps getting hurt."

"Baseball?"

"Right," he kept going. "Look at that one they got now. That long ball hitter."

"Sammy Sosa?"

"No, the one that got suspended. You know, Pat Daly. He oughta hit an iron off the tee. He hits irons farther than those guys hit drivers."

"John Daly," I said.

"I think he just does it for show. I grew up near Oakmont. Now, that's a course."

"John Daly," I repeated.

"Yeah. Go figure," he said.

"Go figure," I replied. "I just don't get some shit." He paused, stared at the clubhouse for a few seconds, and then he continued. "You all raise the prices every year."

"Yeah, I needed a new car," I answered.

"I used to shoot par," he replied.

Luckily some customers coming out of the clubhouse saved me from this exchange. I sprang to my feet and walked over to greet them.

They were four women in their 50s or so. They each wore matching sweaters with the word "golf" embroidered into them. Some golf tees were sewn onto the sweaters as well. They almost looked like fishermen's vests, as if they could just pull a tee right off their sweater if they needed one.

"Hello ladies. Are you playing nine or 18?"

The first lady answered quickly, "Oh, we just play nine. We just do it for our health."

18 Holes of Green

"We just like to walk on the grass," said the second lady. "It's easier on your knees than the sidewalks."

I noticed that all four of them were wearing shiny white walking shoes.

"Really. That's nice," I replied while trying to keep a straight face.

"Are there assigned places to stand?" the first lady asked.

"Excuse me?" I asked.

"I know that when we first hit, we stand up on that mound," said the second lady. "But which colored balls do we hit from?"

"Ladies, if you haven't played before, you might find that the par-three course is a better place to start."

They looked at each other, and then one of the other ladies said, "No, we'll get more exercise on the long course."

"Yes, how long is the course?" asked the first one. "6,790 yards," I answered.

"Is that riding or walking?" asked the second lady.

I just smiled as I tried to control myself.

"You'll want to tee off from the red tee markers."

They seemed satisfied now and made their way toward the tee. I was impressed that none of them were using pull carts. They each carried lightweight bags which looked relatively new. Two of them carried their bags with their hands like suitcases. The other two carried their bags on their shoulders, but the bags were facing backwards. I was trying not to watch them as they prepared to tee off, but one of the ladies came over to me.

"Excuse me?" she whispered. "I shouldn't use my putter until I get to the green, right?"

"Right," I whispered as nicely as I could with a smile.

Timothy McHugh

I turned and walked toward the clubhouse. Old Wes was busy gawking at the group of women. It looked as though he would start drooling soon. It was all becoming too much for me. I tried to suppress all of the sexist stereotypes popping into my head. Maybe I ought to suppose that these four women had just escaped from an asylum. I knew that they were not representative of women golfers in general. Besides, they were very sweet ladies. Despite my reservations about furthering any stereotypes, I could not resist the urge to go inside and give an account of what had just transpired.

When I entered the clubhouse, I found Mark talking to Paul and Charlie in the pro shop. It seemed Paul, who was an amateur club maker, was showing off his latest gem. He had taken a Taylor Made midsize driver, stripped off the finish, added lead tape, and changed the shaft.

"This shaft is a hell of a lot better than the ten dollar job you got with it, Brian," said Paul. The club was originally mine, but when I broke the shaft the year before, I sold it to Paul for thirty dollars.

I proceeded to tell them the story of the four women that I had just encountered. They got a few laughs out of it.

"Which colored balls do I hit from?" said Charlie sarcastically. "I guess I won't be playing today."

"Well, you won't want to play on the front anyway," I said.

"People like that belong on the par three," said Paul.

"I tried. I really did, but they wanted a lot of exercise," I said.

"Mark, you're the pro here. It's your responsibility to make sure people know how to play."

"Yeah, for 40 dollars a half hour," Mark replied.

18 Holes of Green

"What, they weren't cute enough to qualify for one of your free lessons?" I asked.

"Don't you have a job to do?" he responded. "Make sure they don't hold anyone up."

"Yeah, OK," I laughed and walked out the door.

I watched the ladies tee off. To my surprise, they were actually quite quick and efficient about it. They didn't waste any time gawking at each other's shots. They teed up their balls and fired them off the tee one right after the other. Apparently, they really were out for the exercise, because they proceeded to power walk to their balls and quickly hit them again. They didn't hit the ball far, but they sure progressed down the fairway at a good pace. That just goes to show that you don't have to be good to play quickly. In fact, there are plenty of good golfers who are terribly slow.

Feeling a little guilty for assuming that they would be slow, I sat down in the chair at the starter's table. I wasn't sitting there more than two minutes, when a threesome of really odd looking grease balls came walking out of the clubhouse.

Two of the guys were wearing tank tops, and one of those mechanics' shirts that had his name, "Ed," on the pocket. The guy on his right was wearing a Styrofoam visor sort of thing that had wings on each side sticking out about six inches. It looked like something a kid would get at an amusement park. He had a bushy brown beard that seemed to almost hide the cigarette dangling from his mouth. The other fellow sporting a tank top was wearing cut-off denim shorts. He was bald on the top of his head, but the hair that he did have was down to his shoulders.

Ed was toting a bright yellow golf bag with white trim. He had a "Big Bruiser" driver and "877s" irons. He was a typical knock-off clown. Dumb and dumber each had a set of our rental clubs in one hand and a beer in the other.

"Hey there sport, can we hop on over to the back?" asked Ed.

"Afraid not," I replied. "I've gotta keep it open for people making the turn."

There wouldn't be anyone making the turn, but since the front was already going to be slow, I didn't want to screw up the back too.

"You mean we gotta play behind those women."

"I don't think they'll bother you. Just ask to play through if they hold you up," I said knowing full well that it was unlikely the women would hold these guys up.

"They best not hold us up. We hit fast."

"Wonderful," I replied.

Ed, Dumb, and Dumber made their way to the tee. The ladies were nearing the green already. The three guys began doing their baseball warm up swings and their 12-ounce Budweiser curls. They talked about their planned 300 yard drives and punched each other in the shoulders. These were the types of guys that made me dream about working at a private club.

My entertainment was interrupted when a foursome came walking out of the clubhouse. It was a relief to see that they were wearing golf shoes and seemed to know what they were doing. I advised them to go off on the backside for obvious reasons. I checked their receipts and sent them on their way. They were very appreciative. It felt good to get some real golfers. I was starting to wonder if there were any left.

By this time, Ed, Dumb, and Dumber were hitting their second shots, some 20 to 30 yards off the tee. I sat there at my table and watched them zigzag back and forth across

18 Holes of Green

the fairway. A few other groups came out in the meantime, and I naturally sent them to the back nine. In fact, the first of the groups had made it to number ten green before Ed made it to the 150 marker.

It wasn't long before a group coming off nine green shouted over to me. They were a twosome of very large men complaining that their golf cart had run out of gas on number five. They were sweating profusely and appeared to be on the verge of exhaustion from carrying their bags for the last four holes. Both of them were fuming and kept making reference to how it was unfair to make them walk because of their weight. They joked about their size and attacked us for bad golf carts all at the same time. I apologized and sent them in to talk to Mark and said that he would take care of them. After all, that's what golf pros are for. You yell at them and you feel better.

A few moments later, the two guys came walking out of the clubhouse with large beers in their hands. I walked toward them to apologize again and they greeted me with big smiles.

"If I had known we were going to get free beer out of the deal, I wouldn't have bitched at you kid," one of the guys said to me.

I immediately knew that Mark had appealed to their soft spot and hooked them up with a couple of beers.

"Don't worry about it," I replied. "I hate to see a cart break down on anyone."

"Well, for a cart voucher and two free beers, I'd say it was worth the walk," the second guy said.

I laughed and smiled at them as they sat down on the patio to drink their beers. It wasn't long after that when Harley came driving over in a maintenance cart from the practice range.

"I Hear you got a no account mule, Brian, my boy," he said.

"A what?" I asked.

"A broken down cart," he replied.

"Yeah. Mark called you?"

"Yep. Communication," he replied with his usual dry tone.

"Well, let's go," I said. I hopped in the maintenance cart with him and we headed out onto the front nine.

"You know, if those people were physical, they would have pushed their cart in themselves," said Harley.

"I don't know Harley. If you pay for a cart, you shouldn't have to push it in yourself," I commented. "That's bad business."

"Business. That's social," he replied. "No account Mule sitting in a haystack," Harley began to sing. "No account mule, sitting in a haystack. No account mule, sitting in a haystack, all day long."

We were riding down the cart path on number one to get out to where the broken down cart was stranded. As we drove past the first green, we could see Ed and his boys meandering around on the green. The two pull carts were parked on the apron. They had stuck the flagstick up side down in one of the bags on a pull cart so that it pointed into the air hanging over the green. Ed lay on his stomach as he apparently tried to read the break of his putt.

"What the hell is up with those goofs?" asked Harley.

"I don't know man, but the phrase "inbred" keeps running through my mind," I replied.

As we approached the fifth tee, we could see the cart sitting in the middle of the fairway about 200 yards out. It looked as though it was there on purpose, like a target at which people could aim. When we got to the cart, it was

18 Holes of Green

littered with beer cans. The engine cover was hot and the stench of burning motor oil was strong. It had obviously been run very hard.

"No wonder the thing died," I said. "Those fat-ass, beer-drinking chops wore the thing out."

Harley lifted up the engine cover and checked the gas. It still had a half a tank.

I hopped in the dead cart and Harley eased the maintenance cart up behind me. He slowly matched up the bumpers and began to push me forward. After we got up to the maximum speed, the dead cart that I was in began to run. The cart slowly began to pull away from Harley's front bumper. It kept picking up speed as we went. I guess now that the tremendous weight was off the poor cart, it really wanted to move.

Harley and I roared down the path on number one. As I approached the first tee, my mood changed. I suddenly sunk into a depressed and angry state of mind as I saw the frightening scene before me. There were four couples walking around looking over the carts. They were holding cart keys and clubs. My worst nightmare had come true.

I couldn't believe it. It was 7:15. It would take them two hours to play. There was no way that they would finish. I parked the cart and walked over to them. One of the men was much older than the others. He was probably in his sixties. They all appeared to be Asian. The other three appeared to either be sons of or work for the older man. The older man was carrying the large white PING staff bag that we displayed the Ping Irons in. It said, "Andy Pader, White Lake G.C." on the side of it.

The other three men had PING stand bags that looked very familiar. When I met up with them, I noticed that the older man and two of the younger ones all had new Ping irons. The other man had a new set of Titleists. If they weren't just standing still, I would have thought that they were robbing the place.

"Can I help you folks?"

"Yes, we wish to play," said the older man.

The wives stood directly behind each of their husbands holding their golf shoes. The older woman also had a large bag over her shoulder.

"OK, do you have your receipt?" I asked.

"Yes. Here it is," said the older man.

He proceeded to pull out the longest cash register receipt I had ever been presented. These guys must have bought half the shop. It went something like this: four nine-hole greens fees, four carts, three sets of Ping irons, one set of Titleist irons, one staff bag, three stand bags, four-dozen Titleist balls, Four Foot Joy gloves, two pairs of Nike shoes, ten bags of tees, and one ball-mark repair tool. I guess only one of them planned on hitting a green. It was a grand total of $5,548.87.

"OK, well, uh…you can have at it I suppose," I mumbled as I handed him back the receipt and pointed towards the first tee.

I stepped aside in amazement. The women each got in one of the carts and proceeded to pull them up to the first tee. The old man turned to me and said, "They will drive."

"That's…fine," was the only thing that I could manage to say.

The men then walked up on to the first tee and began loosening up. I headed inside to have a little chat with Mark. I let him have it.

"What the hell is this?" I asked as I walked behind the counter.

18 Holes of Green

"Hey man, I was ready to send them packing till I found out that they needed everything," responded Mark.

"They didn't want rental clubs?" I asked.

"I didn't offer them any. When they asked to play at 7:00, I knew we were in trouble. There was no way I was going to let them take carts out this late. I thought that if I told them we didn't have any rental clubs, they'd give up on the idea. Instead, they bought up everything in sight."

"We're going to be here a while tonight you know," I said.

"Yeah, but it's worth it," he replied. I'll have Andy eating out of my hand when he finds out how much I sold."

We sat and discussed our Asian customers. Mark was so delighted to have sold them the works. I could see commission figures running through his head. I had to admit that it was a good sale.

After the excitement had worn off, I went out and started putting carts away. I was just pulling the last cart into the barn, when I heard a voice behind me.

"How am I supposed to play if you put all the carts away?" asked the voice.

At first I was frightened, thinking that we'd never get out of there, but then I recognized the voice.

"You get your lazy ass out there and carry your bag if you want to play," I said as I turned and faced John.

"What's going on, Bri?" asked John.

"Not much. The Toyota board of directors is out on the front with their wives."

"Four carts?" he asked as he noticed them on number one.

"Don't ask," I responded.

With all the carts in except for the Asians', I headed inside with John. The pro-shop lights were off and everything was covered in sheets. With Mark nowhere to be found, John and I headed into the grill. There we saw Mark behind the snack bar with Lisa.

"You guys need beers?" he yelled over to us.

"Oh yeah, I earned it," said John.

"Yeah, me too," I said.

We took our seats at a table by the window.

"I think I might have earned this beer a little more than you did today, John," I said.

John took off his Ping cap and wiped his brow.

"No way," he said. "You wouldn't believe my last lesson."

"I doubt it beats the board of directors and their four chauffeurs on the front," I said.

"It's probably close. It was a guy about fifty years old who had been playing for a long time. Anyway, we get out to the teaching area, and all of a sudden, he looks up at the sky. He says, no, the sun's in the wrong spot. I said, excuse me? Then, he says, I need to be able to see my shadow in order to hit the ball."

"His shadow?" I asked.

"Yeah, he had to see his shadow in front of him in order to swing. I had to take him out to the opposite end of the range and have him hit balls in toward the tees so that he could see his shadow."

"How was he?" I asked.

"His shadow looked great, but he couldn't hit the ball worth a damn."

We could hear Mark say goodbye to Lisa and the outside door behind the snack bar open and close. Then, Mark appeared carrying three cups of beer.

"That's all you got?" asked John.

"Relax, she left the taps on for us," replied Mark.

18 Holes of Green

"That's good, our friends are just making their way to number two now," I said.

"Well, we're set for the long haul now," said Mark.

The sound of golf shoes walking on pavement could be heard coming from around the corner. "No, you don't have time for a quick nine holes," said Mark in anticipation of what was to come.

When the door opened, it was someone carrying a bag of clubs, but it was not a customer. It was Nate Boylan, the 31-year-old attorney, volunteer starter, resident troublemaker and brother of slick Willie.

"What, only three beers?" asked Nate. "You know where it is," replied John.

"Good old Lisa took care of us again, how about that," said Nate.

"So what brings you down here, Nathan?" I asked.

"John said he was going to play, but now I see he's just gonna sit on his ass and drink beer all night," said Nate.

"Play? It's gonna be dark in an hour," said Mark.

"It will be dark in an hour and twenty-seven minutes," yelled Nate from behind the snack bar.

Nate Boylan was a stickler.

"Doesn't she keep any Heineken back here?" He yelled.

"It's locked in the back," shouted John. "You might as well bring a pitcher of Bud Light with you."

Mark lit up a cigarette and Nate returned struggling to carry two pitchers overflowing with Bud Light and a stack of cups.

"I guess you attorneys are good for something after all," said John.

Timothy McHugh

Nate set down the pitchers spilling a cup full onto the table. I got up from the table to go over to the pro shop to get a towel.

"You might as well bring back a stack of singles with you," said Mark as he tossed Lisa's deck of cards onto the table.

"This may not be a wasted trip down here after all," said Nate.

"Yeah, well this is the only way you're ever going to win money off of me," said John.

"Like I said, if you give me three a side, I can take you," replied Nate.

"Three a side?" questioned John. "You're a five handicap."

"I've got another card that says I'm a ten."

"Typical lawyer," said Mark.

I returned with fifty singles from the cash register and we began cashing in our money. We didn't play cards that often, but we usually had a good time when we did. I placed two twenties and a ten on the corner of the table to payback the cash register.

"All right boys, it's time for a little mule train," said Nate as he grabbed the cards and began shuffling them. That was just Nate's name for Texas Hold'em. I started out hot, winning the first three hands. I played with my heart and relied on luck for success.

My winning streak came to an end after a one on one bout with John. By this time we had gone through a couple more pitchers and the conversation was whirling around like a tornado.

First, we were discussing our swings. Then, we moved on to golf in general. We eventually got off of the golf subject all together when Nate laid down his cards to take the

18 Holes of Green

hand and shouted "hoochie mamma!" The Seinfeld reference began an enthralling discussion recounting some of the funnier episodes that we had seen.

But before long the conversation unavoidably came back to golf as it always did. After a few minutes, the card games ceased and the next thing I knew Nate was holding his sand wedge trying to chip a ball off of the tile floor and land it into a beer pitcher about ten feet away. Needless to say he didn't have a lot of luck. His ball kept rolling across the floor banging into tables.

"You're not gonna be able to get it off the ground with it lying on the tile like that," said John.

John proceeded to lay his ashtray on the floor to help tee up the ball. This seemed to help because now Nate's balls were at least getting airborne. However, now they were getting a little too much air and were bouncing off the table tops.

By 9:00 we were deeply involved in a rotation of poker hands and chipping for beers. Our activities were becoming a little too much for the indoors and we were too wound up to sit and play cards. So with our cups of beer in hand, we took Nate's Bertha, a couple of demo drivers and a shag bag out into the darkness. We walked over the patio, down the path and onto the first tee. I could just make out the fairway thanks to the glowing moonlight. The rest of the course was shrouded in darkness and a lone Cessna sputtered overhead on its way to Williams Field.

"All right guys, we each put up a dollar, if you hit the fairway you take your dollar back, if you miss, the dollar stays in," said Nate as though he was making it up as he went along.

"What happens if everybody hits the fairway?" asked Mark.

Timothy McHugh

"Just relax and we'll see as we go," said Nate in his drunken wisdom.

We began playing our little game. As best we could tell in the darkness, none of the balls had hit the fairway after two rotations through the batting order. Naturally, the degree of error was different for each of us.

My drives were slicing low and bouncing off trees and a few other things in the darkness. John and Mark were hitting pretty solid drives, but Nate and I had ruled them all just out of the fairway.

It was nearing 10:00 pm and we were having a good time beating balls and drinking our beers. We had made a few trips into the clubhouse to refresh our pitchers. There were 28 dollars in the pot when Nathan bunted a single up the middle to collect the winnings.

"I think the ball should have to go at least 150 yards," said John.

"What the hell are you talking about? That was at least 200 yards," yelled Nate.

"Bullshit," said Mark. That was 130 at the most."

"Brian, you get to decide. How far was it?" asked John.

I was transfixed by the sound of golf carts coming closer. "You guys hear golf carts?" I asked.

"Holy shit!" said Mark. "The Asians."

There before our intoxicated eyes, were four white carts coming down number nine fairway. It appeared as though they were using flashlights to see what they were doing.

"Who the hell is that?" asked Nate.

"That's our last four carts," I said. "And it's only 10:15."

"An eightsome?" asked Nate.

18 Holes of Green

"Not exactly," said Mark.

Not wanting to alarm the customers, we gathered our gear together and headed back into the clubhouse. We let Nate keep the 28 dollars since he had thought up the game.

We sat on the patio and watched our friends try to putt in the dark. It was wild. Each of the wives was holding a flashlight so that their husband could see to putt.

After three hours and fifteen minutes on the course by themselves, they had finally finished nine holes. I admired their dedication.

They drove their carts out to their cars, unloaded and quickly returned them. They were very polite. Nate, Mark, and John helped me clean the trash out of their carts and put them away. It had been a long day, but just all part of the job for a golf course starter.

Sacrificial Round

It was a quiet Thursday afternoon at White Lake. The morning leagues had just finished, and it was now the slowest part of the day. The middle of the day, right between the morning seniors and the after-work leagues. It was the best time of the day to play. I was sitting on the patio of the clubhouse, putting my golf shoes on, preparing to play a few holes by myself.

It was at that point that my plans changed. Al Harper and Charlie Pendyke, two of the bitterest old men I had ever met, came walking around the corner. When they walked toward me dragging their squeaky old pull-carts, they looked like the best of friends. My first impression was that these couldn't be the same two guys I knew. The Al and Charlie I knew could have been the basis for Grumpy Old Men. Sure, they were always pleasant to me when they would come in and pay for their round, but when they returned, they were always at each other's throats. That particular day was the day that I made the terrible mistake of playing with them.

They had regular game and a regular bet. They played for a dime a hole and allowed each other four mulligans. I later learned that the mulligans were not restricted to tee shots. They acted as though they were playing for big money. Al and Charlie were the two most competitive hackers I had ever met.

They walked past me spitting their old man banter back and forth. That day, it was something about the price of

18 Holes of Green

coffee at gas stations. It was usually always about the price of something.

Then, without any warning, Al turned to me and in true Al Harper fashion, being both demeaning and friendly at the same time, said, "If you don't have anyone to play with, son, you can walk along with us."

No one to play with, I thought. Walk along with you. I don't walk. I couldn't believe him. They just stood there, staring at me, waiting for a reply. I would have much rather played by myself, but for some odd reason, my curiosity got the best of me.

"Well, I was going to practice a little 'till the guys are ready to play," I said. "But, I guess I could play a few holes for practice."

I knew that I successfully conveyed my reluctance to play with them by the looks on their faces. I wasn't about to let them think that they were doing me a favor. I didn't mind Charlie that much because he would actually talk with me once in a while.

"How's it going Charlie?" I asked.

"Haven't made a par in six months," he replied. It was his standard answer. I wasn't sure if it was true or not. I certainly hoped that it wasn't. But it would certainly explain his bitterness.

Al Harper never talked with me. He only talked to me. He appeared to me to be in his mid-to-late 70s. That day he was wearing a pair of ancient-looking white golf shoes with kilties. Those are the tassels or flap that covered the laces, and they were once in style. Beneath pressed, brown shorts he was wearing long black socks, pulled up almost to his knobby, pale white knees. He had on a faded yellow golf shirt with a flyaway collar that was so old and worn that it was nearly transparent.

Timothy McHugh

Charlie Pendyke appeared to be slightly older. Maybe 80. He wore a pair of light blue pants, with a pair of rotten old brown golf shoes. He was wearing just a white undershirt that was so old that it was transparent. It was great that he dressed up for golf. The two men seemed married to each other. They were so happy together. I guess you could say they fit in with each other. They certainly didn't fit in with anyone else.

I followed them to the first tee. As I turned and looked back towards the clubhouse, I could see Andy and Mark staring out at me in amazement. They must have thought I was insane for playing with these guys. When we arrived at the tee, Al immediately began scouring the area in front of the tee markers for broken tees. Charlie soon joined him.

"You better hurry Brian, before we get all the good ones," said Al.

"That's OK," I said. "I've got some in my bag."

This process continued for several minutes. I began swinging my driver to loosen up.

"Hey look, a whole one!" said Charlie excitedly.

"Now, what kind of dumb-ass would leave a perfectly good tee lying on the ground," said Al.

I thought of all the times that I probably forgot to pick up my tee. I walked onto the tee and stood between the tee markers looking for a good spot to tee-up my ball.

"Whoa, Brian, you sure are an eager beaver," said Al as he looked at me.

After five minutes of watching them hunt for broken tees, I guess I was growing a little impatient. I stopped and stepped away from the tee markers. I stretched a little trying not to rush them.

"Just loosening up," I said. "Take your time." I remember wishing someone would just shoot me. I couldn't

18 Holes of Green

believe I actually told them to take their time. I was ready to hit, and these guys were still scavenging for tees.

Charlie seemed satisfied with his newfound treasure. He walked over to his bag and pulled out a driver that appeared to be a Big Bertha. When he got closer to me, I realized it was actually an imitation. I should have guessed. It was actually a "Big Brother". Where it should say Callaway, it said Trident. The words were even spelled in the same calligraphy as on a Bertha. There was even a black dot on the bottom of the head making it appear as though the shaft was bore through like on a Callaway. It was a joke.

"What kind of driver is that?" I asked Charlie.

"Oh, it's one of those big jobs," he said. "Just like yours. Except, I bet you paid a lot more for yours. My friend made it in his basement for me. Only 90 bucks, and it's graphite."

"Sounds like a hell of a deal," I said.

"You better believe it," he replied.

I guess Al had finally found enough broken tees because he made his way over to his bag and unsheathed the ugliest looking wood I had ever seen. It was a swamp green laminated wood that was so old and faded that parts of it were brown. It looked as though it was rotting.

Upon closer review I determined that at one time it had been a MacGregor two wood, but that must have been 40 or 50 years ago. Now the three of us stood there waggling our clubs.

"Age before youth," I said in an attempt to get one of them to tee off. At first, I thought that it worked because Al went over to the tee markers and teed up his ball. However, I learned that this was just the first step in an elaborate pre-shot routine, from which he never strayed.

Timothy McHugh

After he had teed up his ball, he walked behind it and squatted to look at his target. I thought that I could hear his bones creak as he lowered himself. Then, he licked his lips and spit. It almost made me sick. He then slowly raised himself. Again sending a tingle up my spine, as I was almost sure I heard the creaking sound again. He stood there and began staring at a spot on the ground just in front of his ball. He laid his club down behind the ball and pointed the face toward the spot. He was lining up his club before he even got his body into position. While trying not to move his club out of the position he was holding it in, he slowly walked around and addressed the ball with his feet together. He was gripping the club with all of his might. I suppose he was being careful as not to move it off line.

I had seen children try this before, but never an adult. I don't care how careful you are, it's impossible to keep your clubface in the same position as you walk from behind the ball to the address position. It all seemed a little ridiculous to me, but it was entertaining. Once he was certain he hadn't moved his club, he slowly spread his feet apart. First, the right foot. Then, the left.

It was at that point that he began staring at the ball. At first, it didn't seem that strange, but after a full minute, I started to wonder if he had fallen asleep. I couldn't tell if his eyes were open, since his head was practically pointed straight down. I thought that he must be OK, since Charlie didn't seem bothered by the situation.

Now, I know that when you're bored, time seems to go slower. However, I know from glancing at my watch that he stood there and stared at that ball for over 45 seconds.

45 seconds is a long time to stare at a golf ball by anybody's standards.

18 Holes of Green

Finally, he started to move. He picked the club up with his arms and swung the club behind his head, without using any other part of his body. He paused at the top for a moment and then he pulled the club straight down in a chopping motion. His intense concentration was evident in that on his follow through, his body didn't move. His head remained pointed straight down at the ground. His arms swung the club up to vertical, but it stopped there. Then, he lifted his head up to see where his ball went.

"Where is it?" he asked.

"Ought to be about a hundred yards out in two seconds," I said.

His ball finally came down about ninety yards straight out.

"Shit! I popped it up," he yelled.

"I think you lifted your head up," replied Charlie almost out of habit it appeared.

Al's face started to turn red as he glared back toward

"I did not lift up my damn head," he spoke each word louder and slower as the sentence came out.

"You did too. I saw you. You always do," said Charlie as he took his sickly looking wood and teed up a ball.

Al was furious. He was not going to let this die. He stomped around for a few moments like a child. Then, he positioned himself between Charlie and his ball.

"Listen Charlie," he said. "If I would have lifted my head up I would have topped the ball, but I didn't. I popped it up."

"So you must have lowered your head," answered Charlie.

"Must have," acknowledged Al.

I thought I was going to lose it. Al backed off and Charlie addressed his ball. He took a pretty wide stance. It looked kind funny because Charlie was short and a little hefty. He immediately made a quick back swing using a lot of body turn. Then, he swung through using the same amount of speed and turn.

The ball flew straight and low for about 175 yards. Not bad for an old dude I thought.

"Right good shot," mumbled Al.

"OK Brian, let's see how a young whipper snapper does it," said Charlie.

I walked back over to the tee markers and teed-up my ball. I took a couple more practice swings and then, I addressed the ball. I felt pretty good about my swing. I guess it was just one of those days when you just happen to have a pretty positive attitude. I knew that I didn't have to do anything special to upstage these guys. I just wanted to keep it in the fairway. I swung without any other thoughts in my mind. The ball took off a little to the left but then faded back landing near the right edge of the fairway about 230 yards out and rolled about 20 yards more.

"If you would shorten that swing up, you might keep it straight," said Al as if he was instructing me. I just smiled at him and walked over to my bag.

"Shut the hell up, would you, Al!" yelled Charlie. "At least the kid is gonna be on the green in two. You're gonna screw him up."

"I will not screw him up," said Al. "I can still remember a thing or two, unlike Mr. Senility here."

As they began bickering back and forth, I started at brisk pace toward Al's ball. I may not have been able to make them move any faster, but I wasn't about to let them search aimlessly for their balls. They eventually joined me at Al's ball, about 92 yards out, in the center of the fairway.

18 Holes of Green

That was when life ended, as I knew it. Al began his pre-shot routine again. My reaction was something between shock and disbelief. I turned my eyes away from him, hoping that it would ease the pain. I began scanning the nearby fairways for anyone who might be able to rescue me.

I glanced back at him. He was still crouched down behind his ball just staring ahead. I tried to focus on my next shot to get my mind off of them. I stared at the green to determine what the best angle of approach would be. The more that I looked at it; I began to think that I should use one less club than usual. The more that I thought about it, I realized that I usually always went over that green. The green is sloped up in the front but it really levels off at the mid point. Also, it seemed that the wind was almost directly behind me. I had always played to the green using the straight yardage. I suppose that it was about time that I got some sense and used less club on my approach.

My thought process was interrupted by an awful sound. It was one of those sounds where you don't need to see the shot to know it was poor. It was the sound of a vibrating golf club and a stinging wrist.

Al's ball went skidding along the fairway up the middle for about 100 yards.

"Well, you're a little closer anyway," said Charlie.

"Go to hell," answered Al.

I refrained from saying anything and began walking toward Charlie's ball.

"See. It was so bad that it left Brian speechless," I heard Charlie say as I was walking away.

I turned around and said, "Well, it was straight." I continued walking with Charlie laughing in the background.

As I led them to Charlie's ball, I started to think more about my next shot. I became firmer in my notion to use less club than usual. I realized that there was a lot of green to work with below the flagstick. I stopped at Charlie's ball and waited for them. I guess that it was the lack of competition, but I was feeling a hell of a lot of confidence.

I looked back to see what was keeping them. To my surprise, they were standing about 40 yards back having a conversation. I couldn't believe it. We weren't even to the 150 marker yet and they were holding me up. They just stood there talking to each other. They could have at least walked while they were talking. Maybe that was beyond them.

Then suddenly, Al started waving me away. I didn't understand at first, but then Charlie grabbed both pull carts and started walking toward the side of the fairway. Al had a club in his hand and began walking backwards. At the same time, a foursome began walking onto the first tee. It was outrageous. There was a group on the tee and he was going back to rehit his second shot. So, for fear of my well being, I moved over behind a tree in the rough.

Then, with Charlie and I hiding in the rough and a group waiting 100 yards away on the first tee, Al began his pre-shot routine. The group on the first tee was showing their frustration, while Al squatted endlessly behind his ball. I considered taking out another ball, ditching them and playing number three. The tee was open and it was only 30 yards away.

I looked back at Al. He was still squatting. One of the guys on the first tee had already teed up his ball and was making practice swings. Even a beginner should have been able to get that message. Al was still squatting. It didn't seem to bother Charlie. He just stood there watching his friend.

I had never felt so trapped on a golf course as I did at that moment. I then knew why it was that I preferred to ride

18 Holes of Green

when playing. I would have given anything at that moment to have a cart to escape in. As Al slowly raised himself up off the ground, I could hear the guys on the first tee coughing and making noises to speed him up. I turned back towards the green hoping I could think about my own game. I couldn't. Al's pre-shot routine had me so upset that I couldn't concentrate. All that I could think about was how embarrassing it was to be playing with him. I regretted ever agreeing to play with them.

My blood was pumping so fast that I couldn't stand still. I knew this was going to screw up my game. My game. That was a joke. I would be lucky to make it through that round alive, let alone worry about the score. I stared at my ball and then back towards the green. I couldn't stand waiting so long before I hit my second shot. It was like someone was torturing me.

The sound of clean shot startled me out of my thoughts. Al had gotten his ball off the ground. The ball flew straight for about 120 yards and then dropped into the fairway about 35 yards past Charlie's drive.

"Wow! I got all of that one," shouted Al.

"Yeah, a couple more of those and you might make it to the green," replied Charlie.

"It was a good shot. Admit it you bastard," yelled Al. They bickered back and forth all the way up to Charlie's ball. When they arrived at Charlie's ball, they were discussing the status of their bet.

"Well, you just used one of your mulligans. You've only got three left," said Charlie.

"I can keep track of my own mulligans," said Al.

Charlie was slow and deliberate as he prepared to swing. He took three practice swings. Normally this would bother me, but it was a relief after enduring Al's little ritual.

Again, Charlie took a very wide stance and made a quick swing. He thrust his round body through, as the ball flew low and came to rest about 140 yards down the fairway.

"You keep lifting' up," said Al.

"Well, I am closer to the green than you are," replied Charlie.

It was like a race between them to see who could make it to the green first. I took off for Al's ball, hoping to keep things going. I quickly located his ball and signaled to the other two. Then, I walked to the side of the fairway and sat down on my towel. Normally, I was all for ready golf, but I was not walking anywhere in front of those two. With my butt sitting on my towel, I stretched my legs out in front of me on the grass. If I was going to wait for him to hit, I might as well be comfortable. I occupied myself with a daydream about a golf course where they shot people for playing slowly. The next thing I know, Al hit his ball up in front of the green.

It seemed like only a few seconds had gone by, but I knew better. I must have spaced out for several minutes. I set out at a brisk pace for my ball. It had been so long, I almost forgot where it was. I could hear Al and Charlie mumbling to each other in the background. I had planned this shot out so well, I didn't have to think twice about what to do. With 160 yards to the flag stick and the wind slightly behind me, I took out a seven iron.

Al and Charlie were still coming up behind me as I swung. It was one of the first times that I didn't have a swing thought as I began. I was just happy to finally be hitting. It wasn't a pretty shot, but it turned out alright. The ball started out left and low, but luckily it faded back, bounced in front of the green, and rolled up stopping five feet from the hole.

Al and Charlie began yelling and carrying on about my shot. I guess it was nice to be playing with some

18 Holes of Green

confidence boosters for a change. I had caught the ball a little thin, but it worked out all right. I shrugged off the shot saying it wasn't that great to the amazement of that pair. I'll admit I was feeling pretty good as we walked toward the green. So much so that I practically walked past Charlie's ball.

"Hold on there, young fellow. Your ball isn't going anywhere," said Charlie.

It was a little embarrassing to be corrected by one of these guys. At least it wasn't Al. That would have been too much to take. I smiled back to them and waited at Charlie's ball, about 75 yards from the hole.

They eventually joined me and continued to compliment me on my shot. Again, Charlie took his time lining up his shot, and then burst into his high speed swing. The ball flew high and seemed to move in 3 different directions before landing to the right of the green.

"That had to be one of the ugliest shots I've ever seen," commented Al.

"Then, I guess you haven't been watching your own shots today," replied Charlie.

We ultimately made it to the green. I was so happy that I immediately marked my ball and then took a seat on the fringe, on the left side of the green.

Al dragged his pull cart almost onto the apron and took out a wedge. He started making a few hacking motions with his wrists. It seemed that he abandons his pre-shot routine for chip shots. He addressed his ball with a very open stance. His wedge was also wide open. I wasn't sure why he was taking such a stance. It was just a straight uphill 30-foot chip shot. He didn't need a lot of loft, or spin, or anything like that. He must have just been imitating someone he'd seen.

As is so likely to happen in short grass with an open clubface, he shanked it. The ball flew about 15 feet in the air, to the right and stopped about three feet off of the green, in front of Charlie's ball.

"Son of a bitch," shouted Al. "Nice shank," said Charlie.

"It wasn't a shank," shouted Al. "I tried to work it, but I just missed it."

"Work it my ass," responded Charlie. "You shanked it."

Al's face was so red I thought he would explode.

Then, Charlie, who was at the bottom of the slope, made a few chops with his wedge. He addressed the ball like a putt and played the ball off of his front foot. He swung back with just his arms. I could almost hear him thinking, "be a pendulum."

The ball spit off to the left and ended up almost exactly where Al had just chipped.

"You old fool. You're supposed to get the ball on the green," said Al.

"Piss off," shouted Charlie.

Despite Al and Charlie playing chase around the green, my ball was safely five feet from the flagstick. I was content to sit on the apron and watch the spectacle. All of that waiting had worn me out. Al was now meandering around his ball, glancing at the green almost in contempt. As he stood directly across the green from me, he said, "Watch me get inside you, Brian."

Al's ball was about three feet off of the green, where it begins to slope down. Because of the severe slope, his right foot was about eight inches below his left foot. I was hoping that he would get inside of me, if that would move things along. I hoped he holed it.

Al situated himself into the uncomfortable position he needed to make a swing. He wiggled his hips and flexed his

18 Holes of Green

knees continuously, as if he were adjusting his stance. The flexing spread into his arms, wrists and head. After a moment, his entire body was wincing as if being treated to high voltage as he "loosened up" and prepared to swing. Then, he made the same chopping motion he had made on the previous chip. The club head slammed down into the top of his ball.

What had been a 20-foot chip shot suddenly became a 40-foot skull. I was relaxed, leaning back with both hands on the ground to support my upper body. I was not prepared to move.

When I saw Al's ball flying toward me, I could only think, "not in the face." I closed my eyes and tried to raise my hands in time. I immediately felt a sharp pain in my chest and his mangled old Spalding 3 fell into my lap. It stung like hell as I rolled onto my side silently absorbing the pain. It caught me so off guard that the shock distracted me from the pain for a moment. However, as I leaned back up to a sitting position, I felt the bruising sharp pain set in. I had to be in hell, I thought. Surely, I was being punished for something I did wrong. There was no other explanation. One bad decision to play golf with the wrong people led to the worst moment of my life.

"Good thing you're a young fellow. You can take that sort of thing," said Al, as he walked across the green toward me.

"Good thing?" I thought to myself. What are you, Nuts? No "sorry" or perhaps an "are you OK?"

As he walked passed the hole he stepped right on my line. It appeared as though he was dragging his feet as he moved.

That was it. It was insult to injury, literally, and I wasn't going to take it anymore. I was in too much pain and too angry to wait another moment on a green with Al. I didn't say a word to him. I walked over to my ball marker and replaced my ball. They were both still well outside of me, but I didn't give a crap. As I bent over to putt the ball, I could feel the bruise on my chest. Looking down at the ball, I could see where he ripped the green with his spikes.

I took a nice relaxed stroke and just missed the five-foot putt, by an inch. I walked over and tapped the ball in. Then I scooped the ball out of the cup with the back of my Ping putter, so I wouldn't have to bend over again.

Al and Charlie were still standing by their balls, staring at me, with confused looks on their faces. I walked off of the green and stood behind it, giving Al and Charlie room to fire at each other. I needed to escape. I was prepared to sprint into the woods if I had to.

As I stood there, pondering my next move, I heard a whistle. I looked to my left and saw Nate and John walking off of four's green. They motioned to me to join them. I looked back to see if Al and Charlie had noticed, but they were in their own world.

I waved back to Nate and John and I pointed to the fifth tee, which was about 40 yards directly behind the first green through some trees. I was saved. I grabbed my bag and headed to five's tee without looking back. That was the most brutal hole I had ever faced and I had the bruise to prove it.

Nate and John were waiting for me in their cart, by the time I got to the tee.

"What the hell did you do, Brian? Lose a bet?" asked Nate.

"No," I said in embarrassment. "They asked me."
"And you said yes?" John asked.
"Believe it or not, I actually did."

18 Holes of Green

The two of them burst out laughing. I felt like the world's biggest idiot. There wasn't much I could say to defend myself, so I figured I might as well laugh too. As soon as they paused, I gave them the punch line.

"Al hit me with his ball," I volunteered. They broke into laughter again and I joined them. Once I caught my breath, I continued. "He had a 20-foot chip and he skulled it into my chest." They kept right on laughing and I felt a little better. I looked back to the first green Al and Charlie were still putting. They hadn't even noticed that I was missing.

"Does it hurt?" asked John.

"Hell yeah it does, especially when I move around or bend over."

"You want to play for ten bucks a hole?" asked Nate.

"Yeah…screw you," I replied.

Nate laughed. He got a kick out of that. He was always looking for a sucker bet.

"I believe I got you two down," John said to Nate as he took out his old small headed Taylor Made three wood and stepped onto the tee.

"I think I'll press," said Nate.

"What, already?" John responded.

"I'm gonna pull the old hoochie coochie on him, Bri," said Nate.

What Nathan lacked in golf ability, he made up for with his wagering senses. He could feel which way a bet was going to go.

"Should I go for the green or play it safe, Bri," asked John.

"You should probably play it safe, but I'd like to see you go for the green."

"I got twenty that says you don't get there," said Nate.

"I've made it before," John answered.

"Yeah, with the wind," responded Nate.

"You got the distance, but those trees make it tough," I said.

"Yeah. It's not worth twenty," said John.

"A beer then," said Nate.

"A beer a ball," answered John.

"I'll take that all day," said Nate. "And don't forget I'm pressing."

Nate had a grin from ear to ear. He was like a little kid, who couldn't wait to see what was going to happen next.

John walked back to the cart and put away his three-wood. He pulled out his Titleist driver. He smiled as he walked onto the tee box. He used every bit of his long tee to elevate the ball as much as possible. He had a slow and effortless rhythm to his motions. He embodied the grace that all good players carry with them. Number five is a slight dogleg right. To reach the green, he would have to fade the ball around a tree

Once he was in position over the ball, he didn't hesitate. John immediately began his smooth and powerful swing. His club made impact with the usual force. The sound made at impact was that special one associated with the moment when a good player strikes the ball. It is one of the greatest sounds in golf. It wasn't the sweet spot of a nice persimmon, but it was the modern-day version of pure. I looked forward to it every time John addressed a ball.

The ball took off sailing straight down the right side of the fairway. As it neared the dogleg the ball began to fade. Suddenly, it became apparent that the fade began too soon.

"Get through there, damn it!" yelled John.

The ball clipped a branch and veered slightly left into the high grass. It was about 50 yards short of the green.

"That's one beer," said Nate.

18 Holes of Green

"Don't drink it just yet," answered John calmly.

I knew he could do it. I've seen him put a drive on the green before. He had hit that ball well. If it weren't for catching the tree, I think he would have made it. I looked back at the first green and Al and Charlie were still standing on the side of it going over their scorecard. The group behind them was now about 100 yards out waving and shouting at them. I could see two balls just in front of the green and one over it. I guess the fourth had decided to wait for them.

"They still haven't noticed that I'm gone," I said.

"Shut up," said John in disbelief.

"No, I'm serious," I replied.

"You mean they don't know you're over here yet," asked Nate.

"Apparently not," I answered.

"I guess it's not surprising," said John. "Hell, they don't even see the group behind them."

"I couldn't wait for someone to add up their score beside the green," said Nate. "I would have to hit into 'em."

"They wouldn't notice. Unless, you hit them on the head," I said.

John stared out at the hole. "I can't believe a little branch like that stopped the ball," he said.

"That was no branch," said Nate. "That was a leaf that stopped your weak little drive."

"Go to hell," replied John.

John teed up another ball. He was determined to reach the green.

"Going out of turn, now are we, John?" asked Nate.

"Hey, if you were ready," answered John. "You could have gone, but you're too busy watching Al and Charlie. He addressed the ball with the same smooth motions that he always displayed. Then he swung with a picture-perfect swing. The ball flew high and straight down the middle. It made it past the tree on the dogleg and then began to fade.

This ball had the distance, but it didn't quite fade enough. It ended up behind the left side of the green.

"That's two beers," said Nate.

"Fucking tree," said John as he picked up his tee and walked back to the cart.

I looked back and saw Al and Charlie finally making their way toward two's tee. I imagine that they had forgotten all about me by now.

"Now that the stage is set, allow me boys," said Nate.

He took his driver and stepped onto the tee. He had a quick and awkward way about his address. It was as though he were dealing cards and trying to hide something. Immediately, he made his swing. It was flat and abrupt as usual. The ball sailed down the left side of the fairway and sliced back into the middle. The ball looked to be about 50 yards short of the green. Not bad considering it was a lucky slice.

"Good thing it sliced," said John.

"Slice? What the hell are you talking about? It faded just the way I wanted it to," said Nate.

"It was a slice," I said.

"You're full of shit too," said Nate. "It was a fade."

"When the ball starts out heading for the left rough and comes back to the middle of the fairway, it's a slice," said John.

"Either way, it's in the fairway," I said.

"Yeah, sitting pretty," said Nate.

"And you're pressing," I said.

"Hoochie coochie," recited Nate in a high a pitched squeal. Nate was obsessed with betting. He thrived on it.

18 Holes of Green

"You gonna hit, Bri, or are you still in pain?" asked John.

"My chest is still sore, but I'll give it a shot," I replied.

"If you want to sue Al, I'm available," said Nate.

"For what? His gold tooth," said John.

"Yeah, really," I said as I grabbed my driver and walked onto the tee. As, I bent over to tee up the ball, I could feel the bruise on my chest. I straightened up and stepped back a little bit. I took a few practice swings to see what it would feel like. I felt some pain at the top of my backswing, but I was pretty sure that I could handle it. I addressed the ball and relaxed. I didn't have any swing thoughts in mind. I was just worried about being able to swing.

As I took the club back, I decided to try to shorten up my swing. Besides the fact that I usually over swing, I was hoping to keep it as painless as possible. It was one of those shots, where I could feel that it was solid, but I never saw the ball.

"Where'd it go?" I asked.

"Ought to be about ten yards short of mine, Bri," said Nate.

"Didn't hurt too badly," I said. "Next time I won't hold back."

They both laughed at me.

"One more shot at the green, Nathan," said John. "Double or nothing."

"That's fine," said Nate. "I am pretty thirsty."

"So am I," said John as he walked onto the tee one more time. He bent over and attempted to tee his ball up on the end of a pencil. I've done it before, when I was goofing around. I had a feeling he was about to try something new though.

Timothy McHugh

He finally got his ball to balance on the pencil. It was about an inch or so higher than a normal tee.

"What the hell are you doing?" asked Nate. "I'm going over the tree," said John.

The tree that guarded the dogleg was wide, but not exceptionally tall. I couldn't fly it, but John sure had the power to. It looked funny to see the ball teed up so high. Part of his difficulty would be simply getting the clubface to meet the ball at such an odd height. John took his usual address, but stood a little farther away from the ball. I also noticed that he had choked up just a hair on his driver. He swung as smoothly as ever and the ball soared high up into the air. It headed straight toward the tree.

"It's over," said John.

"It sure is," I replied as the ball cleared the tree with about 25 feet to spare. I had never seen a drive that high before. It had the distance as well. John's ball hit in front of the green and rolled up onto the right side.

"Holy shit," gasped Nate.

"I guess we're even on the beers now, huh?" said John.

"That's all right. You earned it," answered Nate.

We all walked off the tee and I strapped my bag onto the back of their cart. We looked like a bunch of hillbillies with three bags on our cart. Their cart did not have a windshield so I took a seat on the front ledge of the cart in front of Nate. I rested my feet on the bumper and grabbed the steering column with my left hand and the right roof support with my right hand.

"Hang on Bri," said John as he gassed the cart.

18 Holes of Green

Where is the seventh tee?

I tightened my grip on the cart and hoped for the best, as we headed for John's first ball. It was somewhere in the high grass on the left.

"It should be a little short of mine," said Nate.

"We'll see," said John as he steered the cart into the rough.

We were driving slowly through the tall stuff. I had a pretty good view, sitting on the front of the cart. The thick grass and weeds could easily swallow a ball. I had let go of the steering column and roof support to get a better view. I was hunched over staring at the ground as we rolled through the tall grass.

Then, without warning, John slammed on the brakes. I fell off the front of the cart and tumbled onto the ground.

"I found it," said John.

I pulled myself to my hands and knees and spit out some grass.

"Thanks for the warning," I said.

"Sorry man," replied John.

"You Okay, Bri?" asked Nate.

"Well, now I've got a sprained wrist to go with my bruised chest," I answered.

John backed the cart out of his way and I managed to climb to my feet. That was when I noticed a cart about 30 yards to the right of the green, but I didn't see anybody in it.

"Hey guys, what's with that cart up there by the green?" I asked.

John stopped looking into his bag and Nate looked up from his beer.

"That wasn't there when we teed off was it?" asked Nate in a confused tone.

"I certainly didn't see it," said John who was now less certain than normal.

"I think I see someone," I said as a person came walking out of the woods. He was wearing a tank top and athletic shorts.

"Looks like one of the maintenance guys," said Nate.

"I don't recognize him. Do you, John?" I asked.

"No, he doesn't look familiar," John responded.

"What? You two know all the maintenance workers?" asked Nate.

"Yeah, I think we do," answered John.

Then, a second person came out of the woods carrying a club. He was wearing a tee shirt and denim shorts.

"Looks like they're playing," I said.

They got in their cart, which was facing towards us. When they turned around, it revealed that they had only one bag strapped on the back of the cart. They then drove to the complete opposite side of the green and parked. They certainly weren't playing ready golf.

18 Holes of Green

"Oh this is just great," said Nate.

"I can't believe someone let them on the course with only one set of clubs," said John. "Who's the starter, Brian?"

"I think it's Mort," I said.

"That figures," he replied.

John's ball was sitting up somewhat. It certainly could have been worse considering where he was. The two guys in front of us were still standing on the left side of the green. Then, the one in the tank top seemed to make a flailing motion with his arms. At first I thought he was waving us through, but then I saw a ball go skipping across the green.

"Damn, we're gonna be here all day," said Nate.

After the tank top hit his chip shot, they both got back into their cart and began driving back toward us.

"Maybe they're going to let us play through," I said. However, they stopped about 30 yards in front of the green. The guy in Denim shorts got out and began making practice swings.

"This is fucking ridiculous," said Nate.

"It's never a good sign when you see the group in front of you heading back toward you," I commented.

"Yeah, you just can't get a decent round of golf in anymore," said John. "I bet they pick my ball up too."

"Oh, I hope so," said Nate.

After each of them hit a couple of more times, they appeared to be on the green. They batted their balls around on the green for a while like it was a hockey rink. Finally, they got them in the hole. They put the flag back in the hole and began walking back to their cart which was still parked 30 yards in front of the green.

"I wish I had taken a video of that," said John as he grabbed his wedge out of his bag.

"Yeah, it probably would make America's Funniest Home Videos," I said.

We settled down and John tried to regain his composure. After going through his normal routine, John hit a nice wedge onto the green. It stopped about two feet short of the hole.

"Good shot," Nate and I said in unison. I climbed back onto the front of the cart and held on as we rode on to John's other balls. We picked them up and headed to Nate's drive and mine. Nate had gotten past me by about nine or ten feet. I was pretty satisfied just being in the middle of the fairway though.

We both managed to hit the green. I was about 20 feet from the hole and Nate was about 25. In a brief demonstration of putting skill, Nate and I each two putted for par. John sank his two-footer for birdie. As we were walking off the green, we were surprised to see that the twosome in front of us was already off the tee.

"At least they've picked it up a little," I said.

"We're still going to have to wait," said John.

Nate tossed his ball onto the ground in front of the cart.

"Closest to the left tee marker for a dollar," he suggested. He couldn't go ten minutes without betting on something.

"Why not? We're not going anywhere," said John.

"Which set of tee markers?" I asked.

"Which set are we playing from?" asked Nate sarcastically.

"The blue," I answered.

"Well then," urged Nate.

"Yeah, OK," I said.

18 Holes of Green

It was about 25 yards from where Nate had dropped his ball to the sixth tee. Nate pulled out his sand wedge and lined up his shot. He made a nice easy swing and his ball flew high into the air. It came down to the right of the tee and hit the cart path. Then, it took a huge bounce and flew 20 yards past the tee.

"I thought you said we were going for the blue tees," I said to Nate.

"He's just partial to the ladies' tees," said John.

"Funny," replied Nate.

I dropped my ball where Nate had hit from and made a practice swing with my sand wedge. I felt pretty good about the practice swing so I went ahead and swung without any further thought. I hit a nice floater that landed next to the right tee marker and bounced immediately to the left a few feet.

"Good kick," said Nate.

"Say it with some feeling," I replied.

John dropped a ball and pulled out his 58-degree wedge. Without making a practice swing, he hit a little knockdown shot that stopped about five feet short of the left tee marker.

"Short!" shouted Nate in excitement.

"Good line," I said.

"Yeah, you don't get much roll on the tees," said John.

"They are a little hairier than the greens," I replied.

I was pretty satisfied with my shot and so began walking toward the tee. Nate and John rode past me in the cart. After they passed, I heard another cart coming up behind me.

I turned around and saw that it was old Paul coming down the path. Paul never liked to miss out on a round of golf. He pulled up next to me and stopped.

"Looks like you could use a ride," he said.

"Hey, thanks old man," I answered. I walked around and hopped in the cart with him.

"How did you get stuck walking?" he asked.

"Oh, it's a long story," I answered.

He seemed satisfied with that answer. That's what I liked about Paul; he knew when to back off. Except of course, when it came to women. Being a widower, he was sometimes starved for attention. We pulled up to the sixth tee and met Nate and John.

"What do you say there, Pauly?" asked Nate.

"Just following my nose," answered Paul. "I thought I smelled someone being hustled, but I must have been mistaken."

"No. You were right, but I'm the one getting hustled," responded Nate.

"That's a switch," said Paul.

"Isn't it though?" commented John.

"A welcome change," I added.

Nate walked toward his ball with a sand wedge in hand. John and I walked onto the tee to compare our shots. It appeared to both of us that I was closest.

"Brian got me," announced John.

"Good. I can't stand losing to you," said Nate as he knocked his ball back towards us with his wedge.

"You ought to be used to it by now," said John.

"What's the game?" asked Paul.

"Well John and I had a game, but I'm up for something new," said Nate.

"I'll bet you are," said John.

"I've got a game," said Paul. "How about if we play a three-man scramble straight up against John," he said.

"That's fine with me," said John.

18 Holes of Green

"Sounds good to me," said Nate. "A dollar a hole."

"John pays each of us?" I asked.

"Or the three of you pay me," he said.

"That's cool," I said.

It sounded like a fair bet to me. We were decent enough players that we ought to be able to beat him in a scramble I thought. The twosome in front of us was about 150 yards out. We stood on the tee and watched them zig-zag back and forth across the fairway. They weren't moving quickly. Finally, they were out of range.

"Mr. closest to the tee marker, you're up," said Nate.

I felt pretty good as I grabbed my driver. There wasn't much pressure in going first in a scramble. Number six is a par 4 that is almost identical to number five. It's another dogleg right, but slightly downhill and a little longer at 385 yards. I teed up my ball and took a practice swing. There was a little pain from my bruised chest, but nothing serious. I was more worried about my wrist pain.

I addressed the ball and began my swing. As I took the club back, I suddenly got one of those mid-swing thoughts that you should never listen to. For some reason, I worried that I was lined up too far to the left. As a result, I attempted to compensate on my downswing by following through a little to the right.

Naturally, my thoughts sparked disaster. It was one of the most wicked slices I had ever seen. My ball flew deep into the woods. Judging by the sounds we heard, it bounced off of a half dozen trees. I could feel the bruise on my chest throbbing now.

"What the hell was that?" asked Nate.

"That's what you call a slice," I answered.

"Yeah, you ought to know all about those, Nate," said John.

"That's OK," said Paul. "We only need one good one."

"I felt a little more pain on that one," I said as I felt my chest.

"What from?" asked Paul.

"First, Al Harper hit me with a ball and then I sprained my wrist when John slammed on the brakes."

"I hope you hit Al back," said Paul.

"I felt like it."

"Go ahead Paul. You're Mr. Automatic," said Nate.

Paul was one of the most consistent golfers I knew. He didn't hit the ball far, but he usually hit it straight.

He grabbed his homemade Golfsmith driver and settled in on the tee. He had a lot of funny quirks about his movements. He wiggled his hips a little and stretched his arms way out to the ball. Because of his belly, Paul stood kind of far from the ball.

"Come on now babe, let's go straight for old Paul now," he said to the ball.

He took the club back with his entire body and swung through almost spinning on his feet. The ball flew straight for about 180 yards and then rolled for another 20.

"Good thing you don't wear soft spikes," said John. "You would have fallen on your ass."

"Soft spikes are for pansies," said Paul.

We all laughed. Paul was one of the only guys I knew who still wore metal spikes. Sure, a lot of the birdie hunters wore them, but I never thought of Paul as one of them. He kept a pair of shoes with soft spikes for the rare occasion that he played somewhere else, but at White Lake he wore metal spikes.

"Not bad Pauly," said Nate as he walked onto the tee with his driver.

18 Holes of Green

"Yeah, now you can really go for it," said Paul.

Nate addressed the ball and made his usual quick swing. His ball was hit hard. It flew straight and high toward the corner of the dog leg. It narrowly missed a large tree, but caught some leaves of another one.

"Looked like it got through," I said.

"Think so?" asked Nate.

"Yeah, it got through, but you might not have a shot," said Paul.

The fairway sloped downward toward the right side of the fairway. His ball looked like it went into the gully just before the woods.

John walked over and teed up a ball. He hit an impressive drive down the middle. His ball stopped about 50 or 60 yards short of the green.

"Nice shot," I told him.

"Thanks," he answered.

I never had a problem being intimidated by John. We were too close for that.

"Onward boys," said Nate.

We hopped in our carts and sped off toward our balls. Paul began asking me about my bruise as we were riding. So, I proceeded to tell him about my experience playing with Al and Charlie.

"I learned a long time ago not to go near those two on a golf course," said Paul. "I thought I told you that."

"You did. I never thought to listen to you though."

"I've learned a few things over my many years, Brian," he said.

"Yeah, I guess maybe you have."

Nate and John headed for Paul's ball and we made a pass by the woods to look for mine. We looked for about 15 seconds before I declared it impossible.

"Don't worry about it. It's no big loss," I said.

"They'll make more," Paul replied.

We headed out to Paul's ball, where John and Nate were waiting for us.

Nate's ball was a lot farther, but it would be a much more difficult shot.

"Is your ball playable, Nathan?" asked Paul.

"Yeah, but I think we oughta go with yours."

"It's about 200 from here. Don't you think we'd have a better chance at the green from closer up?" I asked.

"I think we probably would," said Paul.

"All right, but I don't want to hear any complaints about my tee shot," said Nate.

With that, we picked up Paul's ball and headed toward Nate's.

"Don't feel bad old man, it was a good drive," I said to Paul as we were riding in the cart.

"Compared to yours it was," said Paul.

"That's the last time I try to make you feel better," I responded.

"It's not looking good for us on this hole," said Paul.

"With your short game, we've always got a chance."

"I thought you weren't gonna try to make me feel better anymore," he said.

"I can't help it; I've got a soft spot for ya old man."

We arrived at Nate's ball as he was surveying the situation. His ball had gotten through the trees, but we had an uphill lie because of the gully. We could just barely see the top of the flag stick.

"Oh, yeah. This is a much better position for you guys to be in," said John.

"Screw you. I suggested we use Paul's ball," said Nate.

18 Holes of Green

The twosome was on the green by now, knocking their balls around. We waited patiently, but it was frustrating. John walked up the hill, to the middle of the fairway, to get a better view.

"How far do you think we are?" I asked. "I'd say about 120," said Nate.

"Sounds like an eight iron for me," said Paul.

Nathan and I began rummaging through our bags trying to decide what to hit. Paul was always more decisive. He stuck a tee in the ground next to Nate's ball and flipped it back to him.

We waited a few minutes. Paul moved his feet around trying to get a good stance on the uphill lie.

Then, John yelled down that it was all clear.

Paul addressed his ball and gave it some words of encouragement. He made his trademark swing, flinging his body towards the target. His ball took off like a rocket.

"Be the one baby," yelled Nate as the ball sailed toward the flag stick.

"You're on," declared John who was standing at the top of the hill as a lookout.

"Good shot Pauly," said Nate.

"Yeah, not bad old man," I said.

"Thanks guys," replied Paul modestly.

"How close is he?" yelled Nate.

"He's on the back of the green," answered John.

"All right. Let's see if I can get a little closer," said Nate.

I doubted it, but I didn't say anything. I knew better than to try to argue with Nate.

He dropped his ball next to the tee and adjusted his feet to the slope. Then he made his typical spastic swing. It sounded awful when he made contact. The ball flew low and sliced hard.

"Man, that hurt me just listening to it," said Paul.

"Believe me, it hurt," said Nate.

"Shanks usually do," I said.

"That was not a shank," said Nate defensively.

"Hey John, would you call that a shank?" I asked.

"I don't know what else you would call it," he said.

"Whatever," mumbled Nate.

He wasn't one to admit to a shank or anything else. It wasn't that he was cocky; I think he just liked to argue.

I took my eight-iron and dropped a ball. As I addressed the ball I couldn't seem to get comfortable on the hill. I put the ball towards the front of my stance and took some practice swings.

I kept stubbing the club into the ground behind the ball. So, I tried opening my stance and playing the ball off of my front foot.

Now, I was able to brush the grass. I moved forward to the ball and prepared to swing. As I took the club back, I felt my body fall back away from the ball.

My club barely caught the top of the ball. It went skipping over the hill. I fell backwards down the hill and almost fell over.

"Shit," I said.

"That's OK Bri. We've got one on the green," said Nate. We got in our carts and rode up to John's ball. He was already standing behind his ball surveying his shot.

He had about 63 yards to the green. It was slightly downhill. He pulled out a sand wedge and made a practice swing. I loved to watch his swing. With ease John put his ball five feet to the left of the pin.

18 Holes of Green

"Well, it took a pro to get inside me," said Paul. We all laughed as we got back in our carts.

When we got to the green, it was obvious we had a tough putt ahead of us.

Paul's ball was at the very back of the green. The hole was some 30 feet away, in the front center. There appeared to be two different breaks between the ball and the hole.

John, on the other hand, had a simple straight away five-footer.

We elected Paul to go last since he was the best putter in the group. He'd been putting on those greens for 40 years. Hopefully he would learn something from our putts.

Nate went first. He had a simple shoulder oriented putting stroke that usually worked. He had the right distance but the second break was more than he had allowed for. His ball ended up six feet to the right.

"You guys are gonna have to do better than that," said John.

I lined up, taking into account the severity of the second break. Unfortunately, I paid less attention to the distance. I knew that it was 30 feet, but I ignored the downhill factor. My ball rolled two inches to the right of the hole and kept on going. It stopped about 10 feet past the hole.

"If I could just combine your two putts," said Paul.

"Show him what experience can do," said Nate.

Paul lined up his putt and made a practice swing. His putting motion was an old fashioned all wrist movement.

He struck the ball and it rolled perfectly through the breaks. It first moved left and then back to the right stopping three inches short of the hole.

"Nice putt," I said.

"Too bad. You guys almost got me," said John.

John replaced his ball as Paul tapped his in. He took a moment to line up his putt and then addressed the ball. He made a smooth stroke and rolled the ball straight into the hole.

"I save us a par and he has to birdie the damn hole," said Paul.

"That's life," said John.

"We can't even beat him in a scramble," I said in frustration.

"It's not over yet," said Nate.

"Really. You guys lose one hole and you're ready to throw in the towel," said John.

He was right. We still had a chance to beat him. After all, it was three against one.

"What the hell are those idiots doing?" asked Paul suddenly.

I looked over and saw the twosome riding back towards us from the woods. Number seven, the next hole, was to the left, but they were riding all over directly behind six green.

"Looks like they're joy riding," said John.

"Yeah, they are," said Nate.

They drove up close to us and kind of looked all over the place. We were baffled.

Then, one of them pointed toward the fourth tee and they drove in that direction. They stopped about halfway to the tee.

"Maybe they lost a club," suggested John.

"Hell, at their pace they could at least be halfway to seven green by now," said Nate. "This is bull shit."

"Maybe they'll let us play through," said Paul.

"They wouldn't even know what that means," said John.

18 Holes of Green

"Maybe we could find another hole to go to," I suggested.

"The course looked pretty full to me," said Paul.

It was then that it dawned on me what they were doing. They began driving toward the fourth tee again.

"They're lost," I said.

"You're right, they are lost," said John.

"Good call, Bri," said Nate.

When they reached four's tee, they got out and prepared to tee off.

"They're playing the wrong hole," said Paul.

"What morons," said Nate. "They already played that hole."

"This is perfect," I said. "We've got an open hole now."

"It's too perfect," said John.

"Don't question miracles, John," said Paul.

We all agreed to accept our good fortune and headed toward number seven.

I'll admit that the seventh tee isn't the easiest to find. There's a tree line that hides the hole. You can't see the tee from the sixth green, but they already played number four. It should have looked a little familiar to them. I wasn't going to complain though. It was nice to have them out of the way. We reached the seventh tee, and the hole was completely empty.

"This is what the game is all about," said Paul.

"It is a beautiful sight," I added.

"However, I could go for a drink of water," said Paul who was now staring at what used to be a drinking fountain.

"That is a shame to lose those nice fountains," commented John.

"It's criminal and stupid," replied Paul. "That Cunningham has finally pushed things too far."

"Yeah, he's gone from an annoying nuisance to a sinister villain," I replied.

"He is a villain," added Mark. "He's the evil mastermind out to destroy municipal golf as we know it."

"Somebody has to stop him," continued Paul.

"Have a beer Pauly," said Nate.

"Not while playing," answered Paul. "But I will grab some ice cubes from your cooler."

Paul never drank on the golf course. I suppose that was why he always played so consistently. He did however enjoy a glass of wine from his stash in the clubhouse.

"I'm just glad we got around that twosome," I said.

"They're gonna be stuck in a loop," said John. "They'll be playing four, five and six all day."

"I always wondered why caddies called a round a loop," said Nate.

"You really had to wonder about that?" asked John.

"A round, a loop, out, in," I asked. "None of that reminds you of a loop?"

"A looper," commented John. "A pro jock."

"Big hitter that Lama," I added.

"They use Lama's to carry your bags down under," commented Paul who never got our Caddy Shack references.

"Time is a wasting boys," said Nate.

"I'll give you all something to shoot for," said John.

The seventh hole is a straight-away 460-yard par five. A good chance for us to make birdie.

John hit his usual impressive drive and was on in two. We ended up using a nice drive by Nate and my second shot, which was about ten feet short of the green. Paul chipped up five inches from the cup. We let him tap it in for our birdie.

18 Holes of Green

John two-putted from 15 feet for birdie as well. With our three-man scramble team down by a stroke, we moved on to number eight.

Number eight is a 394-yard par four. There wasn't anything difficult about it.

John made a solid par. We pulled out a birdie, with a beautiful one-putt by Paul. We moved on to the ninth hole even with John.

"I think I'll play this hole Moe Norman style," said John. Moe Norman was a legendary Canadian professional who is said to have been the greatest ball striker that ever lived. He reportedly had played holes by teeing off with a wedge and hitting a driver on his second shot.

"What are you gonna tee off with?" I asked.

"Well, this is kind of a long par four," he said. "I think I'll try a nine iron."

Number nine is a 420 yard par four that runs in along the driving range and bends a little right toward the clubhouse.

"Let's double the bet between us," said Nate.

He couldn't resist the opportunity to increase the stakes.

"That's fine," said John as he walked onto the tee with his nine-iron.

He dropped his ball onto the ground and addressed it. With a picture perfect short-iron swing, he knocked the ball 150 yards straight down the middle.

"Not a bad little shot," said Nathan.

"I'm gonna quit this game if you beat us on this hole," said Paul as he walked onto the tee with his driver.

He hit a simple drive about 200 yards down the middle.

Nate and I hit similar drives cutting the corner down the right side of the fairway and well past Paul.

"I think I might have gotten you on that one, Nate," I said.

"I wouldn't be too sure about that, young Brian," he replied.

"Well, I know it's the first time I've ever out-driven John on a hole," said Paul.

"You sure did," said John.

Paul really did play well for a 72-year-old man. He deserved some encouragement.

We got in our carts and headed down the fairway. The driving range, on our left, was beginning to fill up. I could see Harley out in the Jeep picking balls and Andy giving a lesson on the grass tee.

We arrived at John's ball. After his 150-yard nine iron, he had 270 yards left to the green. He took out his driver and made a few practice swings.

Then, in his usual manner, he struck the ball with tremendous force. The ball flew straight and low. It bounced about 35 or 40 yards in front of the green and rolled all the way up and on. The ball appeared to stop about ten feet from the hole.

"Eat your heart out, Moe Norman," said John.

"I think you rotate too much to swing like Moe Norman," said Paul.

I was amazed at how well he hit a driver off the ground. I had enough trouble hitting my three-wood off the ground. I couldn't believe he got it on the green, let alone off the fairway.

We rode on to Paul's ball. I hated to see him pick up such a nice drive.

"Why don't you play this ball just for fun," I suggested.

18 Holes of Green

"No. I don't want to mess around when there's money involved," he responded.

Paul picked up his ball, and we headed toward mine and Nate's balls. As it turned out, I out-drove him by seven feet or so.

Because my ball had luckily stayed in the fairway as it cut the corner, it was only 160 yards to the green.

As so frequently happens after I hit a good drive, I screwed up the next shot. It was a chunk that went only 20 yards. The divot went 30.

"That's OK, Bri," said Nate. "You got us this far. I'll get us on and Paul will sink the putt."

"Sounds good to me," I said.

Ironically, Nate pushed his shot way right and Paul hit the green with one of his homemade seven woods.

Nate stormed off to his cart mumbling about his shot. I thought we were doing pretty well, but he always beat himself up over his bad shots.

Paul and I followed them in our cart towards the green. He was feeling pretty good about himself.

"Not bad for an old man," I kidded him.

"I've always had a lot of luck with that club," he said. "I'll have to make one for you."

"That would be great," I said.

I couldn't turn down his generosity. I still had some room at home with all the other clubs he had made me.

We picked up all of our stray balls and arrived at the green. John was seven or eight feet to the right of the hole and Paul's ball was ten feet short.

"You better putt first, Nate," said Paul. "You're getting kind of wild on us."

"Wild?" he whined. "I am not getting wild, am I Brian?" "

No way," I answered. "But maybe you oughta go first just the same."

Nate rolled his ball within three feet. "Good try," I said.

"Wasn't too wild for you was it?" he responded.

I, on the other hand, left my putt a good five feet short.

"Hike up that skirt next time, OK Brian," said Paul.

I swatted my ball out of the way and shrugged it off. Paul lined up his putt and begged his ball for help. "Come on babe. Go in one time for old Paul."

He rolled the ball to just three inches right of the hole.

"Not too shabby from that distance," said John.

We let Paul tap it in for our par. John picked up his ball marker and set down his ball. He took a moment or two to get his line. Then slowly he addressed the ball.

He hit the putt a little hard, but it caught the center of the hole and dropped in.

"Slam dunk," said Nate.

"Good putt. You earned that birdie," I said.

Even though we lost to John, I had a lot of fun. I still had my bruised chest and a sore wrist, but that would get better. I wasn't as confident in my swing.

As we pulled up to the clubhouse to settle our bets, Leo, the ranger, came over.

"You guys will get a kick out of this," Leo said.

"What happened?" asked Paul.

"I was out riding around, checking on things," he explained. "I got to number five's tee and noticed that there were six people on the tee."

"A sixsome?" I asked.

"No, it turned out that a twosome in a cart, with one bag mind you, cut in front of the foursome on number four,"

18 Holes of Green

he continued. "Not only did they cut in front of the foursome, but they held them up the entire hole. But the funny part was that one of the fellows claimed that the guys in the foursome had hit into them on number five while they were approaching the green."

I looked at John and Nate, who were trying not to laugh as Leo continued the story.

"So I asked them, if they were hit into while approaching the fifth green, what were they doing on five's tee?"

The four of us burst into laughter, but we urged Leo to go on.

"As it turned out, they thought they were standing on the eighth tee. I finally figured out that they missed the turn off to number seven and accidentally got onto four instead. Obviously, the group behind them got pissed and must have hit into them. So, I escorted them over to seven and suggested they try the par-three course next time."

"You're a hell of a man, Leo," said John.

"They were clueless," said Leo. "But it was strange, they were convinced that someone had hit into them the first time they played number five. What's even funnier is that they claim the guy hit into them from five's tee as they approached the green. That's too big a poke for anyone around here. I guess they're just nuts."

"Must be," said John.

Leo was about to drive away, but then he stopped and turned back to us.

"Oh yeah, I almost forgot the big news," said Leo. "There was a gator sighting."

"Someone saw Vader?" I asked.

"Yeah, and you know I might have as well," answered Leo.

Timothy McHugh

"Where was he?" asked John.

"Well, while I was watching those yahoos on four, I was parked by the edge of the woods next to number five," said Leo. "A group on five approached me and said they saw him while they were on number four. They claim that while they walked toward the woods to look for a ball, what they thought was a log on the ground began crawling into the woods. I tried to find out more but they apparently didn't stick around to see where he went."

"I don't blame them," said Paul.

"Were they drinking?" asked Nate.

"No, it was two married couples," answered Leo. "They seemed pretty credible."

"I still don't believe it," responded Nate.

"What did you mean when you said that you might have seen Vader as well?" asked John.

"Well, before I stumbled across those yahoos, I was looking for balls from the maintenance path that goes through the woods," said Leo.

It was more like he was taking a nap back there, I thought to myself. Leo was notorious for taking naps while on duty.

"So, I see what looks like a bright, shiny Nike lying on top of some leaves," he continued. "I get out of the cart and walk passed a couple of trees to take a look at it. As I get closer, all of a sudden, a wild turkey springs out of the brush and starts carrying on and squawked at me. I figured that I was a little too close to its nest and trying to defend its eggs, but that Nike looked unblemished. So I quickly stepped forward, bent down and grabbed the ball. As soon as I did, the thing charged me. I haven't run that fast since I saw 50,000 Chinese coming over the hill in Korea."

18 Holes of Green

We all broke into laughter, but then John tried to get back to the point.

"What about Vader," he asked.

"When I got back to the cart, I turned back to see if the turkey was still chasing me. But it had stopped after a few feet and seemed to be flapping and squawking at a log on the ground. I didn't think anything of it until those folks on five told me about the log that crawled away."

"I guess that turkey was more worried about the gator than it was you," said Paul.

"And the Gator was more interested in the turkey than you," said John.

"Yeah, you were lucky," I said.

"More like bad luck," said Leo. "The Nike had a big cut on it."

Timothy McHugh

Night Golf

I had no idea of what was to come when we decided to start a night-golf tournament at White Lake. It started out innocently enough. Mark and I read about a night-golf charity tournament in Golf Digest. The concept immediately excited us both. I loved playing at dusk, and the idea of playing at night sounded even better. We weren't even interested in a tournament at first. We just wanted to go out and try it ourselves. It sounded like a blast. If for no other reason, it would be a chance to play without the nuisance of other golfers being on the course.

Within 15 minutes we had ordered ourselves a dozen glow balls and two dozen glow sticks online. Andy thought we were nuts.

The balls arrived on a Friday afternoon. John and I were closing the course together. Mark was giving lessons down at the range. We were like kids on Christmas morning, anxious to play with our new toys. As John opened the box, I was surprised at their strange appearance.

"They're clear," I said.

"What'd you expect?" asked John as if I was a moron.

"I'm not sure, but I guess it makes sense."

18 Holes of Green

John just laughed at me. He dropped a couple of them on the carpet and grabbed his sand wedge. We began putting and chipping with them behind the counter.

"Boy, these things are hard as rocks," I said.

"Yeah, I gotta get used to their feel. The short game is gonna be the secret," he said.

He and Mark were planning a money game. Both of them were habitual gamblers. They couldn't even play golf in the dark without betting on it.

We needed a fourth, so naturally John called Nate Boylan. If anybody would be interested, it would be Nate. He had an appetite for the unusual.

It was about 8:00 pm when things started winding down at the course. Mark had finished his last lesson, and we only had two more golf carts out.

Oscar, our starter, was on his way in with the score cards and tee sheet.

"We're almost there, Brian. Almost in the barn," he said as he entered the pro shop. "Hell, even the editor in chief over there is getting ready to leave," he laughed in reference to news junkie Fred.

Fred had been there all day, and we didn't hear much from him. Must have been a slow news day.

"Did John tell you what we're doing tonight," I asked him.

"Yeah. You boys are crazy. Playing golf at night. Shit."

It was then that Nate Boylan arrived. Oscar and I could see him walking towards the door.

"Now I know you're crazy," said Oscar. "You invited that crazy-ass boy."

"He's harmless," I said.

"He's a crazy-ass nut."

I laughed in acknowledgment. There was some truth to the statement.

The pro shop door swung open and in came Nate, lugging a full size cooler.

"What say there, Brian?" asked Nate.

"Not much, stranger. How you doing?"

"Shitty. Just finished three weeks of depositions, man."

"Bummer," I said.

"Yeah, bummer," he said. "I haven't seen the outside of my house in three weeks, and the first time you dick-heads ask me to play golf, it's in the fuckin' dark."

"We think it's best if you don't come around during the daylight hours," said Oscar. "Wouldn't want you to scare anyone."

"Well, hello Oscar," responded Nate. "Where've you been hiding?"

"I ain't been hiding," said Oscar. Been in the same place for 17 years. Getting folks off this tee. You the one who ain't been around for three weeks. At least you showed up with a cooler full of beer."

"I never go anywhere empty handed," said Nate.

"Shit," said Oscar as he turned around laughing to himself.

"I'm impressed, you remembered the beer," I said to Nate.

"I don't forget the necessities," he said as he set the cooler down behind the counter.

"Well, are you gonna share 'em or keep them all to yourself?" I asked.

"Relax; I've got you one here. Where's Mark?" asked Nate.

"He's still down at the range."

18 Holes of Green

He handed me a beer.

"You guys got the balls?" he asked.

"Yeah, I'll get you one," I answered as I reached into the box.

"One? I'm gonna need a couple."

"Just take one for now," I said to him. "We've got extras."

"What about flashlights?" he asked.

"I'm sure we can find some."

"What you all need is some bug spray," said Oscar. "They gonna eat you up tonight."

"Oh yeah. Good call, Oscar," I said.

"Definitely," said Nate.

"I think we have an open can in the back," I said.

"Yeah...we got some," Oscar mumbled as he walked back outside.

"Oscar never changes," said Nate.

"He's cool to work with," I said. "I just stay out of his way and he gets everybody off the tee on time."

I tossed Nate a glow ball and he checked it out.

He got a funny look on his face and turned to me. He looked puzzled.

"There's...a hole in it?"

"You slide a glow stick in it," I said slowly.

"That's how it glows?" asked Nate.

"That's how it glows," I said.

"Alright," he said excitedly. "Let's see how this baby rolls on a green."

"John's got a head start on you. He's out on the course with one now."

"He oughta be on the practice green," said Nate as he smiled and walked out the door.

Timothy McHugh

I rummaged through the drawers in the back room for a few minutes before I found a bottle of bug spray, almost full. That would help.

It was getting dark quickly. The last foursome with carts was now on 18 green. Oscar was anxiously awaiting them by the starter's table.

I was closing out the cash register. After about 15 minutes, I finished counting the money. It was then that I began to hear shouts and laughter coming from outside. I put the money in the safe and walked out to see what was going on.

It turned out that Mark had joined Nate on the putting green. They were putting for quarters.

"Is it dark enough yet, Brian?" asked Nate.

"Is that a question you really need to ask?" said Mark.

"I think we need just a little more time," I said.

"Besides, you obviously need a little more practice," said Mark as he picked their balls out of the hole.

"I haven't left the house in three weeks, and now you want to take my money," responded Nate.

"Well, yeah. Two more quarters and I can get a car wash," Mark answered.

I laughed and walked out to the green. "How's the glow ball roll?" I asked.

"Well, you have to place the ball so the hole running through it is vertical," said Mark. "Otherwise, it'll be lopsided."

"It rolls kind of goofy either way I think," said Nate.

"Not if the hole is vertical," said Mark.

"Let's see you putt one," I said.

"Vertical," interjected Nate.

Mark squatted down and adjusted his ball on the green. It would be about a ten-footer.

"It looks lopsided," I said.

18 Holes of Green

He gave me a scathing look, and Nate laughed. Mark then rose to his feet and addressed his ball. He glanced once at the hole and then stroked the ball furiously.

I couldn't believe it. He hit the ball so hard I expected it to go 30 yards past the hole and off the practice green.

Instead, the ball hardly rolled in comparison to his stroke. It slowed down quickly and wobbled unevenly. The ball stopped four inches short and about six inches wide right.

"I thought you killed it," I commented.

"Oh, yeah. You have to hit it a lot harder, Bri" said Mark.

"I guess so," I replied.

"It still rolled goofy," said Nate.

"Yeah, it was a little squirrelly," I added.

"Where the hell is John?" asked Mark.

"He's still out there I guess."

"It's almost dark enough," said Nate.

"Yeah, I'm gonna go in and grab a beer," I said.

"Sounds good after four beginner lessons in a row," responded Mark.

The three of us walked back to the clubhouse as Oscar was coming out.

"Are we there yet?" I asked him.

"They all in the barn," he said. "That last bunch of factory pros came in when they ran out of beer. They ran out of daylight 20 minutes ago."

"Who needs daylight?" I said.

"Not no crazy fools like you all. I know that."

"Thanks Oscar."

"I'm gone Brian," he said as he walked toward the parking lot.

"See ya Oscar," said Mark.

"'Bye Freddy," said Oscar.

"Freddy?" asked Nate.

"He thinks I look like Couples," explained Mark.

"Hey, yeah you do," said Nate. "I just never noticed it because of your swing."

I laughed and walked inside for another beer. I opened the cooler and heard more laughter as John pulled up in a cart. Surely, he would want a beer as well. In fact, they all would. After briefly fumbling through the cooler attempting to grasp several bottles at once, I put my college education to work and decided to carry the whole cooler outside.

"Alright." said Nate. "Look at Brian."

"Yeah, but don't we have a cooler for each cart?" asked John. "What kind of operation is this?"

"Hey mister, this is the big time," replied Mark.

"Yeah, we've even got bug spray," I said as I set the cooler down on the patio. I began passing out beers and wondered out loud, "Are we gonna play the front or the back?"

"You'll have to ask the starter," said John.

"Not unless you want to piss him off," replied Nate.

Nate and I looked at each other and then recited together our favorite starter's line, "The game of golf begins on the first hole."

"We've got 18 holes of green all to ourselves," said John. "We've got to start on number one."

"Yeah, it's been a while since I've started on the first hole," I said.

"No shit," said Mark. "We never get to play without interruptions anymore."

"Well let's get going then ladies," said Nate.

I carried the cooler over and set it on the passenger side floor of our cart. Mark walked back inside the clubhouse

18 Holes of Green

and gathered up the remaining glow ball paraphernalia. Nate began strapping his bag on the back of John's cart as the lights inside the clubhouse went off. A few moments later, Mark came out carrying a box and locked the door behind him. He carried the box to John's cart and set it in the rear basket. "If we've got the beer cart, you've got the supply cart," he said.

"I think we're getting screwed already," said John. Mark walked toward our cart, where I was standing.

"You need clubs, huh?" he asked.

"Yeah, if you don't mind," I answered.

"Think they'll help you?" he asked.

"Screw you," I said. "Drive me to my car."

We rode out into the parking lot. My car was parked behind the clubhouse next to the dumpster. I quickly kicked off my shoes and opened the rear hatch on my Jeep. There were four shoeboxes in line with several dozen balls. The oldest pair seemed appropriate for the dark. You never know what you might step in out there. I took a drink of my beer and then set it on top of my car. I pulled out my clubs and slammed my Ping stand bag onto the ground. As I sat on my bumper, sliding on an old pair of Foot Joys, Mark thought of Vader.

"I wouldn't want to run into the gator at night," he said.

"I don't think they come out at night," I said.

"What do you mean, they don't come out at night?" he asked. "When do you think they would come out?"

"Well, all the reported sightings have been in the daylight," I said

"That's because there's no one to see him here at night," said Mark.

"Well, I wouldn't worry about it," I replied.

"I'm not worried; I'm just not going in the jungle after any balls in the dark."

"Then don't hit any in there," I said as I strapped my bag onto the cart. I quickly shut my Jeep, grabbed my beer and hopped into the cart. Mark drove us back towards the tee where Nate and John were waiting.

As we approached the tee, I could see John shaking his glowing ball. Its yellow tracer streaked through the darkness. When we stopped, Nate was trying to squeeze a glow stick into the hole in his ball.

"Having some trouble getting it in the hole?" asked Mark.

"My stick is too big for the hole," said Nate

"He's a little excited," said John.

As I ripped open the packet and looked at the glow stick, I doubted its effectiveness. I bent the stick until it snapped. Suddenly, a greenish yellow glow began emanating from its center. I shook the stick a few times, and its glow spread more evenly. I had to admit that it was a tight fit trying to get it inserted in the ball, but I suppose it needs to be tight to stay in there.

"It says to shake it vigorously," suggested John. "You don't want it to stop glowing after you hit it."

"All right, will do," I replied.

Once I had forced the stick all the way into the ball, I joined the others on the tee. They were peering down the fairway into the darkness.

"Hey man, I can't see the green," said John.

"Oh my, that's terrible," I said. "Would you like a rain check?"

"No, I want a refund."

"You better go see the county commissioners," I said.

18 Holes of Green

Mark walked onto the tee next to John.

"You tried them, how far did your drive go?" he asked. "About 75 yards shorter," John answered.

"So, about a hundred," said Nate.

"Fuck you," said John.

"Well, if these balls are that much shorter, we should play from the forward tees," said Mark.

"Don't you always?" asked John.

"Yeah yeah," replied Mark.

"I'm all for it," I said still shaking my ball.

"Ok ladies, let's do the forward tees.

I walked up about 20 yards as the others moved the carts up to join me. I could hear Mark and Nate bantering back and forth. They would be going at each other all night.

"You should have warmed up putting," said Nate. "I've got the groove going with this ball."

"You'll lose it on the first hole," said Mark.

"Tee it up, Bri," said John.

"Yeah, knock it out there," said Mark.

I started to walk to the tee markers, but Nate interrupted me.

"Wait a second fellas," he said. "What kind of game are we playing?"

"I'm playing Mark straight up," said John. "Two bucks a hole."

"That's fine," said Mark. "We oughta have a team game, too, though."

"Ten a man, best ball teams," said Nate. "John and Brian, and me and Mark."

"That's fair," said Mark.

"Ok with you, Bri?" asked John.

"Yeah, fine, as long as we win," I said.

"No problem," said John.

"Our boys are a little cocky," said Nate. "Let's see it, Brian."

I started walking toward the tee markers again. Ten bucks wasn't nothing to me like it was to those guys. I had a pretty good chance though with John as a partner.

I wasn't sure what to expect when I hit the ball. It seemed awfully strange. It was just clear plastic. I teed it up kind of high. I was worried about hitting the ground, since I couldn't see it in the dark very well.

"You oughta balance your glow stick," said Nate.

"I oughta what?"

"Your ball is lopsided," said John.

It took me a second, but then I saw what they were talking about. The glow stick, which runs through the ball, was at an angle. I moved my ball so that the stick was parallel to the ground.

"I think it should be vertical," said Mark.

"I don't think so," said Nate. "You don't want the glow stick rotating end over end. You want it spinning like an axel."

"That would only make sense if your ball was spinning perfectly parallel to the ground, but it doesn't," replied Mark.

"It's physics," said Nate.

"Exactly," said Mark. "And according to physics there would be less room for error if the glow stick was vertical."

"Just so it's straight," said John.

I adjusted my ball to make it vertical, which seemed like the best idea to me. I could almost make out the fairway in between the tree lines. Picking a general area out in the shadows, I swung and seemed to catch it a little thin.

The ball flew low through the air with a nice yellow tracer. It came down about 150 yards out and appeared to roll pretty well.

18 Holes of Green

"Roll baby!" shouted John.

"It's nice and hard out there," I said. "It oughta be ok."

"Hitting it low is the only way to get distance with these things," added Mark.

The ball was just barely visible as a small yellow dot, nearly in the middle of the fairway.

"It's gonna have to be better than OK," said Nate as he walked over and teed up his ball. He had a Cobra driver that he loved dearly.

"At least we can't see how ugly that thing is in the dark," said John.

"I was gonna say the same thing about your face," said Nate. "Watch how positioning the ball on the tee correctly improves the trajectory of the ball."

He placed his ball on the tee with the glow stick horizontal and took his stance.

"Don't let the glow throw you off," said John. "The ball is really an inch lower than you think."

"Oh, OK," said Nate.

He swung quickly like he was trying to kill it. The ball took a sharp right into the trees about 50 yards out.

"That's a definite improvement in the trajectory," said John.

"Damn, that felt weird," said Nate. "Yeah, it looked weird too," I said.

Mark and John laughed. I grabbed another beer out of the cooler and sat down in the cart.

"All right boys, watch how it's done," said John as he teed up his ball.

"A buck says you miss the fairway," said Nate.

"Make it five or it's not worth the effort," said John.

"Five it is," answered Nate.

Timothy McHugh

John set up and made his usual smooth swing. The ball whistled as it streaked through the dark sky with a yellow tracer. It hung for a moment and then dropped down so far past my ball, it couldn't be seen from the tee.

"That's five," said John.

"We'll see when we get there," said Nate.

"You mean after your third shot," said John.

Mark laughed as he walked over to tee his ball.

"You want the same bet?" asked Nate.

"Hell no, I don't know where this thing is going," answered Mark.

"That's nothing new to you," said John.

Mark laughed as he addressed his ball. He hit a liner down the right side.

"That may stay in," I said.

"No, I think it's in the trees," Said John.

"It stayed in," said Mark.

"We'll see," said John as he quickly sat down in his cart. Nate joined him and they sped off.

"Hell of a drive, Bri," said Mark as he walked towards our cart.

"Thanks, but I did catch it thin. I was just trying to make contact."

"That's all you gotta do," he replied

Mark got another beer and sat down next to me. We headed out into the darkness after John and Nate. The cart bounced as we hit ditches and holes that Mark couldn't see in the darkness. Full speed in a golf cart seems a lot faster in the dark.

We narrowly missed a few trees as we tried to find Nate and John. One small branch did manage to catch my head.

"Shit, watch out, man!" I said.

18 Holes of Green

"Sorry," replied Mark. "Where the hell are they?"

"I think they're up farther," I said straining to see them in the shadows ahead.

As I was leaning forward, Mark cut the wheel hard to the left, and I went flying out the right side. I tumbled onto my hands and knees and rolled over once.

Mark stopped when he finished the turn and looked back at me.

"They're back there," he said.

"Oh, I'm fine, thanks," I said to him.

I stood up and brushed off my now grass-stained khaki pants. I got back into the cart, and we headed back through the trees towards the old lake.

Nate and John were standing about 20 yards into the thick tall grass that occupies the old lakebed. They were each smoking a cigarette.

"We wanted you guys to see this," said John. "This is the farthest anyone has ever hit into the jungle without losing their ball."

"Was it sitting up?" asked Mark.

"No, it's down pretty deep," said Nate. "Glows right through that tall shit."

"You can't lose these things," said John.

"I'm sold," I replied. "Better hit it before Vader gets you."

"Take a stroke and drop it out," said Mark.

"Hell no, I'm playing it," said Nate.

"There's no way," said Mark.

"Fuck the stroke," said Nate. He was never one to be conservative. Not your typical attorney.

Nate pulled out his seven Wood. "You're nuts, man," said John.

Nate quickly took his stance and waggled the club a few times.

"Watch out boys," said Nate.

He took a big swing, and the ball flew out low and fast. It stayed under the tree branches and rolled into the fairway.

"Good out," I said.

"You lucky son of a bitch," said John.

"It's not luck, it's balls," said Nate.

"Good shot," said Mark as he turned the cart around.

"You still with me Bri?" he asked.

"Right here."

We headed back through the trees and into the fairway. Nate's ball was right in front of us. Mine was about 30 yards farther in the middle of the fairway. Mark's ball was in the right rough even with my ball. We couldn't see John's ball yet.

It looked strange to see the three yellow balls glowing in the grass. They looked like something out of Star Trek.

Nate still had about 210 yards. The way these balls flew, he didn't have a chance to get there. They were awfully hard, like Pinnacles. Nonetheless, he decided to hit a driver off the fairway.

"You can't get there with these balls," said Mark.

"Watch me," said Nate.

He took a big cut at the ball. You could tell he was trying to kill it.

Nate must have caught it thin because it never got more than 20 feet off the ground. Naturally the ball rolled pretty well, but he was well short of the green.

"You wuss," said John.

18 Holes of Green

Nate yelled back at John and they began to argue. They always argued. We drove on to my ball, and I surveyed the situation. I had about 180 yards, but I would need more club than usual. I pulled out my three-wood and swung it a few times.

"Let's go, while we're young," said Nate from behind me.

"How old are you again?" I asked.

"I'm still young." Replied Nate. "Yeah, OK," I said.

"I am," he said, as I addressed my ball.

I found it easier to focus on the ball for some reason. Maybe it was because the ball was the only thing I could see. With its yellow glow against the dark ground, I could see the ball better than I ever had before.

I smoothly swung concentrating only on the ball, and it flew right at the green.

"Good shot, Bri," yelled John.

The ball landed just in front of the green and appeared to roll up next to the hole. At least I thought so. The flag wasn't exactly visible from where we were. The yellow dot was visible on the front of the green.

"There you go, old man," I said to Nate as I walked back to the cart.

"I'm not old," said Nate.

"He's just older," said John.

I sat down next to Mark in the cart and we drove across the fairway to his ball.

"Maybe you play better in the dark," said Mark.

"I guess so. We'll have to make this a regular thing"

"I'm thinking we should start a league," he replied.

We stopped at his ball. Mark stood up out of the cart and pulled a club from his bag. Then he turned to me and said, "Or a tournament."

Timothy McHugh

I smiled and said, "A skins game."

We both knew that we were on to something. Either that or we were starting to get a buzz. Mark focused on his shot and addressed the ball. As Nate and John were pulling up behind us, he swung. The ball rocketed through the sky with a bright yellow tail. It hit the green and rolled to the back.

"Almost too much," I said.

"Yeah, I still don't have a good feel for these balls yet," said Mark.

"You beast," said John as they parked next to us.

"You're next, man," I said to John.

"Yeah. I'm last, aren't I?" he said. "Wonder what that means?"

"It doesn't mean shit if you don't win the hole," said Nate.

He and John began arguing again. Mark and I drove on to John's ball. He was on the edge of the left rough with only 155 yards left.

John and Nate pulled up behind us. "That's five,' said Nate.

"You're full of shit," replied John. "That is completely in the fairway."

Nate got down on his hands and knees to stare at the ball. "It's touching the rough," he said.

"We need a ruling, Mark," said John.

"Hell, the way they mow here, you can't tell the difference. Carry over!" shouted Mark.

John took his stance and made his typical graceful swing. He swung his eight-iron as easily as he could. The ball landed on the front of the green and rolled about six or seven feet to stop about a foot short of the hole.

"Well, maybe next time," I said.

"Yeah, it might go in next time," said Mark.

18 Holes of Green

"Screw you guys," said John.

He was ready to gloat, but Mark and I weren't going to stick around. We drove to Nate's ball, which turned out to be about 30 yards short of the green. Not too bad with a glow ball and a driver off the ground.

Nate and John arrived quickly. Eager to hit his third shot, Nate sprung from his cart. He already had his wedge in one hand and a cigarette in the other. With his smoke hanging from his lips, he took a practice swing brushing the fairway.

I heard John hold in a laugh behind me. As I turned back to look at him, Nate hit his shot.

"Sit damn it!" screamed Nate.

I spun around to see a yellow tracer go flying over the green.

"How far did you think you were?" I asked.

"I thought you had to hit these balls harder," replied Nate.

"Yeah, but you took a full fucking swing," said John.

"Is that what you were laughing about?" I asked.

"Yeah, he took a full cut for a practice swing, so I knew that one was going long."

"Well, you guys said they don't go as far," said Nate.

"You were 30 yards out," said John. You should have played 50, not 100."

I couldn't help but laugh at Nate.

"Now you might need that full swing," said Mark as he and I drove off.

Mark and I parked to the left of the green, while Nate and John drove around and past it looking for Nate's ball. Mark opened another beer, as I sat on the cart watching the dark images move around behind the green. I couldn't see Nate's ball, but it looked like they had found it.

It was a beautiful evening. A multitude of stars filled the sky, while moonlight glistened off the waving flag. Its rustling and the chirping of crickets were all I could hear. It was quite peaceful. Then, there was the smack of a ball being hit. I saw the yellow tracer of Nate's ball fly up from behind the green. It landed short of the green and took one bounce stopping a foot short of the fringe.

"You woman!" I shouted.

Nate said something but I couldn't hear what it was. More than likely it wasn't complimentary. I took a drink of my beer as Mark walked toward the green with his putter. Having a moment before the others were ready, I sat on the cart and soaked it all in. There was enough of a breeze to rustle the flag and the leaves. The course really felt different at night.

"Looks like a full moon," said Mark, as Nate and John pulled up.

"I don't think it's quite full yet," I said following him toward the green.

"It sure looks full," said Mark.

"I think it's a waning moon," said Nate.

"No, it's waxing," I said.

"Right, it's past full," said Mark.

"No, waxing is going toward full," I said.

"But it's waning," said Nate as he cleaned his putter.

"Who cares?" screamed John.

Nate was up first. He had a 20-footer from the fringe. He spent a moment trying to position the ball so that the glow stick was running parallel to the ground. Once he was satisfied, he addressed the ball.

"You have to hit 'em harder than normal," said Mark.

"Screw you," answered Nate.

Nate hit the ball pretty hard. It looked as though it was going to roll well past the hole, but it slowed down a lot

18 Holes of Green

faster than you'd expect. It stopped five feet short of the hole. Just at the top of the crest in the middle of the green.

"You pussy," commented John.

"I couldn't see the ridge in the dark," Nate answered.

I was up next. John's ball had me stymied as it sat one foot short of the hole.

"Let me finish this off," said John as he tapped it into the hole.

As the ball sat in the bottom of the cup, it illuminated the entire hole.

"That's awesome," said Mark.

"Yeah, leave it in there so I can see where the hell i'm going," I said.

"Yeah, I propose a night golf rule that we use one of the extra balls to light the hole when putting," said Mark.

"Agreed," replied Nate. "A hole-ball on every green."

"Hole-ball," I shouted to concur. It was a funny sounding phrase to me.

Squatting down behind my ball, I realized how difficult it was to read the green in the dark. The moonlight created shadows on the green that added to the deception. My ball was on the front of the green about 25 feet short of the hole. I had to reach the second tier and it looked as though it might break right. After Nate's display, I wisely struck the putt very hard. It made it to the second tier, but actually broke left rather than right

"I told you guys that you can't see the break in the dark," said Nate.

"That's why you have to get it close like I did," said John.

"Screw you," was the natural response that came forth from Nate. Being an attorney, you might expect something more thoughtful from Nate. However, night golf was a new experience for him, and he was getting defensive.

Mark had been quietly studying his line as he waited. He addressed his ball without saying a word. With his usual confidence, he struck the ball hard and it rolled about 12 feet. The ball started left and the broke back toward the hole. It stopped two inches short.

"They're not so difficult to read," he said with a smile.

"It's only the first hole," said Nate.

Nate and I each three putted. We walked off the green with a birdie for John, a par for Mark and a bogie for me. Nate ended up with a snowman.

The four of us were overcome with excitement. It had been one of the most enjoyable holes I had ever played. Even Nate was glowing after his dismal performance. We were not exactly out there to try to post low scores. We were out there to have a good time.

Just being on the course at night was interesting because of the feeling it gives you. You notice the trees and their movement more. As we pulled up to the second tee, an old imposing oak tree towered above us. Its branches swayed making moon shadows across the tee box. The tree line that borders the left side of number two was twinkling with fireflies.

Number two is a short par three that is straight away with two bunkers guarding both sides of the front of the green. There wasn't much to the hole during the day, but we had no idea what to expect in the dark.

"Are we still playing from the forward tees since it's a par three?" asked Nate.

"No, not on the par threes," said Mark.

We all agreed.

"Let's see..." said John. "Who has honors?"

18 Holes of Green

"Let's see it birdie man," I replied.

John put his tee shot onto the center of the green. Mark hit a nice shot that landed on the right side. Possibly on the fringe. I caught my tee shot a little fat, and my ball rolled into the front left bunker. I got some shit from the others for it, but I didn't feel bad. After all, it was dark. I can catch the ball fat in the daylight just as easily. Nate, on the other hand, caught his ball very thin. It was a liner that rolled across the green and just off the back.

We all seemed content to be either on or somewhere near the green. We hopped in our carts and headed down the cart path.

I grabbed my sand wedge and putter and walked toward the bunker. Nate appeared to be close enough to putt from just off the back fringe.

"Putting from the rough?" asked Mark as he and John stood on the green.

"I'm not taking any chances," he said. "Now, put a ball in the hole so I can see where I'm going."

"Oh yeah," said Mark.

"Hole ball," replied John.

"Hole ball," I shouted from the bunker.

I tried to find a stance as Nate whacked his ball onto the green. It stopped within about five feet.

"Not bad," said John. "Now let's see what you can do Brian."

I went through my usual routine of opening the club face and aiming a few inches behind the ball. However, the darkness played havoc with my perception. I swung and hit way behind the ball throwing nothing but sand onto the green.

Mark and John scattered to avoid the sandstorm.

"Whoa, easy now," said Nate.

Still calm, I took another swing and missed the ball again.

"Shit," I exclaimed as I grew frustrated.

"What's the matter down there," asked John.

"It's darker down here," I said.

Again, I took my stance and concentrated. I swung and this time I caught the ball thin causing it to hit the lip of the bunker and stay in the sand.

Now I was pissed off. I walked a few steps to my ball, picked it up and tossed it onto the green. It rolled to within a foot of the hole.

"There you go,' said Mark.

"I propose a second rule that when sufficiently pissed off, one may throw the ball," I said.

Everyone agreed, and we all putted out quickly. John and Mark each made par. Nate had a bogie, and I had a seven.

Even after a bad hole, I was still having a good time. It was pretty cool to be playing at night with no one else around. As we pulled up to the third tee, I noticed that the course looked in better shape than during the day. Like many things, White Lake appeared better at night. The fairway looked impeccable in the dark. The wear and tear of the day's 350 rounds of golf was masked by the beauty of night. The divots and bare spots were not visible from the tee. In my mind, we were playing on a lush rolling fairway.

"Guess I'm up again," said John.

"Don't get used to it," said Mark.

John stepped onto the tee and prepared to address the ball.

Number three was a par four dogleg left with a fair number of trees guarding the dogleg.

"Make sure that your glow stick is level," Mark said.

18 Holes of Green

"I think it needs to be vertical," John replied as he bent down and rotated the ball on the tee.

"Horizontal would be better," said Nate. "It's all physics."

"This is physics," answered John as he addressed the ball. He made an easy swing and roped a low screamer right up the middle of the fairway that drew left. The yellow tracer seemed to curve around the trees.

"Nice shot," I said.

"Too bad these things won't roll," said Nate.

"It will roll when you hit it that hard," said John.

As John stepped away from the tee, we could hear footsteps coming towards us from the fairway.

"Who the hell is that?" asked Mark.

"Sounds like they're running," I said.

"Whoever it is, you must have scared the shit out of them," said Nate.

It was then that we could see a pair of eyes glowing in the moonlight and coming right for us. We could then see that it was followed by two more sets of eyes.

"Umm...guys," I mumbled.

"I think they're pissed," said Nate.

"Great, you got us into a brawl, on the golf course, in the dark. Way to go, John," said Mark.

"Relax," answered John.

"I'll take the big one, and you guys take care of the smaller ones," suggested Nate.

Nate then walked towards the front of the tee and raised his driver like a weapon. Mark picked his club up and prepared himself.

"This is crazy," I said.

"We've got them out numbered four to three," said Mark.

Timothy McHugh

All kind of thoughts were running through my head at that moment. Who would be out in the fairway at this hour anyway? Were they really going to fight us over it? Having never been in a fight in my life, I was too afraid to think about how bizarre this really was. Never the less, the eyes were getting closer and were closing fast. Whoever it was, we would be face to face with them in a moment."

"Get ready boys," said Nate.

Just then, the body of a large deer became visible as she leaped towards the tee. Nate screamed and dropped to the ground in the fetal position. The rest of us were frozen in awe. She and her two babies darted to the right of the tee and then off into the woods in a flash. It happened so fast that I couldn't react.

The three of us broke into laughter as Nate looked up from the ground.

"I thought you were going to take care of the big one," said John.

"She looked pissed off," said Nate.

"You wuss," said Mark. "I think she was more scared of your face than you were of hers."

"Yeah, she changed course in a split second when she actually saw your ugly mug," I said.

"That was just odd," said Nate.

We were all still breathing hard from the excitement. Nate got up and brushed off his pants. We heard a few sounds from the woods. The deer were likely trying to get farther away.

"Who knows what else is out here tonight," said Mark.

"I bet Vader comes out at night," I said.

18 Holes of Green

"Yeah, we found that deer carcass early one morning last year by the creek," said John. "Boy, he did a number on that one."

"Wonderful," replied Nate.

"You wimp," said Mark as he walked to the tee markers with his driver.

"Try not to rile anything up out there," I said.

"I'll do my best," he replied.

Mark hit a nice high drive down the fairway. Nate and I followed with decent drives ourselves. The excitement must have had us pumped up because we both had swung with confidence. We all drove on to see where our balls had wound up.

We approached two balls, both roughly 150 yards from the green and on the right side of the fairway. That was when we realized that we had an unforeseen problem.

"So who's who?" asked Nate as we all stopped next to the two balls.

"Beats me," I replied. "I guess we should have marked them."

"I think mine was more toward the right of the fairway," said Nate.

"They're five feet apart," I replied.

"But mine has a better angle around the dogleg to the green," objected Nate.

"I'm going up to look for my ball while you ladies powder your noses," said John. He walked across the fairway and up the left-hand side toward the tree line.

"Well, they're close enough that it doesn't matter this time," said Mark.

"Yeah, but we better mark 'em now," replied Nate.

"I've got a permanent marker," said Mark as he turned to rummage through his bag.

Timothy McHugh

Mark tossed me the Sharpie, and I wrote a capital "B" on each side of one of the balls. Nate marked his ball with his usual dollar sign. He was so cocky sometimes.

"I'll go first," said Nate.

"Always the Boy Scout," Said Mark.

"Ladies first," I replied.

Nate chuckled as he addressed his ball closer to the right side of the fairway. I didn't give a damn which ball he chose. He took his time and swung with a nice tempo, but the ball flew dead left into the trees guarding the dogleg.

"You pulled it," said Mark.

"No, I was trying to draw it," Nate answered.

"You can't draw the ball in the daylight," said Mark.

"Yeah, yeah," moaned Nate with disgust. He turned away from us and flung his club through the air in frustration.

"That was brilliant," I said.

"Yeah, good luck finding that one," said Mark.

I walked to the remaining ball, took my stance and aimed just right of the green. I wasn't taking any chances. I thought about the fundamentals of just making contact and hit my ball straight, but shorter than I had hoped. At least it would be in front of the green.

"Not bad," commented Mark.

Nate walked after his club, and I returned to the cart where Mark had sat down. We each opened another beer and relished the view of Nate pacing back and forth looking for his club. As we watched him, the trees behind him again glistened with lightening bugs. I had never seen so many at once.

"Those fire flies are amazing," I said.

"It's a natural Christmas tree," said Mark.

"That's exactly what it is," I replied.

18 Holes of Green

Mark and I were both amazed by the clever phrase he had coined. It may have been the beer, but it seemed momentous to us.

"I'm just glad that Oscar suggested the bug spray," said Mark.

"Yep, I haven't been bitten once," I responded.

"Can I get a little help over here," yelled Nate.

"I think it's to your right," I replied.

"Gee, thanks," said Nate.

He kept pacing in some kind of grid pattern. This was apparently the third rule of night golf: don't throw your club into the darkness.

"Come on guys," shouted Nate.

Mark grudgingly drove the cart slowly toward Nate. As the cart inched forward, we both peered forward looking for his club. We weren't about to put too much effort into it.

As we slowly crept up on Nate frantically searching the same area over and over, it seemed hopeless.

Just then we felt the front left cart tire roll over an object. Mark and I each looked at each other with the same thought on our minds. He reached down and pulled Nate's seven iron out from under the cart.

"I found it," he announced.

As he handed the club to Nate's outstretched hand, its shaft was obviously bent. I was trying not to laugh, but couldn't contain myself.

"You bent my damn club," said Nate.

"You probably bent it when you threw it," said Mark.

"Bullshit," said Nate. "It didn't hit anything but the ground."

"Either way, it's bent and needs to be reshafted," I said.

"Yeah, and either way Mark is going to reshaft it for me," replied Nate.

"Yeah, all right," said Mark. "Now, let's go. John is probably on the green by now."

Nate jogged over to his cart carrying his wounded club. Mark and I headed toward the trees on the left to look for Nate's ball.

"Great, first we have to look for his club, now his ball," I said.

"At least his ball glows," replied Mark.

"That's true," I said.

Sure enough, when we entered the tree line, Nate's ball was glowing like a beacon just ahead of us. We parked just to the right of his ball. Nate quickly arrived behind us and hopped out of his cart.

"Well, hot damn," he shouted. "I've got an opening." His ball was sitting in a clearing with an opening to the green about 50 yards away. He had gotten a lucky break.

"A little six-iron ought to keep it under the trees," said Nate.

"I'd use a seven if I were you," said Mark.

"Funny," he replied.

Mark and I sat patiently in our cart as he took a few practice swings choking down on his six-iron and playing it in the back of his stance. Then, he addressed the ball and knocked it through the opening and onto the green.

"Great shot," said Mark. "Thanks," replied Nate.

Just then, I winced with shock as a hand reached out from the darkness and grabbed my shoulder. My beer spilled onto Mark's lap as I screamed the "F" bomb.

Nate broke out into laughter as I turned and saw John standing beside me.

18 Holes of Green

"What the hell happened to you ladies?" he asked. "Lawyer-boy threw his club and then couldn't find it," said Mark.

"Nice," said John as he lit a cigarette.

I leaned back in my seat and gasped for air as they all laughed.

"You scared the shit out of me," I said with my heart still pounding.

"You spilled your beer all over me," said Mark.

Nate and John were both laughing at me.

"I can't believe you guys didn't see me standing there," said John. "I wasn't hiding."

"It's pretty dark out here," I said.

"Yeah, dark enough to run over a club," added Nate.

"Really?" asked John.

"Yeah, that's how we found his club for him," I answered.

"Yeah, thanks," replied Nate.

We gathered our composure and pressed on. Mark drove us to his ball in the fairway, while John and Nate headed to the green. I watched Mark put his approach shot on the green and then we moved onto my ball.

I chipped my ball on as Nate inserted the now famous hole-ball into the cup. We all putted out. Nate saved a five to tie me. Mark and John both made par. That kept John and me one up on team score after three holes.

We rode down the windy path to the fourth tee and could hear something howling in the distance as we parked.

"This is really pretty cool," I said.

"Yeah, we have to set up a night golf tournament," said Mark.

"We've had some trouble, though. And we know the course better than anyone," replied Nate.

"You have to set it up with glowing markers on pins and yardage markers," Said John. "You can use those paper bag candle lanterns as tee markers and yardage markers."

"What do you use on the pins?" asked Nate.

"They make longer glow sticks that you hang on them," answered Mark.

"They're kind of like those glow in the dark necklaces you see at concerts," I added.

"Cool," said Nate. "Now, who's up?"

"I believe I still have the honors," said John.

"Naturally," responded Nate.

John walked onto the tee and prepared to hit. Number four was a very sharp dogleg right, and he appeared to be trying to distinguish the outline of the hole.

"It's pretty dark out here," he said.

"Wise beyond your years," replied Nate.

John ignored the comment and addressed his ball. He made his usual high arching swing and followed through holding the pose. However, the ball seemed to whistle in the air. It was a sound we had not yet heard. Then, to our surprise, the yellow tracer disappeared as the ball was still rising.

"That was weird," said Mark.

"Yep, a real shame," added Nate. "I hope it's lost."

"Why would it stop glowing?" asked John.

"Maybe a large bird snatched it," I suggested.

"No bird grabbed a golf ball out of the air," responded John.

"A whooping crane might have," said Nate.

"What the hell do you know about whooping cranes?" said John.

"It would have had to have been something large, like a buzzard or hawk," said Mark.

18 Holes of Green

"Or two African swallows flying in tandem," I suggested.

"Exactly," said Mark with a laugh.

"I better hit a provisional," said John.

He broke out a spare ball and began preparing the glow stick as Mark got ready to hit. Mark and Nate both hit good shots. I on the other hand, caught mine thin, and it only went about 100 yards. I stayed calm and opened another beer. John hit his provisional ball around the dogleg. This time there was no whistle, and we could see the yellow tracer clearly turn the corner.

We rode onto my ball, which was still short of the dogleg. I lined up as Mark had showed me to hit a draw, but the ball didn't draw. It went straight into the trees guarding the corner.

"You need to swing on line with your imaginary target," said Mark as I got back into the cart.

"I'll try next time," I said.

"Quit screwing up my partner," shouted John from his cart.

We started down the fairway again and saw something small glowing in the fairway just 30 yards away. We followed John and Nate to inspect it and were surprised to find it was John's glow stick. However, there was no ball, just the tiny stick.

"You knocked the stick right out of the ball," I said.

"Son of a bitch," said Nate.

"Don't worry, Nate; you don't hit it that hard," said Mark.

"I don't think we're going to find that ball," I said.

"Nope," agreed Mark. "John lies three."

We drove onto my ball which was stuck in a tight grove of trees right at the corner of the dogleg. I only had about a three foot wide opening to go forward, but I wasn't about to play it safe in the dark. I quickly addressed the ball and tried to punch it through the opening with my three- iron. Unfortunately, I struck the ground first and the ball rolled about two feet.

"A little fat," said Mark.

I decided to invoke rule number two, so I picked up my ball and threw it through the opening as hard as I could. Mark drove me to the ball and without much thought; I jumped from my cart and heaved it again with all my might.

"Damn, that hurts my shoulder," I said.

"You can't throw very well," replied Mark.

"What the hell is going on over there," shouted John from his cart ahead of us.

"Rule number two," I replied.

"OK," he answered.

Nate hit his second shot onto the green and so did Mark. I finally used a club and managed to get my ball onto the right-hand fringe. I was pretty frustrated with this hole.

John's provisional tee shot was only 30 yards from the green. He easily knocked a sand wedge close to the pin.

We finished that hole with Mark and Nate getting back a skin to even the match. We played the next few holes without anything crazy happening. Most of the time, we were arguing over whether Andy and the county park board would allow us to have a night golf tournament. Hugh Cunningham, the director of golf for the county, was a major weasel. He micro-managed everything that happened at the golf courses, and he didn't have the balls to try anything new.

By the time we reached the seventh tee, Mark was sure that he had a plan to sell both Andy and Cunningham on a night golf tournament.

18 Holes of Green

"You just want to talk about a tournament because y'all are down two skins," said John.

"It's simple," said Mark, ignoring John. "We bring up three big points to Cunningham, and we'll win him over. First, we're gaining revenue at a time of day that we currently don't. Second, we're gaining exposure for the course and county golf courses by promoting it big time. Night golf is sure to get some free publicity with the local media."

"Nice," I said.

"And third," Mark continued. "We tell him that some proceeds will go to the county junior golf fund."

Junior golf was near and dear to Cunningham's heart. Not because it gave kids a chance to learn the game but because it got his name in the papers. We had the largest junior golf program in the state at White Lake. We actually taught them etiquette and the spirit of the game, in addition to how to swing. Cunningham was more interested in producing college scholarships for a few stars that were bred to play the game.

"That's perfect," said Nate. "A drunken night golf tournament and poker party will help the kids."

"Poker party?" asked Mark.

"Yeah. If you add a poker party after the tournament, it will be out of sight," said Nate.

I could tell already that this night golf thing was going to become larger than I had thought.

"We would pull 'em in with an afterhours poker party," said John.

"It's a good draw, but the county will never go for it," said Mark.

"We'll see," said Nate.

We played number seven arguing the whole time about how best to put on a night golf tournament. I think that

Mark and I were so into planning it that we lost interest in the match we were playing. That was fine with John, but it didn't sit well with Nate.

"You're supposed to be a damned golf professional," shouted Nate. "How about concentrating on the match."

"It's night golf," replied Mark. "

Bullshit," rebutted Nate.

"It is night, and this is golf," I commented.

"Go to hell, Brian," said Nate.

He always was a sore loser. We waxed them badly by the time we finished the ninth hole, thanks to John. It was a wild time out there, and we all had played enough for one night. We sat out on the patio under the stars and finished the remaining beers as we recounted the evening's strange events. After a few more drinks, Nate stopped whining about losing. Mark was confident enough that he couldn't care less about losing at night golf. We were all just enjoying the moment. Nate moved onto the theory that a night golf tournament would require at least a few strippers. None of us were opposed to the idea, but no one really took him seriously.

The moon was moving quickly across the horizon, and it was getting pretty late. Mark was juggling three of the glow balls, creating a nice light show for my blurring eyes. I was impressed by his coordination at that point. After some more bantering, we began to wind down. It had been a fun evening, and I had a feeling that there was more night golf to come.

<u>18 Holes of Green</u>

The Fifth of July

It was Friday, July 5th. The week had been unseasonably cool for July; a welcome break from the typical hot and humid days we were accustomed to. The beautiful weather combined with the day after Independence Day falling on a Friday was sure to make it one hell of a day for us. Everyone and their brother were taking Friday off to enjoy the long weekend. Our tee times were booked solid until 3:00 PM. In fact, we had set up two waves of starting times that would cross over from one nine to the other. This helped maximize the number of groups we could accommodate.

While this plan worked well from an efficiency standpoint, it always caused us some problems. The inevitable walk-ins would be sure to wonder why we could not get them off the back side for just nine holes.

Things had started out smoothly enough. Mark and I had opened the clubhouse while John and Hank worked the tees to make sure everyone was where they were supposed to be. The early players were never much hassle. These were usually the guys from our regular skins game and other serious golfers. My biggest problem was explaining our tee time situation to people calling us on the phone. By 8:30 AM we had made it through most of the first wave without incident. It was a perfect day outside, and players had been teeing off since 7:00 AM. All was going well as I answered the phone.

"White Lake golf course, Brian speaking," I said.

"Yeah, I have a tee time for Ferguson, but I can't remember whether it's at 9:30 or 10:00 AM?" the voice on the other end said.

"Well, I don't see a Ferguson listed, and we..."

"I know. It was 9:45, my wife just reminded me," the man interrupted.

"But sir, we don't have a 9:45 tee time," I replied.

"Well, it's probably 9:44 or 9:46, or something like that," he said.

"No, you don't understand," I said. "We don't have any tee times between 8:45 and 10:45 AM due to the cross over. You must have the wrong golf course."

"What the hell is a cross over?" he asked.

"We start players on both number one and number ten and they cross over," I said.

"Oh yeah, I must be on number ten," he said.

"Sir, we don't have your name or even a tee time anywhere near the time you mentioned."

"How about if I just come down there. Can you get us off the back?" he asked.

"No sir, but it is first come first served on the par-three course," I said.

"Alright, thanks for nothing," he said as he hung up.

I just shook my head and answered the next call. The clubhouse was full of boisterous regulars bantering in their different cliques. There were the old guys from the Birdie Hunters League checking their standings on the bulletin board and sitting at tables in a corner of the clubhouse they claimed for themselves. Though they all appeared to be from the same demographic of elderly white men, they had

18 Holes of Green

somewhat of a tribal structure. The hunters stood by the bulletin board to talk statistics. The gatherers sat at the tables making conversation and hoping to draw the name of a good hunter for their foursome.

At the three tables directly in front of the big screen were the middle-aged guys from the skins game. They were already passing around pitchers of beer, enjoying the free pass for the morning from their wives. Scattered around these two local tribes were the unrelated foursomes of weekend warriors. Some talked on their cell phones while others looked at their watches impatiently wondering if it was their time yet.

Lisa and Missy were working their asses off over at the grill. Both the Birdie Hunters and the guys from the skins game were high maintenance for them. They all expected the world, flirted like fools and tipped like they were destitute.

The next call I answered was Ashley, Mark's fiancée. It was the third time that she had called that morning. The first time was to argue about the reception. The second time was to get directions to the possible reception hall. This time, she had to either be lost on her way to the hall or on her way back. My money was that she was still on the way.

I handed the phone to Mark and took his place at the cash register. A foursome from the skins game was at the counter rifling through our jars of cheap balls and messing up the displays. This was a complex ritual that some golfers had to go through before they decided to pay.

"How much for those Titleists?" asked Mike, a roofer who always had dirty hands.

"A sleeve or a dozen?" I asked.

"Just a sleeve," he responded. "$12.95," I answered.

Timothy McHugh

"You don't need any Titleists," said Pat, one of the larger and louder members of the game. "You're just going to lose them," he said.

"It's nice to have such good friends," I said sarcastically.

"Yeah, you're right," said Mike. "I'll take six of these dollar balls."

I just shook my head at Pat and began to ring-up Mike's balls.

"Are you paying for your round too?" I asked.

"Unless you want to let me go for free," Mike replied.

"Sorry, you're not cute enough," I answered as I rang up his 18 holes walking.

About half the guys in the skins game walked. They didn't walk because it was the way the game was supposed to be played. No, it wasn't for exercise either. There were no principles involved other than economics. Ironically, it was the heavier ones that always rode in carts. Pat was one of our worst offenders of driving down the middle of the fair- way or parking too close to a green. You would think guys that played here regularly would be more apt to take care of the course, but some of them just took it for granted. Pat had been told a dozen times, but he didn't give a damn. He liked to park so close he could almost step onto the green.

I could hear Mark giving Ashley directions to the interstate over the phone. The pro shop door opened, and I saw a pair of light blue pants shuffling into the threshold as an arm from behind held open the door. Paul was helping old Wes into the building. Paul was my favorite old-guy, but it wasn't fair to call him old around Wes.

"It's nice of you to help that young man in the door," I shouted to Paul.

18 Holes of Green

"Just trying to earn that citizenship badge," Paul replied. "It's not every day that the founder of the Birdie Hunters visits. It's every other day."

Wes said something to me, but it was too soft for me to hear what it was.

"He said that I'm just helping him because it's the only thing that makes me look younger," said Paul.

"Wes, you're still better looking than Paul," I shouted, hoping he would hear me.

Wes smiled and nodded his head in acknowledgement as Paul helped him through the pro shop. The foursome that I was helping turned and loudly welcomed Wes as he approached the counter. They didn't quite yell "Wes" in unison, but it was awfully close to a "Norm" moment from Cheers. Everyone knew Wes, and we were all very fond of him. I think most of these guys just hoped that they'd make it to his age someday.

After a brief exchange, Paul continued to walk Wes into the grill where he could sit down. I could see that Paul took him to his usual seat at the center table by the window. It was right next to News Junkie Fred. I finished taking care of the foursome at the counter. I gave them their cart keys and wished them well as they headed back to their comrades in the grill.

With no one else at the counter for the moment, I turned to the window and looked out at the tees. Poor Hank was working both tees as John sat in a cart smoking and holding court with a group of Birdie Hunters. He had a putter in one hand and appeared to be espousing his view on the fine art. They seemed to be eating up everything he said, hanging on each word. Behind me, Mark finally finished his painful conversation with Ashley. As I turned toward him, he wiped his brow as if it had drained him.

"Better get used to it," I said. "Marriage is forever."

"We'll see," said Mark. He liked to talk as if it wasn't a done deal. It must have been a deeply rooted masculine drive for saving face that caused him to disavow what was clearly inevitable.

"So, was she lost going to the hall or coming back from it?' I asked.

"Both I guess. She really just wanted to tell me all about the reception hall. I think getting lost was just an excuse."

"So will there be an open bar or what?" I asked.

"Man, don't get me started," he replied. "I'm lucky that we're having a bar at all. She's got aunts and uncles who are Pentecostals. You know, real backwoods snake-handling kind of shit."

"Damn," I replied. "Did you tell her that no one would show up if there wasn't alcohol?"

"Yeah, I think that's what got her convinced. The one thing that scares her more than disappointing her family is not having any friends show up."

"I don't know how you do it," I said as I walked around the counter to straighten up the displays.

Paul had left Wes in good hands as his table was swarmed with Birdie Hunters, and he was now walking toward the pro shop. Mark answered the phone again and took his turn at explaining the cross over to a caller. Paul was singing Fly Me to the Moon as he approached. He was always singing, and it was usually Sinatra. He had played the bass in a big band dance band back in the day. His pants were neatly pressed, and he wore a Polo golf shirt and saddle shoes. He was one of the few widowers I knew who still dressed well.

"How's it going old man?" I asked.

18 Holes of Green

"We have 18 holes of green and it's a beautiful day," he replied. "Nothing wrong except for the yahoo downtown."

Paul was referring to Hugh Cunningham, our much-dreaded director of golf for the county. Paul had been at odds with him for years. Paul had served on the citizens' golf advisory committee ever since he retired. He served for 18 years until Cunningham came to power and disbanded the committee.

"But Paul," I sarcastically protested. "He's looking out for the health of all our customers. There's lead in the water pipes."

"There's lead in his head," responded Paul. "He just wants to sell more of that damn bottled water from that company his wife works for."

"He's brilliant," I said.

"He has an MBA you know," replied Paul.

"Yeah, everyone knows."

"I guess I don't speak MBA, but I think that bottled water is for pussies," Paul said.

"I prefer mine to have some malt and hops in it," I replied.

"He's a damn fool," Paul went on. "Taking away the drinking fountains is a health hazard. You remember when old Ted from the Birdie Hunters died of a heat stroke last year."

"Yeah, but Ted was 102," I said. "It may have just been his time to go."

"Well, if he takes them out this month as planned, and we go into the August heat without water fountains, there's going to be Birdie Hunters dropping left and right. They won't pay $2.50 for a bottle of water."

"I think the cheapest bottle they have over there $2.89," I said.

"I don't care what size it is, the Birdie Hunters wouldn't pay 50 cents for water," responded Paul.

"You're right about that," I said. "They won't pay 50 cents for a golf ball. They only play with the ones they find. The cheap old farts."

"Easy Brian, most of those guys grew up when times were tough and you had to know how to stretch a dollar," Paul replied.

"Yeah, but there's some of them that have serious money," interjected Mark, who now appeared to be back on the phone with Ashley.

"Right and how do you think they got it?" asked Paul.

"By being cheap," I said.

"By saving," said Paul.

"Some do it by cheating hardworking people out of their money," said Mark, who appeared to be simply listening on the phone.

"That's just Ralph," said Paul. "Rain check Ralph," I added.

We all laughed about Ralph. He was a Birdie Hunter who drove a new Mercedes but had a ratty old leather golf bag. He always had a wad of cash, but he'd try to scam you out of something each time he played. He never played more than nine holes at a time, but he was notorious for paying for 18 holes and then asking for a rain check after nine. He would say that something had come up or that his back was sore, but we figured out that he was just trying to get the price break. An 18-hole round is cheaper than two nine-hole rounds.

Andy Pader finally called him out about it and put a stop to it. But Ralph never shied away from an opportunity to save a penny. Apparently, he wasn't the most ethical lawyer, but he sure did profit from other people.

18 Holes of Green

Mark finally broke away from the phone and came over to the counter to join us. He seemed a little tired.

"That woman will be the death of you, son," said Paul. "Take my advice and end it. You have 18 holes of green here, why settle for..."

"Just one?" asked John appearing from around the corner.

We all laughed.

"I'm afraid it's too late," replied Mark.

"She's not pregnant, is she?" asked Paul as I turned with interest.

"No, it's worse," Mark answered. "She's spent too much money on our joint credit cards. I'm in debt up to my ass, and I didn't spend a penny of it."

"But you sure do have nice window treatments and furniture," I said.

"Go to hell, Brian," replied Mark.

"Like I keep saying, you have 18 holes of green here, why would you want to ruin it by marrying that girl." said Paul. "18 holes versus one, sounds like a no brainer."

I choked laughing at that one. I headed over to the grill to see what was going on. I knew that Paul would help answer the phones if Mark got busy. He enjoyed stepping behind the counter and helping. It made him feel needed. Andy had offered to hire him several times, but he didn't want to be on the payroll. He preferred being a volunteer so he could come and go as he pleased.

I passed a couple of Birdie Hunters and smiled at them as I walked through the tables toward the grill. Most of them had teed off by now, and the last group was leaving their seats with Wes. As I approached the grill counter, Missy was filling two pitchers of beer for a couple of guys. Lisa was at the end of the counter trying to check her inventory list and fend off Harley's advances at the same time. He was a subtle guy. He never directly hit on Lisa, but he sure tried to show off around her.

"It's good to be physical," he said to her. Lisa kept from looking up and stayed focused on her clipboard. "These guys all prefer to be social and drink their beer, but I prefer to be physical."

Harley immediately dropped to the floor and did ten push-ups right in front of the counter. Many of the golfers at their tables turned and stared at him briefly, but then returned to their conversations. Harley had been known to do that from time to time no matter how much we discouraged it.

As he returned to his feet, Lisa walked over and flipped a sausage patty and egg off of the grill and onto a bun.

"Here you go," she said as she handed it to Harley. He handed her a dollar tip and walked out the back door toward his maintenance golf cart. Harley preferred to eat outside.

"He better watch it or I'm going to get physical on his face," said Lisa.

"Sounds interesting," I replied,

"Just a sausage biscuit Brian?" she asked.

"Yeah, that will do," I replied.

Lisa flipped a sausage patty onto a bun for me and poured me a Mountain Dew. That was my version of coffee. She smiled and went over to help Missy deal with the morning beer hounds.

I slid two bucks onto the counter and turned to walk away. All of the Birdie Hunters were now gone, and there were just a few groups of the skins game left inside. Most of the players left in the clubhouse were your typical weekend warriors. Old Wes was sitting at a table by himself now, gazing out the window. Fred was relaying the highlights of

18 Holes of Green

the latest Donald Rumsfeld news conference to him, but Wes didn't appear to be listening. Seeing Old Wes by himself made me feel charitable, so I reached behind the counter, poured a cup of coffee, grabbed a doughnut, and headed over to his table. He was still staring out the window when I arrived. His face lit up when I placed the coffee and doughnut in front of him. I dumped two packets of sugar in the coffee for him.

"Just remember who took care of you when you're deciding whom to leave your millions to," I said.

"You can have all my left-over food stamps," he whispered. I began to eat my sausage biscuit as old Wes continued to gaze out the window. I could tell he wanted to say something, but he couldn't quite get it out. That gave me the minute I needed to finish my sandwich. As I took my last bite he coughed a couple of times. That was the sign that he was about to speak.

With doughnut glaze around his lips, he gasped in his hoarse voice, "People just don't know how to dress anymore."

I looked out the window and nobody looked too crazily dressed. Not even any t-shirts or jeans. That's pretty good for White Lake.

"Golfers used to coordinate. Our slacks used to match our tops," he said. "Don't any of these guys have wives." It was then that I noticed that old Wes was wearing purple pants and a white shirt with purple stripes. Naturally he had a white belt on to match his white shoes.

"They just don't have your fashion sense," I said.
"You're exactly right," he replied. "No common sense."
"That too," I said.
"That's why there are so many car accidents these days. No common sense," he coughed a couple of times and

sipped his coffee. "Everyone drives these big monster trucks, and you can't see around them. And those minivans aren't any better. What the hell ever happened to a station wagon?"

Wes gasped for air after that long tirade. For a moment, I thought I was going to have to run to get the oxygen tank. That happened about once every other week for someone.

He coughed a few more times and then continued. "They all oughta be illegal. It's just not safe." By then, Paul had walked over to our table to save me.

"Now Brian, how'd you get Wes so excited?" he asked.

"No one drives station wagons anymore, and they don't match their outfits either," I replied.

"Sounds fair enough to me," replied Paul with a smile.

News junkie Fred turned in his chair and announced that both Fox News and CNN had been broadcasting from Williams Field next to the golf course. He claimed that to celebrate a reunion, the 82nd Airborne was going to have 250 paratroopers jump at noon.

"The sky over us should be full of them when it happens," he added.

"You're crazy," said Paul. "If the 82nd Airborne was going to have a reunion at Williams Field and drop 250 paratroopers, we would have heard about it ahead of time."

"Rick Leventhal and Anderson Cooper are both here," Fred replied. "I just saw them reporting from the airport."

"That's the big time," I said to humor Fred.

"Hell, this might even be on O'Reilly tonight," He added. "I just wish they sent a couple of those broadcast

18 Holes of Green

beauties. Just wait and see. They'll do it again. The damn news always repeats itself over and over."

Fred was usually infallible in his sources, but this seemed ridiculous. He had embellished things in the past and was known for being opinionated, but he had never made something up out of the blue like this before. Maybe he was starting to lose it. He had been sitting in that chair a little too long.

"This coffee is awful," Wes said.

Paul reached across the table and grabbed the box of sweetener. He took out about ten sugar packets and started dumping them into the coffee.

"I put two in already," I said.

"Two?" said Paul with a laugh. "When you get old, you lose your taste buds. It's a terrible thing, Brian." He continued to pour sugar packets into Wes's coffee. It had to be thickening into slush I thought.

After dumping all ten packets into the coffee, he slid the cup back in front of Wes, who took a sip and smiled.

"That's good coffee," said Wes as he smiled and slid a flask out of his pants pocket. I don't know how he fit the thing in there. Then, without saying a word, he slyly poured a little whiskey into his coffee cup as if it was second nature. It was as though he was too good to waste his whiskey on the coffee when it only had two sugars in it. Now, it was coffee deserving of his special ingredient. He never looked at us during this performance and continued to gaze out the window as if he had not done a thing.

"Brian! I need you buddy," shouted Mark from the pro shop.

I quickly hopped up from the table and headed toward the counter. There were two groups waiting to pay him, and the phone was ringing. I quickly grabbed the phone and hastily answered it expecting a simple question.

It turned out to be Hugh Cunningham of all people. He wasn't at all happy that the phone had rung 15 times before I answered it. He was notorious for counting the rings every time that he called. It was really annoying. He went on for a while about the importance of good customer service, and I explained that I was helping an elderly man to his car and couldn't just let go of him. He actually commended me on my act of kindness and said he would be coming by that afternoon for a visit.

That meant we had to be on good behavior for a while. No chipping balls at the garbage can. No drinking beer while on the clock. No fun of any kind, and we had to wear our nametags. I informed Mark and then went out- side to warn John and Hank. John would have to refrain from wandering to the practice green for the time being. That was where he spent most of his time when he was starter.

When I got outside, I found John and Hank discussing the value of a good short game. John's was one of the best in town and Hank's was very strong for an amateur.

"That's the problem with the average golfer," said John. "They only practice how to get off the tee, and they never practice how to get it in the hole."

"Getting it in the hole has never been my problem," replied Hank.

"Nice," I commented. It was really amusing to hear how the old guys likened everything to sex. They were hornier than teenagers.

When I warned them about Cunningham, John went off on a tirade, and Hank joined in. We all had stories to tell about our run-ins with him.

18 Holes of Green

I sat down at the starter's table with John, while Hank went inside to use the restroom. We continued for a moment discussing Hugh Cunningham's bullshit. I told John what Paul said about Birdie Hunters dropping like flies without water fountains. He agreed and had a few choice words for Cunningham's wife. Then, our conversation drifted to another easy target. We chatted for a while about Mark's impending doom. I told him about Ashley's latest trouble navigating the city she grew up in.

"I'm from out of town, and I know my way around this city better than she does," said John.

I agreed as John rose to greet a young man and woman who were approaching us. They appeared to be walk-on hopefuls, but they didn't have any clubs with them. They may have left them in their car while they checked to see if they could get off. The woman was carrying what appeared to be a bottle of liquor or perhaps perfume that she was selling. John and I were both a little perplexed.

"Maybe they're gypsies," I said.

"This oughta be good," replied John as he stepped forward.

The man and woman walked right up to John. They were dressed too well to be gypsies, and they didn't appear to be selling anything. They were exactly the opposite of sales people. They were quiet and reserved in their manner.

"Hello," said the man who appeared to be in his late 20s. "I'm not sure who we should talk to, we kind of have a strange question."

"What is it?" asked John, who was never one to beat around the bush.

"Well," said the man. "Our father liked to play here and...well he..."

Timothy McHugh

"He played here for years," said the woman, who must have been a few years older than the man and by now was obviously his sister. "He passed away recently and well...it was his wish to have his ashes sprinkled on the golf course."

I slid back in my chair as if to back away from what was apparently an urn containing their father in her hands. I wanted to get out of my chair to get further away, but I didn't want to be rude.

"I see," said John. Nothing seemed to faze him. "I'm sure we can make arrangements for you to do that sometime."

"I take it that today would not be a good day?" asked the man.

John explained how busy we were with it being the day after a holiday and that there would not be any privacy for them. Although they were visibly disappointed, they were very nice. I just sat there in shock, frozen and afraid to move. John suggested that they come back in the evening or early morning, and they agreed. They thanked him and walked away.

"Well, that was a new one," said John.

"Yeah, just when you think you've seen it all," I said. "I could just see us holding up play while they sprinkled their father's ashes on the fairway."

"It's not a bad idea for when you go, but I wouldn't want to be sprinkled anywhere near a tree," added John. "Some bastard would end up pissing on me."

I laughed at his deep thought on immortality and headed back into the clubhouse. When I got inside, Andy was there talking to Mark and Paul. He was there to bring us some fresh change for the cash register in between his lessons. Andy was a good guy to work for. He loved the game and

18 Holes of Green

knew how to teach. Although, I think he liked selling merchandise more than he liked to play. At least he made more money that way.

I told them of the encounter that John and I had outside, and they nearly lost it. Paul proceeded to give us specific instructions on where to sprinkle his ashes when he goes.

"I want a little of me on each of the 18 greens," he went on. "That way, each time they cut a new hole, I'll be the first one in it. I'll also be able to screw with everyone who tries to sink one."

"You'll be cursed when we miss them and blessed when we make them," commented Andy.

"Amen," replied Paul.

"What were they thinking?" asked Mark.

He couldn't believe that the guy's kids wanted to sprinkle his ashes while the course was packed. I think it was a situation where they didn't know golf well enough to know any better. You got that a lot at White Lake. Until that day, I thought I had seen it all. Every question, every problem, every possible scenario that could occur while running a golf course. Severe weather, slow play, and wild tournaments. I had dealt with and mastered it all, but I had never had anyone ask to sprinkle their deceased father's ashes before.

Andy walked to the office behind the counter area of the pro shop to make change and take a deposit to the bank. He usually brought us back lunch on bank runs. It was a nice break from Lisa and Missy's usual fare. I think he was hurrying so he could avoid dealing with Hugh Cunningham.

The phone on the wall behind the counter rang and I stepped forward and picked it up. It was someone wanting a tee time for Sunday morning. I asked how many would be playing and the man said, "Two, possibly three." We were booked through 10:46 AM already, but we just had a foursome call that had an 8:30 AM time and say that they were going to be down to two due to an emergency. When I explained that I had room for a twosome at 8:30 or the threesome at 10:46, the man jumped on the early time.

I confirmed back to him, "A twosome at 8:30 Sunday for Kelley." He replied that "We might still show up with three." That threw me for a moment. I made the quick decision between reacting as a smart ass or a dumb ass and responded with a second attempt to explain the two options.

"Sure, we can get you off as a threesome at 10:46, or I do still have an opening for two players only at 8:30 AM on Sunday," I said. "Do you want to pick one now, or do you want to try to call back?"

"So, you wouldn't be able to get us off if we show up at 8:30 with a third?"

"No sir, I already have a twosome scheduled for 8:30, so that only leaves room for two more players."

"Oh, well we don't want to play with anyone else, so I guess we'll take the 10:46 time."

Mark and Paul looked at me with smiles as I beat my head on the monitor of the tee time computer. After going around and around a few more times, Mr. Kelly agreed to take the 10:46 time. He also assured me that he would have at least three players. I made it very clear to him that if he showed up with just two players; he would be paired up with another twosome. We always had walk-ons waiting for an opportunity.

Mark began taking care of another group of players who were paying and signing for carts. They were the last of the morning tee times. The crossover was about to begin.

"The first groups off of each side should be making the turn soon," I said to Paul.

18 Holes of Green

"That is as long as they kept moving out there," he replied.

That was always the concern. A smoothly run crossover requires that the early groups move around fast enough to make it to the next nine shortly after our last tee time. However, if they made it around too quickly, they'd be waiting for the tee. The former would be more likely than the latter at White Lake. Our ranger this morning was Leo, so anything could happen. He was a nice guy and knew what to do, but he had a habit of falling asleep out on the golf course. He had been the weekend morning ranger for years. He was doing it long before Andy or any of us were here, so we couldn't just change his shift. The nice part for us was that we wouldn't have any new customers for the next two hours. There'd be nothing to do but answer the phone.

The phone rang again, and I quickly answered it in less than two rings. Cunningham would have been proud of me. It was Dr. Anderson on the line. He was a regular player at White Lake and had taken many lessons from Andy. He was calling from the golf shop up by the mall. He asked if Andy was available because he needed some advice on a new set of golf clubs. I was shocked that he would be so bold. I put him on hold and yelled back to Andy.

Mark had just finished with the last player in the foursome. I nudged him in the shoulder and said, "Listen to this." I hit the speaker phone on the line that Dr. Anderson was holding and hit mute. Paul came closer to hear as well. A second later, Andy picked up the line from the office.

"This is Andy," he said in a friendly tone.

"Andy, Doc Anderson here. How you doing?"

"I'm great Doc, what can I do for you?"

"Well I'm up here at Golf Galaxy looking for some new clubs. They have me trying the Titleist and the Callaway."

"Uh huh," replied Andy cautiously.

"I've hit them into the net a few times, and they both feel pretty good. I just can't tell how straight they are because they only go about 20 yards into the net. With my tendency to fade or even slice, which set do you think I should buy?"

"Well Doc," said Andy before a brief pause as he thought. "Honestly, I think you're in the wrong damn golf shop."

Andy immediately hung up the phone. I quickly dropped the call on our end and we all burst out laughing.

"Did you guys hear that shit?" Andy asked as he stepped out of the office.

"Yeah. That takes nerve to ask someone for advice on how to buy equipment from their competitor," said Mark.

"Nice tactful response," said Paul.

"I've had it with that place stealing our customers," said Andy as he walked back into the office.

Mark walked outside to tell John about Dr. Anderson and to see how the crossover was working. Lisa and Missy both would stay busy for the next two hours and then some. While we had less to do in the pro shop during the crossover, they would have a steady flow of customers. After nine holes, every group would want food whether it was breakfast or dogs and burgers. And after nine holes, every group would buy beer whether it was the first round or a refreshing of the cooler.

Old Wes was still sitting at the same table gazing out the window. The first group of Birdie Hunters came in the door as they were making the turn. They each stopped and said hi to Wes as they passed. Some sat with him for a

18 Holes of Green

moment and others patted him on the shoulder and dashed for the restroom. Wes would be in his glory for the next hour as the Birdie Hunters came through talking to him as they turned. It was always the bright spot of his day.

I looked out the window and saw Mark and John pitching balls to the putting green from in front of the first tee. They were lobbing balls out of the mulch about ten feet into the air over a small hedge and a brick walkway to the fringe of the putting green only 15 feet away. The green had five different target pins on it, so I wasn't sure which one they were aiming for. However, it was clear that they were trying to land the shots on the fringe, which suggested they were going for the closest pin. They were just pins stuck in the ground with no hole. It was supposed to be better for the green, but it didn't seem ideal for a chipping contest. It certainly threw a wrench into any gambling that might be involved. It was a situation where the best way to practice wouldn't necessarily be the best way to approach the bet. To avoid bouncing off the pin and being farther away, one would want to be short of the hole or at worst next to it.

I watched them for a moment trying to discern who was winning. They paused for a moment to let the group exiting the ninth green make their way across the path to the clubhouse.

Paul came up from behind and stopped beside me. He glanced out the window and asked, "Who's winning?"

"I don't know yet," I replied.

Just then the phone rang. I turned and stepped toward the wall to answer the phone. As I turned, I saw Hugh Cunningham standing behind the counter of the grill harassing Lisa. He must have slipped in the backdoor of the clubhouse by the dumpster and the employee parking. He was a pretty lively guy who must have been in his late 40s or maybe 50. He was just over six feet tall and had light hair that was still more blonde than it was gray. Cunningham gave the appearance that he was very engaged in everything. He was very energetic and had a habit of repeating things to you with emphasis to stress a point.

Paul slipped out from behind the counter and sheepishly made his way over to the table where Wes was sitting. I couldn't blame him for getting the hell out of there. He didn't get paid to put up with Cunningham's shit like the rest of us. Besides, it was safer for us all if we kept Paul away from Hugh Cunningham.

I answered the phone, but kept my eye on the director of golf watching for any hints at a problem. He was scrutinizing everything behind the grill. He checked the grease trap and the condiments bar. He even poured himself a Coke out of the fountain machine. I'm sure that he wasn't thirsty and that he was actually checking the level of carbonation in the fountain machine.

After my distracted greeting, the caller on the phone, a middle-aged sounding man, said, "Yeah, I'm out here on the fourth hole, and there's a foursome of old men in front of us that are so slow that there is an open hole in front of them."

I was still more interested in the movements of Cunningham, so I responded out of habit with the same thing I've said all day. I'm sorry sir; we don't have any open tee times until 3:16."

"Aren't you listening to me," the guy said. "I'm not trying to get a tee time, I'm on number four tee right now, and there are four old guys in front of us holding up the whole course."

Cunningham seemed to be finished with the grill. Lisa and Missy were frantically scrubbing the counter to please the bastard. He made his way around the corner and

18 Holes of Green

glanced at the thermostat on the wall. He took off his glasses and peered at it to ensure it was set at 77 degrees.

Realizing the guy was on a cell phone and feeling pretty stupid, I replied with a question to appear concerned, "So you're on number four tee?"

Cunningham turned and began walking toward the pro shop.

"Yeah, it's pretty bad," the caller said.

I glanced all around behind the counter to make sure it was in order. I looked for anything we wouldn't want him to see. "We'll get someone right out there," I replied.

"I sure would appreciate it," the man said.

I hung up the phone and wanted to go outside to warn John and Mark about Cunningham, but he was walking right toward me. He still had to wind his way through the maze of tables and chairs in the dining area of the grill. I decided to chance appearing to be in a panic and walked right outside to tell them what the guy on the phone said. Hopefully, I would catch them before Cunningham was close enough to see them pitching balls at the green through the window.

I saw Cunningham's face show concern as I left the pro shop counter and walked out the door. He was about halfway to the pro shop and almost close enough to be able to see Mark and John through the window. I took long steps so as to move quickly, but not appear to be running. After three long steps, I heard the clubhouse door close behind me. With the director now unable to hear me, I shouted toward Mark and John, "Cunningham is here!"

They went into crisis mode. John immediately turned, walked toward the starter's table and began pointing to the tee pretending to be doing something. Mark headed straight for me to return to the pro shop.

Timothy McHugh

I stopped him and told him of the guy who called about the slow foursome of old men. He took the opportunity to avoid Cunningham and turned back toward the line of carts saying that he'd take care of it himself. He got in a cart and headed out onto the first nine.

I turned around to find Hugh Cunningham standing in the doorway of the clubhouse looking out at me. He was holding the door open with one hand and had the other propped up against the doorframe so as to get control of the situation. I walked toward him, quickly thinking of what to tell him. I could simply tell him the truth, or I could try to think of something better in the next two seconds.

As I approached him, I was getting more nervous with every step. He seemed to be looking for a problem today. Had he seen Mark and John pitching balls to the putting green? What would he say?

He greeted me as soon as I neared him. "Hello Brian."

"Hi Mr. Cunningham." Everyone called him Hugh, but I always laid it on pretty thick. You've got to have an edge.

"What was that all about?" he asked in his high browed tone.

I proceeded to tell him of the customer service emergency on number four. I explained to him that there was a report of some extreme slow play and that Mark was going to coordinate with the ranger on the scene to investigate. Basically, he was going out to wake up Leo.

"Well I hope so," he replied with vigor. "We can't have slow play on the busiest day of the year."

"No sir," I agreed.

"Could be that crossover thing confused someone," he said. "I'm not sure that it's really the best way to go."

18 Holes of Green

I couldn't believe that he was actually blaming the crossover format for slow play. It's not like we were asking people to play the holes in any different order, it's just one nine holes and then another.

"Probably someone who keeps losing balls," I replied trying to steer the conversation back to a sensible line of reasoning.

"I've told all the county greens keepers that I want the tall grass reduced on our courses," he said. "Way too much tall grass here at White Lake. Way too much."

So much for a sensible line of reasoning. Sure, reducing the amount of tall grass on the course would speed up play, but so would putting the ball in the hole for the players. Where do you draw the line? While reducing the number of people who have to look for their balls, it would also reduce the character of the golf course. We don't have a lake anymore. Very few fairway bunkers. The tall grass was one of the only challenges that White Lake could offer. It resembled Scottish heather. To cut it to the ground or shrink its size to nonexistence would seem a sacrilege.

Cunningham turned away from me and walked back into the clubhouse without saying a word. He was likely going to talk to Andy. I turned and looked toward John who was now holding a clipboard and talking to a group making the turn. I gave him a thumbs-up and he smiled in acknowledgement. When I entered the clubhouse, I glanced over to the office and could hear Andy and Hugh talking. Andy never took any shit from the director, but he always talked to him in the most diplomatic way. Andy had a way of telling you "no," but making you feel like you won some- thing. He could be charming, professional and courteous as hell, if he either worked for you or was trying to sell you something.

Timothy McHugh

I saw that the phone was not ringing for the first time all day, so I headed toward the grill to get away for a moment. I pushed a few chairs into their tables as I made my way to the grill. Missy was busy helping someone at the counter, but Lisa was wiping off the tops of bottles in the cooler due to the inspection. I approached her and asked how he was today.

"His usual anal-retentive self," she replied as she wiped bottle tops. She paused from her work for a moment, turned and looked toward me. "What was he looking at outside?"

"I had to warn Mark and John that he was here. He almost saw them chipping balls to the putting green." I went on to tell her about the guy who called from his cell phone to complain about some slow play.

"Probably one of them old Birdie Hunters," she suggested.

"More than likely," I agreed. They had a few old guys who would never give up on a lost ball. They'd look for it until the sun went down if they could.

I walked around behind the counter and poured myself a Mountain Dew. Lisa asked if I wanted anything to eat and I told her that Andy was going to pick us up some burger's. I grabbed a Snickers Bar to tide myself over.

"Do you want anything from Wendy's?" I asked.

"Yeah, I'll take a Frosty," she answered.

That's what I figured. Lisa was never one to turn down a Frosty. I don't remember her ever getting a burger or fries, only Frosties. Missy never wanted anything. She hardly ate a thing and was skinny as a rail. I guess if I slopped together greasy food all day for ungrateful men, I wouldn't eat either.

"Does Missy want anything?" I asked. "No, she's dieting again," Lisa replied.

18 Holes of Green

I chuckled with a smile and turned away from her. As I headed back toward the pro shop, I could see Hugh Cunningham and Andy talking behind the counter. They were laughing and smiling as if they were the best of friends. Andy sure was good at kissing ass. I didn't exactly want to resume my post with Cunningham still behind the counter. It appeared that Paul had vanished from the clubhouse so I stopped at Old Wes's table to check in on him. He appeared tired from talking to each group of Birdie Hunters that came through the clubhouse. He was just gazing out the window when I stopped next to him.

"How's it going Wes?" I asked loudly to announce my presence.

"When I was playing in the league," he said with hoarse voice and a cough. "We never went inside the clubhouse at the turn; we went straight to number ten. We drank from the water fountain and we didn't have to eat because our wives had fed us a big breakfast before we left the house," he continued. Wes loved to tell us how things used to be. "If we had to take a piss, we did it behind a tree. There was no reason to come inside the pro shop after nine holes. That's what letting women play has done to the game. It has to be domestic. We have to wash our hands and watch our mouths. That's not what golf is supposed to be about."

There was something that he said toward the end of his tirade that seemed to make sense despite his otherwise wild and sexist ranting. I did enjoy going straight from nine green to 10 tee.

It looked like Andy had successfully appeased the Director's concerns. Cunningham began walking out from behind the counter, but he stopped suddenly as he rounded the corner. He stared down in disgust at the display that held scorecards and pencils. The pro shop phone rang so I headed to the counter. Andy stepped toward Cunningham to see what was troubling him. As I passed the corner where Cunningham was standing I heard him lecture Andy on the pencil box. Apparently, not all the pencils were pointed in the same direction. Some were pointing up and some were pointing down.

The chaos that this created was unfathomable to us but all too real to Hugh Cunningham. He appeared to be genuinely disturbed in an unhealthy way by the non-synchronized stacking of each and every pencil.

Once behind the counter, I picked up the phone and answered it. Although I was explaining our tee time policy the caller, all my attention was on Andy's face. I was looking for a smile or a sneer, but there wasn't any crack in his armor. He remained stone-faced toward the Director.

After all, the pencils all start out pointing the same way. We should be pleased that some of them actually get recycled rather than upset about the manner in which they are returned.

Finally, after a brief moment of silence, Andy looked right at him and said, "Hugh, you have got to have something more important to worry about. Like stopping that reverse pivot."

Cunningham smiled and agreed as I recited our open tee times for Sunday afternoon. He was so self-involved that any interest in his game brought forth an unwarranted level of confidence. Andy liked to feed his ego about his golf game because he knew that he'd always have the edge there. Cunningham was a hack and Andy's advice went a long way. I couldn't hear what else they said to each other, but Andy had definitely lightened the Director's mood. He seemed so pleased with himself that he didn't bother to inspect Lisa's progress behind the grill on his way out. He walked right by her and out the back door.

As soon as I hung up the phone, Andy began cursing Cunningham's existence. He didn't just say the Director was full of shit, he questioned whether he was worthy of being deemed human. Kissing Cunningham's ass so well came at a price. It was difficult for Andy to forgive himself. Nevertheless, the Director's scrutiny had been deflected one more time. That just meant that he would be harder on the other golf courses that he visited later that day.

As usual, Andy quickly changed the subject to something positive. He said he was going to stop at Wendy's on the way back from the bank and asked me to get everyone's orders. We all looked forward to lunch. Then, he returned to the office to finish putting together the morning deposit.

Just then, John called in on the radio that we used to communicate between the pro shop and the starter and ranger.

"Where the hell is Hank?" asked John.

"I don't know," I replied. "Last time I saw him, he was heading for the men's room."

"That was twenty minutes ago," responded John. "Go check on him."

"I'm not going in there," I replied.

"We have to make sure he's ok," said John.

"Uh huh," I answered as I turned to look for Paul. It would be much better to send another old guy in there after him, I thought. But he wasn't sitting at the table with Wes anymore. Wes wasn't an option. He would get lost in the Men's room by himself. Fred was still sitting at the table next to him, but he was transfixed by the news. Fred would never get up from that table to check on Hank. Not unless I told him there was a TV in there with the news on it.

I looked out toward the tees, but I didn't see him out there. It appeared that I was going to have to go check on Hank myself. I looked at the phone on the wall, hoping that it would ring and get me out of this. Unfortunately, it remained silent. With no one presently at the counter, I headed though the grill and toward the bathroom hallway. As I approached the door, I started to think that it was no big deal. Some older people just take a while to go to the bathroom. There was no way he was lying on the floor helpless or anything. If he was, I sure hoped he still had his pants on.

I reached the door of the men's room and briefly paused. I placed my hand on the door as if to test for the warmth of a fire. After a moment, I got up my nerve and pushed open the door. As I took one step inside, I was greeted with the most devastating odor I had ever smelled. The overwhelming stench of death hit me like a breaking wave. It was so wretched that I started to gag. I quickly turned around and hurried back out of the bathroom gasping for air. It felt as if I had been sprayed in the face with mace as tears began to run out of my eyes. I had encountered some awful smells in the bathroom over the years, but this one was beyond belief.

I bypassed the pro shop and quickly walked straight outside for some fresh air. I coughed a few times and took some deep breaths. After hanging my head low and closing my eyes for a few moments, I looked up to see John facing me.

"You sound like you're dying," he said. "You didn't eat a hotdog, did you?"

"No, you asshole," I said. "I went in the bathroom to check on Hank and it smelled like something died in there."

18 Holes of Green

"Was Hank OK?" he asked.

"Hell, if I know. I got the hell out of there," I replied as I coughed a few more times. "It was like tear gas," I added.

John finally seemed to sense the seriousness of the situation. He offered to get me the oxygen tank. Now, he was just being a jerk. I assured him that I would be all right in a moment and he suggested that we switch places for a while. That sounded great to me. I needed the fresh air. It was the only thing saving me at that moment.

He went inside to take care of the pro shop and I walked toward the starter's table. I sat down to catch my breath and enjoy the brief moment of peace. Then Harley came riding around the corner and parked his maintenance cart next to the table.

"What's the matter Brian my boy?" he asked in a friendly way. His appearance at that moment was unwelcome, but I could tell that he was genuinely interested.

"I just encountered the nastiest smell in the world."

"What was it?" he asked.

I walked in the men's room while Hank was taking a dump."

"That's messed up," replied Harley.

"Yeah, it was awful," I said.

"There sure are a lot of people hitting balls at the range," said Harley. "It's good that people want to practice, but I wish they'd take their time. For so many of them, it's rapid fire. They hit one right after the other without any breaks. You can't work on your swing that way. Besides, if they slowed down, I wouldn't have to pick up the balls so fast."

He laughed at his own joke without shame. No one would ever say that he lacked self-confidence. He was oblivious to the fact that I was not in the mood to listen to him rant. I felt like the wind had been knocked out of me and his story was giving me a headache. He just went right on telling me about his day.

Harley had a unique philosophy. He got along well with all of us, but he had a deep disdain for people in general. He was divorced and that combined with the loss of his parents made him act a little peculiar. He apparently had a nervous breakdown a few years ago and luckily his brother stepped in to take care of him. Now, Harley had a trust fund to live off responsibly. That enabled him to work at the golf course and have fewer worries. He often spoke at length about the importance of nature and the benefits of being outside.

I certainly enjoyed being outside half the year, but this wasn't Florida. I wouldn't want to work outside year-round up here. I guess that's why I went to college. As eccentric as Harley was, he was still a pleasure to work with. He worked hard and was the most honest fellow you would ever find. My stomach and my head started to feel better. It must have been the fresh air.

It was then that I saw Mark returning in a cart from out on the course. He drove in from the cart path on hole number nine, parked his cart at the end of the line and walked over toward us.

"What are you doing out here, Bri?" asked Mark.

"I needed some air," I responded.

"Hank dropped a stink bomb in the men's room," added Harley.

"Is he still in there?" asked Mark.

"Yeah, I think he died in there," I answered.

"Wonderful," replied Mark. "It was a mess out there on number four. Roscoe and Stew had an open hole in front of them and were looking for balls in the trees."

18 Holes of Green

"No wonder the guy called us on his cell phone," I replied.

"Yeah, I would have been angry too if I were behind them," added Mark. "And you can't reason with them," he went on. "They just don't want to ever give up on a lost ball. I gave them each a handful of balls that I had been chipping with. That seemed to satisfy them for the time being."

Harley had come to the clubhouse for a purpose. He quickly changed the subject because he knew that Andy would be leaving soon and he wanted to place his lunch order. I told him and Mark that it would be Wendy's that day and they both became eager to write down their orders. Harley got back in his maintenance cart and proceeded to drive it around to the back of the clubhouse. Mark and I both headed inside to place our orders. As I opened the door, I saw Paul talking to John at the counter. Naturally, he had returned in time to place his lunch order.

"Andy wants to know why you don't have the lunch list going yet," John said to me.

"Umm, maybe it's because you made me go in that gas chamber to check on Hank," I replied.

"Has he come out yet?" asked Paul.

"Not yet," answered John.

"Somebody ought to check on him," said Mark.

"I wouldn't recommend it," I commented as I grabbed a yellow legal pad and a pen. I began writing down everyone's order. I liked taking the orders because I wanted to make sure that mine was right. I was a little picky about what I ate. Everyone else was pretty straightforward except for Paul. He was as picky as I was. Old men could be very particular.

First, I wrote down Lisa's Frosty. Paul gave me his order next and then I was on a roll. A "number one" with a diet Coke for Mark. Harley had arrived and was bouncing up and down he was so anxious to give me his order. He was afraid that we'd forget him. Such an act would be impossible considering his determination to make himself known.

He shouted to me and I acknowledged that I was ready. I didn't need to hear him recite his order. I knew it by heart. He got the same thing every time.

"Brian, I'll take a Double Combo with a Coke," he recited like a poem. "And Biggie Size it because I'm a hard-working boy."

"Got it," I replied in a monotone of annoyance.

Andy walked out from the office just at the right time.

"I see that my staff has doubled in size now that it's lunch time," he said.

"Yeah, and it shrinks in half when Hugh Cunningham shows up," said John.

"Well, I can't blame you all for that," Andy replied. John proceeded to give me his large order. He was a big guy and he sure ate like one. He wasn't fat, just tall and stocky. He wanted a double with everything, a spicy chicken sandwich and fries. Next, I meticulously wrote down my order: a single with pickles, onions, ketchup and bacon only, no cheese and biggie fries.

I handed the list to Andy as he zipped up the brown canvas bank pouch. He gazed at the list with an animated look of dismay. He liked to make us all feel guilty for his generosity.

"Where's the cash?" he asked.

Paul and Harley walked away from the counter toward the grill. John, Mark and I looked away and acted busy as if we didn't hear him.

"That's what I thought," he replied as he walked out of the pro shop and toward the backdoor.

18 Holes of Green

There were a few people congregating around the starter's table so John walked back outside to assist them. As Mark and I talked to each other behind the pro shop counter, Roger Merchant exited the men's restroom with a sick look on his face. Roger played in the skins game and must have been making the turn.

Mark and I turned to each other and chuckled when we saw him approaching.

"What the hell happened in there?" he asked. "It's Hank," I replied. "Did you see him in there?"

"I heard someone moaning in one of the stalls," he answered.

"You guys need to do something about that," he said. "Call homeland security or something."

"Yeah, we'll get the chemical response team in there," Mark replied.

Roger walked toward the grill to join his group who were at the counter getting some food. I turned to answer the phone which just started ringing. As I picked up the phone, I saw Hank emerging from the men's room. He was headed toward the pro shop with a grin on his face. Mark glanced at me to see if I had also seen him and then he turned to face Hank. They spoke to each other briefly as I explained our tee time situation to the guy on the phone. After a moment, Hank walked back outside toward the tees as if nothing happened. I walked closer to the window stretching the phone cord as I watched Hank approaching John. He spoke to John for a few seconds and then sat down at the starter's table.

John grabbed his sand wedge that was leaning against the split-rail fence and walked toward the practice green. I finished my conversation with the guy on the phone and turned toward Mark.

"What did Hank have to say?" I asked.

"He just asked how the tee was moving and wanted to make sure you had ordered his "number three."

"Nobody told me to order him a "number three,"" I replied.

"Well, he thought you should have known," Mark answered.

"That's bullshit," I replied. "This isn't a retirement home. I'm not a caregiver."

"Just call Andy's cell," said Mark.

I went ahead and called Andy while he was still in his car. As I was giving him Hank's order, I saw a few more golfers who were making the turn walk over to talk to Mark. I couldn't hear exactly what they were saying, but they appeared to be complaining about something. After Andy took another opportunity to jokingly claim that his generosity was being exploited, I hung up the phone.

Mark told me that two more players had complained about the men's room. We argued over who was going to do something about it for a moment. Naturally, I ended up being the one who had to go in there. I grudgingly walked to the back hallway and grabbed a can of disinfectant spray from the janitor's closet.

As I walked back through the grill toward the men's room, I could feel the eyes of everyone in the clubhouse watching me. They all knew what I was on my way to do. I stopped at the door for a moment. Then, I took a deep breath and quickly ran inside the restroom. I held my breath as I continuously sprayed pine scented industrial disinfectant all over the room. After making my way toward the window, I slid it open with one hand and continued spraying with the other. I kept my finger on the nozzle without any pauses. About 30 seconds I exhaled, but did not inhale. Then, after about 30 more seconds, I could feel my lungs begging for air. I

18 Holes of Green

quickly ran back outside the restroom and inhaled once the door had closed behind me.

The clubhouse immediately erupted in applause and rowdy screams then turned in to laughter. I started to turn red with embarrassment, but I quickly progressed into a proud confidence.

"Hey, I'm the only one young enough here to take it," I pronounced as defensive fire. They returned fire with more laughter. However, this time they seemed to be laughing with me rather than at me. Sometimes respect can only be earned through verbal combat.

I made my way back to the pro shop with the excitement dying. Mark was smiling with glee. He took pleasure in sending me on such a humiliating task. It was just more friendly combat. I'd get him back sometime.

"Way to go Brian!" shouted Roger Merchant from the grill. "I hope you got hazard pay."

His buddies from the skins game all laughed and I waved in acknowledgement. I gave Mark a friendly punch in the shoulder as he answered the phone. It made him fumble in his greeting on the phone and I smiled at him to rub it in. He turned away from me and glanced at the tee time computer.

Paul and Harley were returning from the grill. They appeared to be involved in a serious debate. I could hear them better as they got closer to the pro shop. Paul appeared to be trying to convince Harley that hitting balls at the range was hurting his game.

"You're at your best when you're playing on the course with your friends," Paul said to Harley. "You are in a rhythm when you're playing a round of golf. You're a physical player. You shouldn't be analyzing your swing for hours at a driving range. You should be muscling the ball straight out of a crooked swing."

Harley seemed stunned from the moment Paul said the word "physical." That was music to his ears.

"I should be playing rather than thinking. Not bullshitting," said Harley, as if Paul had made a revelation. "I'd rather be a player than coach," he added.

"That's the way," responded Paul, who seemed grateful to be taken so seriously.

There was never a dull moment around the clubhouse. Paul and Harley both stepped behind the counter and grabbed my clipboard to look at the tee sheet. They were looking for an opening as Mark hung up the phone with a huge grin on his face.

"Must have been a girl," I said.

"She laughed when I stumbled answering the phone," he replied. "It was the best laugh.

"You sucker," I commented. Mark was notoriously vulnerable to a cute girl with a nice voice. He'd do anything for them and get trampled on in the process. That was his problem with Ashley.

Paul turned away from Harley to face us. I thought that he was surely going to join me in ridiculing Mark, but instead he changed the subject.

"Fred says that the C130s have already left Wright Patterson," he stated sincerely. "They should be overhead soon. The jump is scheduled for twelve noon."

"You actually believe him?" I asked.

"Well there was something on about a paratrooper reunion," Paul responded. "But I couldn't see where it was. Fred seems pretty adamant though."

"I think Williams Field would have notified us if something like that was happening," added Mark.

18 Holes of Green

"Jumping out of C130s, now that's physical," said Harley.

"I think Brian is the hero of the day for going in there after Hank," said Paul.

"It was dangerous," I replied.

"Whatever," responded Mark.

"Paul, you are playing with Harley?" he asked.

"Well, I might if it's not too slow out there," he replied.

"Your idea of not being crowded is one group on each nine," I replied.

I was exaggerating, but Paul could not stand to have a group behind him or in front of him. I hated to be pushed from behind, but I could handle a slow group in front of me. That's life. I'll count my blessings all day long if there is no one pushing me. I'll follow a slow group of golfers and take my time to practice a little and cherish the fact that no one is behind me. Usually when we played, we'd find the slowest group on the course and jump in front of them. Sometimes you could find an entire open hole in front of a really slow group.

"Well, we'll see what it looks like after three o'clock," said Paul. "If those paratroopers cause a spectacle in the air, it could back up the whole course."

"I don't think you have to worry about that," I responded.

"I'm going to be a player," said Harley.

The phone rang and Mark answered it. He began explaining our tee time situation as a group of weekend warriors came into the clubhouse. They were apparently making the turn. They were in their thirties and looked like yuppies. They were dressed very well, but seemed a little unfamiliar with golf in general. They stood a few steps inside the door of the clubhouse gazing toward the grill. Then all four of them turned toward the pro shop and slowly approached the counter. I walked up toward the front of the counter to help them as the most assertive of the four approached.

"How are you doing?" I asked.

"Well, we have a complaint to register," the tall, skinny gentleman replied.

"Oh, what is it?" I asked assuming it would be regarding the slow play.

"Well, you really shouldn't let the sprinklers go on while people are playing," he said. "It made it very difficult to play out the hole."

I explained to the man that the summer was very hot and we did have to water the course several times a day to keep it in good shape. I went on to explain that if we didn't water the fairways at all during daylight hours that the grass would burn out.

The gentleman acknowledged that he understood and the four of them walked over toward the grill. As soon as they were out of earshot, I turned to Paul and Harley and expressed my frustration.

"What the hell was that?" I asked rhetorically.

"The holiday weekends bring out all types to play," replied Paul.

"That's messed up," said Harley.

I agreed with him and went on to vent about the complaint. I didn't mind if someone complained to us for a valid reason. Slow play and course conditions were fair game, but to bitch about the sprinklers coming on was absurd.

Mark hung up the phone and asked what was going on. When I explained, what had happened, he was in awe. It wasn't often that a new one came our way, but that was White

18 Holes of Green

Lake. As soon as you thought you had seen it all, something crazier came along.

"I remember when they used to have to pump water out of the old lake to water the course," said Paul. "They didn't put in the irrigation system until 1972."

"That's getting back to nature," commented Harley.

"Yeah, poor Ron Walden, the greens keeper, had to keep moving the hoses and sprinklers every day to water the fairways and greens," added Paul. "He had a whole network of hoses and connections spanning most of the golf course.

"That's wild," I said.

"Sounds pretty physical," said Harley.

"I'm sure you would have loved it," added Mark.

"Definitely," responded Harley.

Paul laughed and took his hat off of his head. "Harley, you were born 30 years too late," he proclaimed.

That was a deep statement that seemed to perplex Harley for the moment. Something like that was bound to keep him thinking for hours. I answered the next phone call as Paul settled into the chair by the window. On the phone was Alice from the driving range. She was looking for Harley. She had a stack of empty baskets that needed to be filled.

"He just left here a minute ago," I said as I glared at Harley. "I'm sure that he'll be back down there soon." I hated to lie to Alice, but I had to cover a little for Harley. Alice had run the driving range forever. She was as sweet as could be, but she knew what made the driving range work. Being nice to people and having plenty of golf balls were essential. Alice was always nice, but having enough balls was sometimes a challenge. In the spring, the range would be so wet and swampy that the mud would literally swallow the balls. In the summer, there would be so many people hitting balls that a picker would have a hard time keeping up.

Timothy McHugh

I hung up the phone and looked at Harley. Everyone knew who had called. Harley was a hard worker, but he loved to slip away from Alice occasionally and hang with the guys. He claimed to despise being social, but he was notorious for sitting down with news junkie Fred to discuss current events. Those two had some wild discussions.

"Guess who's looking for you?" I asked him.

"My dear sweet adopted mother," he responded.

"I thought she was my mother, "said Mark.

"She's everyone's mother," I answered.

The others laughed in agreement. Paul might have been more of a brother to her than a son, but the love was there nonetheless. Harley turned like a dutiful farm hand and headed toward the back door where he had parked his maintenance cart.

As he walked back through the grill, Fred turned away from the television and shouted to Harley.

"Keep an eye on sky," he said. "Those C130s should be overhead soon."

"Will do," Harley responded. He'd have Alice restocked on baskets of range balls in no time and be back up at the clubhouse in time for lunch. None of us paid much attention to Fred's insistence that the 82nd Airborne was heading to William's Field.

John walked in the door and took his sunglasses off. He had worked up a sweat practicing his short game while he worked the tee.

"Where's Andy?" he asked. "Hank is getting pretty hungry out there."

"That's because he's doing all the work," Mark replied.

"I think it's because he's running on empty after his trip to the Men's room," I added.

18 Holes of Green

John and Mark laughed as Paul chuckled trying to stop from laughing.

"Hell, he's lucky that he got his order in at all," added Mark.

That was true. I couldn't believe that he expected me to automatically order his lunch. I work with the guy one day a week and he thinks I should remember his eating habits. He was a nice guy and all, but he never did anything for me to warrant that type of expectation.

All of a sudden, the sound of someone snoring came from the grill. We all turned slowly to confirm our suspicions. There was Wes still sitting at the closest table facing the window. His head was bowed straight down and his mouth was wide open. He was out for the count. It was a common occurrence when Wes was at the clubhouse.

"Wow, it's not even noon yet," said John.

"Yeah, he's a little early," I commented.

Paul went on to tell us that Wes was tired because his daughter had him over to celebrate some family birthdays the night before. A group of golfers came in the door while they were making the turn. They couldn't help but slow down and gaze at Wes snoring away as they walked past him. It had to be an unusual sight for someone new to White Lake.

It was then that the door facing the first and tenth tees opened and Nate Boylan walked in grinning from ear to ear. Behind him came the rest of his foursome. They were making the turn and no doubt refilling their coolers.

"I have two skins for sure and maybe a third," Nate proclaimed. "I talked to Willie a few groups back and no one has me beat on three, five or eight. There were only two groups behind his. Hell, this game is getting easier every week."

Willie, Nate's brother, was an even bigger hustler than he was. I wouldn't trust the two of them when it came to any type of gambling. Nate proceeded to summarize his excellent round for us while his three teammates went on to the grill. John and Mark took turns attacking him and raising doubt about his score.

Paul joined the fun by making his own observation. "You talk a great game, but you've never measured up to the talk when I've played with you."

"That's because it wouldn't be polite to show up an old man," answered Nate.

"Well, this old man will gladly keep taking your money," replied Paul. "After all, I am on a fixed income."

"Y'all better keep moving along out there," said John. "I don't need a bunch of our employees slowing down the course. You guys should have turned twenty minutes ago."

"It's all those Birdie Hunters out there," responded Nate. "They have the whole course backed up. What are they doing playing 18 holes anyway?"

"It's a holiday," answered Mark. "I was out there moving along old Roscoe and Stew."

"Roscoe and Stew, that figures," said Nate as he turned and walked into the grill to join his teammates who were loading up on beer.

"Make sure you get enough Bud Light," he yelled as he approached them. "I'm not drinking that Miller that you guys think is so great."

Nate Boylan was outlandish, but theatrical enough to be entertaining. Playing with him was always an experience. You had to watch his score keeping, but his camaraderie was usually a confidence boost. Confidence goes a long way on the golf course. I would speculate that it is the most key ingredient to playing well. There was something about Nate's

18 Holes of Green

blatant directness that actually made you feel better than someone who might be more of a cheerleading influence. I'd rather my playing partner poke fun at my bad shots than hear the words "good shot" out of sympathy.

That's probably the real reason that Nate's team wins the skins game so often regardless of whom he's playing with. The teams are relatively equal every week, each with an A, B, C and D player. Nate just inspires people to play well for some reason. It's his personality that invites everyone to explain it by saying that he cheats. Even though no one has caught him and often it's his teammates that play the best, it's more fun to harass him about it. That's the way the skins game is. Everyone bitches except for the team that wins and anyone who grabs a skin.

The phone rang behind me so I turned to answer it. As I picked up the receiver, Mark was smiling and bullshitting with John. He looked like a kid enjoying life. That was until I answered the call and he heard me say, "hi Ashley" to his loving fiancée. The expression on his face went from youthful exuberance to despair and gloom. It was if the sky had darkened and the smell of death was in the air. Maybe it was somewhat due to the rolling of my eyes as I greeted her or John's laughter at the sound of her name. However, he too must have had a deep disdain for her at least on some levels in order to go through such a visible change in expression and demeanor.

Mark did his duty and picked up the phone. John smiled at me and turned toward the computer to print a new copy of the tee sheet to take outside. Paul was leaning up against the counter facing the big screen in the grill. Fred had actually gotten out of his seat in front of the television and was walking toward the pro shop. Paul stepped away from the counter and slowly approached Fred.

Timothy McHugh

They met next to the table where Wes was sitting all alone. There they could see out the large picture window toward the tees. Fred squatted and bent at the waist to look up through the window. The patio roof obscured most of his view, but he must have been able to see some of the sky. Wes was oblivious to the fact that they were standing next to him. Fred gazed out the window for a few seconds obviously looking for the 82nd Airborne. Paul bent down beside him to take a look for himself. I fully expected them both to get stuck in that position and need help straightening back up.

After a moment, Fred stood back up and Paul followed his lead. Without saying a word, Fred hurried back to his seat in front of the TV. Paul said something to Wes, then slowly turned and made his way back toward the pro shop.

"Fred says that to honor World War Two veterans, the 250 paratroopers are going to use the vintage style chutes," said Paul as he stopped in front of the door. "You know the big round ones that you can't really steer. Hell, that should be a sight."

He smiled and backed himself out the door to the patio smiling and humming. Such behavior might seem odd in most civilized parts of the world, but Paul and Fred were not at all acting unusual for the golf course. I had become accustomed to such behavior. Once they got a thought in their heads that they found amusing, you might as well forget about having a conversation with them. Sometimes they were almost childlike in their glee.

From behind the pro shop counter, I could see out onto the patio and most of the first and tenth tees. I watched Paul slowly stroll out toward Hank who was back working the tee after his rest and relaxation. Hank was standing next to the starter's table holding his clipboard. He was staring at

18 Holes of Green

something near the tenth tee when Paul reached him. They both turned and gazed toward the back nine. They appeared to be discussing whatever it was they were watching.

"What's going on?" asked John as he walked up beside me.

"I don't know. They seem to be looking at something," I replied.

"Let's check it out," suggested John as he stepped out from behind the counter and toward the door. I immediately followed him leaving Mark on the phone with Ashley. He was in a world of his own and never noticed us leave. I would much prefer Paul's world to Mark's.

I was with John step for step as we walked across the patio and then onto the brick walkway that led to the starter's table. As we approached Paul and Hank, they appeared to be in absolute awe of something we could not yet see. Their mouths were both open wide enough to hold a golf ball and they were as still as statues. Hank had removed his hat and placed his hand on his head in some primal attempt at processing the information his eyes were receiving.

I assumed that we would find them gazing at a deer or a cardinal. Something you might expect to see on a beautiful summer day. To my surprise, it was not Mother Nature they were appreciating, but rather the dazzling display of a gyrating female form on the fifteenth green.

John and I both stood silently as we took a moment to register our own sensory input. After a moment, I was sure of what I was seeing. Within a small opening in the tree line, there was a completely naked young lady dancing on the fifteenth green. There was a group of golfers sitting on the green in a half circle watching.

Finally, John broke the silence with a reasonable explanation. "Must be that bachelor party that's out there," he suggested.

"Oh, that makes sense," said Paul as he continued to gaze at the sight.

Hank continued to stand silently in amazement of what he was witnessing. I stood still as well. Frozen in place I simply agreed, "Yeah, that's the bachelor party."

"I guess I'll have to make sure they move along," said John with a smile.

"I may be better suited for the job," said Paul. "I was a police officer."

"Paul, you'd have a heart attack if you got too close to that action," said John as he turned and started walking toward the front cart in the line.

Fred had walked out to join us while we weren't paying attention. "Do you see the planes yet?" he asked.

"No Fred," said John as he continued to walk. "What we see is far more entertaining than any paratrooper jump."

"I'll go with you," I suggested as I started to follow John. As I took a couple of steps I could hear the rumbling sound of a large plane approaching. The deep low roar grew louder than that of the typical plane we were used to hearing overhead.

John and I stopped in our tracks as we began to consider the possibility that Fred had been right all along. The approaching plane sounded like a humming subwoofer on a surround sound system. It grew louder even still as we could almost feel the vibrations. Just as the noise contin- ued to become more intense, a low flying military cargo plane roared overhead. It wasn't flying low enough to be on an approach to land, but it was low enough to suggest a local purpose.

18 Holes of Green

"I knew they were coming," shouted Fred. "Both Fox News and CNN were saying so. I can't wait to see them." The rest of us were motionless and silent for a moment. We all knew at that point that Fred had been right all along.

As the lumbering giant passed over the golf course and approached Williams Field, we could see objects coming out of the side of the plane. It felt like the Thanksgiving episode of WKRP for a moment. Unlike the Turkeys that Mr. Carlson had dropped, this Holiday skydive involved parachutes. Just as Fred had promised, the sky was soon filled with World War Two style parachutes drifting to the ground.

"Oh my, is it beautiful," said Fred.

"It sure is," said Paul.

Within a moment, another plane roared overhead and more of the 82nd Airborne jumped out. One by one, three more of the giant planes flew low over us. It was so loud that we didn't bother trying to speak. The group of us along with everyone else in the vicinity was staring upward.

After the last plane pulled up and away, there were more paratroopers in the air than I could have imagined. They were floating down in all directions.

"It feels like a war zone," said Mark. "It's like Red Dawn," I added.

"Wolverines!" shouted John.

"It's World War Two," said Paul.

"And no damn Germans to shoot holes in them like they did us when I was jumping out of those things," added Hank.

"I thought you worked on the engines?" asked Mark.

"I did," answered Hank. "But I went on several missions as a flight mechanic."

"You never jumped," said Fred.

"I did in training," responded Hank.

"Well, you served and that's enough," said Paul.

The C130s had all moved out of earshot at that point. While most of the Airborne were sailing toward the airport, many of them were drifting over the golf course. It became clear pretty quickly that there were going to be paratroopers landing all over the back nine.

"Well, this is all very interesting," said John. "However, I have a job to do." He turned and began walking toward the cart again.

Realizing what he meant, I chased after him to assist. We reached the cart at the front of the line together. I slid in next to him as he pulled out his set of keys that had a cart key in addition to keys for his car and house. We all kept golf cart keys on our key chains. It just made things easier. As we pulled away and headed toward the back nine, I turned and looked into the sky to see the paratroopers. They were slowly drifting toward the ground.

The others all turned their eyes skyward as well. I could see Fred with a smile of satisfaction on his face. Mark, Hank and Paul all appeared to be in awe. I turned around and faced forward to see several of the Airborne descending over the back nine. While most of the 250 paratroopers were safely making their way to Williams Field, there were about forty to fifty that had been blown short of their destination. The vintage style chutes apparently weren't very accurate.

As John and I approached the fifteenth green, we could see that even the female entertainer had noticed the unusual visitors. Two of the Airborne were close to landing on the fifteenth fairway just in front of the green. This whole evolving situation had the words "incident report" written all over it. The county commissioners would flip out about either of these events by themselves. The combination of

18 Holes of Green

paratroopers swooping down on a dancer doing a strip tease on the fifteenth green would surely get someone in hot water.

By the time, we arrived on the scene, the paratroopers had landed and disconnected themselves from their equipment. They had approached the green and were checking out someone else's equipment. John parked our cart and we approached the green.

"I'll take the lead," John said to me as we walked.

"It's all you," I replied.

When we reached the cast of characters, John was cool as ever. He acted as if this was nothing new and quickly took control of the situation. He joked that the paratroopers had landed here on purpose when they saw what was happening. Then, he ignored the presence of the stripper as an issue by itself and simply told the guys that they were holding up the pace of play. He amused me by implying that if they had kept moving along at a better pace, the dancing would not have been an issue.

After a bit of friendly banter, John had the golfers moving on their way and the dancer was going to ride in with us. She quickly dressed and sat down next to John. I had to stand hanging on the back of the cart and hang onto the roof supports. John told the paratroopers that we would send someone out to pick them up and we headed in toward the clubhouse. John made small talk with his new friend as he drove us down the cart path. It turned out that her name was Star. It seemed to fit her pretty well. She certainly had John captivated for the entire ride.

We pulled up to the clubhouse and I hopped off the back of the cart. I found Paul and asked him to head back out to help me pick up the two paratroopers. John, of course, escorted Star to the patio and helped her take a seat. Paul was eager to help me assist a couple of America's bravest.

I hopped back in the cart and Paul got into another. He followed me out toward number fifteen to meet the paratroopers. They had just finished rolling up their chutes into manageable bundles when we arrived. Paul was relishing the moment as he introduced himself. He lavished praise on their performance and asked them about their jumps. He was like a little kid meeting his favorite ballplayer.

We offered them rides back to Williams's field and so one of them hopped in the cart with each of us. My passenger was named Patrick and Paul's was Eric. They were very friendly and casual with us so we didn't bother with military rank. We drove west through the tree line and around the maintenance barn. From there we took a maintenance road that wrapped behind the sixteenth green and headed toward the airport. As we proceeded past the seventeenth tee, we saw a large group of paratroopers walking from the golf course to the airport. They were each carrying their cumbersome equipment, but all appeared to be jovial and having a good time. After all, it was a beautiful day for a jump and they were all still able to walk after being blown off course.

As Paul and I pulled up to the group, they immediately laughed and gave our two guests a hard time. The comrades made fun of them for being chauffeured in on golf carts. Patrick and Eric fired back at their peers that they had seen quite a show on the golf course. They graciously thanked us for the rides and said they would walk the rest of the way. They seemed eager to tell their story to their buddies, so Paul and I bid them farewell.

Paul began following me back in toward the clubhouse, but I couldn't wait for his cautious driving. He quickly fell out of sight as I took short cuts across fairways and through tree lines. Normally I wouldn't be in such a rush to

18 Holes of Green

get back to work, but I was getting hungry and Andy would be back soon with lunch.

When I pulled up to the clubhouse, John was sitting on the patio chatting with his new friend. Star now had more clothing on, but still appeared out of place at the golf course. The other guys on the patio were all gawking at her and debating John's prospects as I walked past them and headed inside. Not only did they envy John's golf game, but now they envied his charisma. He had the Kavorka as they said on Seinfeld.

The clubhouse was all a buzz about the day's excitement. Everyone had a different story to tell. There were tales of putts, chips and drives interrupted by the sudden sight of 250 paratroopers descending to the ground. Apparently, a few actually landed on the driving range. The poor guys didn't know that they would be jumping into enemy fire. Alice had to make an announcement on the PA asking everyone to stop hitting balls until Harley could help them get to safety. After a few more beers for everyone, the stories were sure to grow even more outrageous. Mark and I didn't have a lot to do while the crossover continued. Andy would make it back with our lunches soon. Hopefully, we had seen an end to all the excitement for that July Fifth.

Don't Drink the Water

The dog days of August were upon us and the humidity seemed to suck the life right out of people. We had seen a record setting heat wave for several weeks with the heat index well over 100 degrees. The golf course was virtually abandoned between 11:00 am and 4:00 pm. I think we saw more golfers on days in November during those five hours than we had been seeing that August. A few of us would brave the heat to avoid the crowd, but most everyone else stayed indoors. There were a few Birdie Hunters and other assorted elderly who were so stuck in their routines that they just couldn't stay away. Andy Pader actually got into a few arguments when he recommended that some of the old guys not play in the heat.

Hugh Cunningham had made things worse by following through on his threat to remove the drinking fountains on the golf course. The first week after the Fourth of July holiday weekend, he had the water works out on the course tearing out all the drinking fountains. There were bright yellow dump trucks all over the golf course for two days as the backhoes smashed the drinking fountains into pieces. These weren't the modern steel drinking fountains built for functionality. They were the original turn of the century ornamental fountains. They had circular bases made of a stone wall about three feet wide and four feet tall. There was a 12-inch-deep reservoir on top that was filled with round pebbles for drainage. Stainless steel fixtures protruded out of

18 Holes of Green

the pebble drain. They didn't make drinking fountains like these any more.

Paul was so enraged that he drove out in a cart to try to stop the water works crew. He tried to convince them that they should at least leave the stone bases to be used as decorative planters. When that failed, he returned to the clubhouse and immediately called downtown to the County Park board office. He demanded to speak to Hugh Cunningham, but only got as far as his voicemail. Paul left a message strewn with his extensive vocabulary and ended with the decorative planter suggestion.

The worst part was that some of the fountains had plaques on them memorializing deceased birdie hunters. Paul went back out on the course in an attempt to retrieve the plaques, but he was told that he would have to remove them himself. The waterworks apparently did not have the right tools for the job. Paul contained his anger and used his charm to buy one hour from the crew's supervisor. Paul immediately tracked down and enlisted the help of Harley who had access to a variety of tools and knew how to use them. In less than the allotted one hour, Paul and Harley successfully removed all seven memorial plaques. Paul brought them into the clubhouse, set them on a table near the Birdie Hunter bulletin board and proposed a toast with his beloved Makers Mark.

When the water works was finished demolishing the historic landmarks, the rubble was hauled away. Then, the water lines were capped and fill dirt was poured leaving virtually no trace of what were once very functional, very beautiful and very convenient water fountains. There would be no decorative planters and amid a heat wave there was no water on the golf course.

Timothy McHugh

Mark, John and I had successfully used our new-found passion for night golf as a way to beat the heat. It was the marketing achievement of the year. After all, if it was too hot to play golf during the day – why not play at night. We had weekly night golf events on each Friday and they were an instant success. The local paper and a television station each did a story on our night golf extravaganzas. Each Friday we would have a shotgun start at 10:00 PM. There were two separate tournaments all in one: a four-player scramble for those who wanted to party and a four-player best ball for those who wanted to play their own ball throughout and try to win some skins as well.

We had a quarter barrel of beer on every other tee box and paper bag candle luminaries served as tee markers and 150 markers. Long glow sticks hung from the flags to show players their target. It was a unique atmosphere that captured the fun-loving child in all who played. Paul put us in touch with an old friend of his who played the bagpipes. The guy marched the course every Friday night in full regalia wailing Amazing Grace and other traditional songs. He only stopped long enough to down a beer each time he made it to a keg. The occasional incoming or outgoing aircraft from Williams Field added to the light show.

Nate and Willie Boylan were regulars at the night golf events. Each week more and more of their friends showed up to play. What started out as an unofficial skins game soon turned into a full-fledged late night gambling festival. When the golf concluded and the official tournament was over, the diehards were just getting started.

The White Lake Clubhouse became the home to the largest regular Texas Hold 'em tournament in the area. Virtually every table in the grill was busy with cards flying across them. It got so large that poker players were showing

18 Holes of Green

up just to play cards after the golf was over. It was as if the golf had become incidental to the event. However, the golf did provide the perfect cover for using a building owned and operated by the county for a poker tournament. Besides, we all made a little money from the deal and sure had a lot of fun at the same time.

I spent my time taking the entry fees and playing banker to make sure everything was on the "up and up." Mark and John on the other hand immersed themselves in the gambling. Lisa had her own side business going selling beer to the masses and cooking burgers and dogs. She would use cups, napkins, condiments and other accessories from the County's supply at the snack bar, but she picked up meat and beer at a Sam's Club to keep her prices down.

Andy never asked too many questions because he was making a killing himself. The extra golf revenue helped to increase his cut from the County and the publicity made him the star of the County Park District. Hugh Cunningham was pleased by what he thought was an innocent and profitable enterprise. After all, the distinguished Director of Golf was too busy with his own exploits to explore the details of our night golf events.

Cunningham had commissioned another study by his brother-in-law to find a new standard temperature for the County Clubhouses during the heat wave. Apparently 82 degrees was enough of a change to reduce the monthly electric bills by 20%. He could show the County Commissioners that he was saving the taxpayers money and earn a kick back from his wife's brother at the same time. After managing to have all the drinking fountains on the golf course removed just in time for the heat wave, Cunningham scored the big deal for his family. His wife's company had all the County Courses fully stocked with bottles of water ranging from $2.50 for a shot glass to $6.75 for a one gallon "Super Jug." It seemed that his in-laws were profiting quite a bit from their connections with the director of golf.

While we had the public night golf event on Fridays, a few of us would get together on Saturday nights to play night golf the way it was meant to be played. We didn't have any candle luminaries, but we all knew the course well enough at night by then that they were not needed. Although we couldn't allow the public to drive carts in the dark, Mark, John, Nate and I permitted ourselves the luxury. We'd take a couple of coolers of beer and play by the moon and starlight. The only thing glowing when we played was the ball itself.

On about the Fourth Saturday in a row, we had Nate's brother Willie Boylan and Roger Merchant from the skins game join us. We were getting pretty used to night golf and were finding ways to enjoy it as much as possible. Roger was always a nice guy to have around and the combination of Nate and his brother Willie was sure to add some excitement to our night. I had volunteered to work the closing shift at the clubhouse on Saturdays in order to provide some cover for our unofficial outings. The worst part about it was that I had to deal with Ashley calling for Mark a half-dozen times each night.

That particular night, I had made a point to keep the evening play to a minimum. I warned prospective players of the slow play that didn't necessarily exist. The sun had just given us a break for the day and dropped below the hillside. I was trying to get off the phone with someone asking about tomorrow's weather forecast when Nate, Roger and Willie walked in.

"Well sir, I'm not exactly sure," I said. "But if you stay up and watch the 11:00 news, I'm sure you'll catch the forecast."

18 Holes of Green

Nate stopped at the counter with a big grin as Willie and Roger headed over to the grill. Nate could tell I was getting frustrated on the phone so he made a talking motion with his hand to mock me. I quickly grabbed a used ball out of the bucket on the counter and threw it at him. He laughed as he turned and ducked. The ball bounced on the floor and then banged off of a few of the tables and chairs.

"What the hell is going on?" yelled Willie from the grill as I finally hung up the phone.

"That guy must have thought I had my own Doppler radar system to look at," I said to Nate.

"You should have just told him that it was going to rain all day tomorrow," responded Nate.

"I should have just told him that it was going to be too damned hot for his fat ass to play golf," I responded.

"Where're the boys?" asked Willie as he and Roger returned with two beers each. Willie handed one to Nate and Roger handed one to me.

"Mark is outside talking to Ashley on his cell phone," I answered and took a drink of my beer. "And John is down at the range giving a lesson."

"What the hell is John doing giving a lesson this late in the evening?" asked Roger.

"Must be some hot little number," responded Nate.

"I think that it's Al Harper," I said. "John won't give any lessons in the heat of the day. He should be finished pretty soon."

"You guys couldn't have had too many players out there today," said Nate.

"No, it was pretty slow for the most part," I said. "But you'd be amazed by how many old guys who went out and braved the heat and humidity."

"Old people are always cold," said Willie matter-of-factly.

"Yeah, but it's not safe out there now that the county took out the water fountains," I said.

"No shit," said Nate. "There's a damn heat emergency in effect and no water fountains on the golf course. The least the county could do is put water jugs on every other hole like the new courses do."

"Then Mrs. Cunningham wouldn't be selling her high priced bottled water," I said.

"Ain't that the truth," responded Roger. "It's pretty bad when beer is cheaper than water."

It was then that Mark walked through the door after having finished lying to Ashley. He had her believing that we had a night golf event on Saturdays as well as Fridays. She would never allow him out at night if she didn't think he was working. She would get angry enough if he just went out for a beer or two after work with us. I can't imagine what she would do if she knew he was playing 18 holes with us in the dark. Nate, Willie and Roger were giving Mark some shit about Ashley calling, while I started to close out the cash register as I sipped on my beer. They traded insults for a while until they began arguing over who was the better putter with a glow ball. Within minutes, the four of them were headed out to the practice green to put their claims and wallets on the line.

It was getting dark and I began to shut down the clubhouse. I took the cash drawer back into the office to count the money and put it in the safe. I sat at the desk, licked my fingers and flipped through the stack of cash. Two hundred dollars stayed in the drawer, and the rest went into a money pouch. Once that task was complete, I got up from the desk and sat the money on top of the safe. The golf

18 Holes of Green

course safe was an archaic contraption that had letters rather than numbers and required some jiggling to get the tumblers to drop. It always took me a few tries to get it open. Somewhere in the middle of my second attempt at it, I heard the clubhouse door open. I figured it was one of the guys so I just continued with the counting in my head as I tried to get the combination just right.

As I pulled on the lever fruitlessly, I heard a customer's voice call out, "Anyone back there?"

"Yeah, I'll be right there," I shouted.

With the pressure on me, I quickly cracked the code, pulled the lever and swung open the door. I tossed the money in the safe, locked it back up and headed out front to the counter where I found a rather large man in his mid to late 40s and his son who appeared to be about 12 years old.

"What can I do for you?" I asked.

"Hey buddy, I seem to have lost my head cover out on the back nine," the man said. "I just need to borrow a cart so we can run out on the course and find it real quick."

It was now officially dark and there was no way I was letting this guy and his son take a golf cart out onto the back nine with all the ravines and drainage ditches. It would be my ass if they got hurt or worse yet, damaged the cart. Besides, I was ready to get out and play some night golf.

"I'm sorry sir, but the carts are locked up and we can't let them out in the dark," I said. "It's too dangerous."

"I'll keep it on the path," he replied. "It will only take a few minutes."

"We only have cart paths around the greens and tees. I'm not allowed to let a cart out in the dark. It's a liability issue with the county. I'll be happy to take your name and phone number and when the greens crew finds it in the morning, we'll call you."

Timothy McHugh

The guy wouldn't take no for an answer. He became visibly upset as he wiped his brow and huffed.

"It's a Chicago Bears head cover that my son gave me," he said. "It's really important to me and I don't want to go hiking around out there in the dark."

"But that's why we can't let you take a cart out," I replied. "It's too dark out there." I felt a little funny saying that knowing full well that I was planning on taking a cart out that night, but I knew the golf course. Hell, I've almost gotten stuck out there in the dark, so there was no way I was letting this guy and his son go joy riding. Besides, Mark and John would kill me.

"This is bullshit!" he shouted. "What the hell do we pay taxes for if we can't get any help here? What fucking service."

With that, he turned and walked out the clubhouse door and stood on the patio staring out at the golf course. His son, obviously impressed by the fine parenting and example his father set then took it upon himself to plead their case. I was turning off the display lights throughout the pro shop as the kid followed me.

"Please man, my dad really loves that head cover," he said. "Can't we put a down payment on the cart until we get back?"

"That would be a deposit," I said as I walked back behind the counter.

"Yeah, let us give you a deposit on the cart until we bring it back."

"We can't send a cart out in the dark," I replied politely. "There are ravines and ditches out there. It's just too dangerous."

"Come on, don't be a jerk," replied the kid.

18 Holes of Green

I was not about to be called names by some punk kid following his father's example, so before I lost my cool – I leaned onto the counter and very sternly but calmly said, "kid, there is no way you are taking a cart out on that golf course. Now get out of the clubhouse while I lock it up."

The kid went running out of the clubhouse to his dad and started screaming. I was glad to be finished with him and checked the other doors. I figured that if I locked up and headed over to join Mark and the guys at the practice green, the fat ass and his loud mouth son would go home. I was wrong.

As I stepped out the clubhouse door to the patio, I was met with a verbal assault the likes I had never heard. The father was screaming at me that nobody talks to his son that way and that he ought to kick my ass.

Naturally, I responded and escalated the verbal confrontation with my own string of profanities describing his obesity and lack of intelligence in a colorful way. I had argued and traded profanity with irate customers before, but nothing had prepared me for what was about to happen.

I was trading insults with the father face to face when he suddenly reached out and grabbed me by the head. It seemed to happen in slow motion. I was so shocked that I did not react. I could feel him trying to pull my head forward into a headlock between his arm and body. I was in total fear as I felt his big meaty hands squeezing around my head. Just as I had learned to do when wrestling with my older brothers, I turned my head to an angle and slipped out of his grasp. I thought seriously about throwing a punch knowing that I had plenty of backup nearby, but I opted to keep my high ground as the victim and quickly turned and ran. As I bolted for the clubhouse door, he chased after me. I wasn't sure what to do, but the instinct to flee to safety was directing me. I darted inside the door and turned the corner behind the counter. The guy was right on my ass and started to follow me behind the counter as I picked up the phone with one hand and a sand wedge with other. I swung the sand wedge toward him as I dialed 911. He stopped in his tracks just in time to avoid being hit by the club. Within seconds Mark, Nate, Willie and Roger burst through the door.

"911, what is your emergency?" the voice on the phone asked me.

"I've just been assaulted by a fat ass over a golf cart," I replied.

"Do you need medical attention?" the dispatcher asked me calmly. I'm sure she had heard much stranger stories.

"No, just the police," I replied. She confirmed the address, took my name and a description of the father and said someone would be right out.

By the time, I had gotten off the phone, the father had retreated out from behind the counter and was acting much less aggressive now that he was outnumbered. John arrived quickly and wanted to know exactly what happened. As I began to tell my story, the father walked out onto the patio to join his son. Mark, Roger and Willie followed him out to make sure that they didn't leave.

"Hugh Cunningham is not going to like this," said John.

"Screw Cunningham," I replied. "I was attacked."

"I know, but I better call Andy just to give him a heads up," replied John.

"I guess that's not a bad idea," I said.

I walked toward the front window to look for the police as John made the call. I heard him laughing as he

18 Holes of Green

spoke to Andy. I guess it was funny now that I had time to look back at the incident.

When the police arrived, I was comforted by the fact that one of the officers was big Jack. Jack Kelley often played on weekends with his wife or other officers. This was a prime example of why we let police and firefighters play golf for free. I knew that I was on the right side of the law in this case, but it never hurts to have an edge.

Jack said "hi" to John and me and introduced us to his partner, Officer Ryan. Mark, Nate, Willie and Roger walked inside from the patio. They quickly took seats at the closest table to watch the events unfold.

Officer Ryan asked me to tell my side of the story and so I started at the beginning. By the time, I got to the part about the father attacking me, the peanut gallery at the table was giggling and snickering. Upon hearing the story, the police officers appeared to find some humor in the story as well.

"You grabbed this kid by the neck over a head cover?" Jack asked the father.

"I admit I made a mistake, but he was being verbally abusive to my son," answered the father.

"I was not!" I interjected.

"Brian is not the type to be verbally abusive," added John who could come across as very professional when he wanted.

"It doesn't matter what he may have said to you or your son," said Officer Ryan. "You can't physically attack someone. That's assault."

Jack then asked if I wanted to press charges and of course I said that I did. Unfortunately, though, they weren't going to take him away in handcuffs. They explained to me about some citizen mediation hearing I had to go to first.

Timothy McHugh

Apparently, it was an effort to solve disputes out of court but I was going to see the thing all the way through no matter how many hoops I had to jump through. This fat ass was going to be the martyr for every rude and obnoxious golfer who ever insulted a golf course employee. At least that was how I felt that night. I was pretty worked up.

The police had us sign the paperwork and then they escorted the father and son to their car. By that time, Nate had brought me over a fresh beer which was just what I needed. Now that the incident had reached a safe conclusion, the guys were free to taunt me.

"Why the hell didn't you just kick the guy's ass?" asked Willie Boylan.

"I was afraid that he might sit on me," I replied.

"You should have yelled to us for help," said Mark.

"When did you guys notice, what was happening?" I asked.

"We looked over when we heard the two of you yelling at each other," replied Mark. "We started walking over to see what it was all about and then we saw him grab you. That's when we all started to run."

It was then that Jack and Officer Ryan walked back inside the clubhouse with smiles on their faces.

"Sorry to drag you guys down here for this," I said.

"Not at all," answered Jack. "It was a nice break from the domestic disputes."

"That guy is crazy," said Officer Ryan.

"Yeah, some example he set for his son," commented John.

"So, you guys playing night golf tonight?" asked Jack.

We said that we were and invited them to hit a couple of tee shots with us. Jack informed us that he had been telling

18 Holes of Green

his partner all about night golf. Officer Ryan was eager to hit a glow ball so I locked up the clubhouse and we all headed to the first tee.

I found it ironic that 30 minutes earlier I was being attacked by a nut who wanted to take a golf cart out in the dark to look for his head cover and now I was standing on the first tee in the dark with: three golf carts, two coolers of beer, two police officers and a bunch of glow in the dark golf balls.

"I can't believe how well those things glow," said Officer Ryan.

"Yeah, it's amazing," answered Willie.

"Don't I know you from somewhere?" Officer Ryan asked Willie.

"Spend much time at the horse track?" asked Willie.

"No, must be from somewhere else." replied Officer Ryan.

"Must be," replied Willie with an uncomfortable look on his face. Then he slowly stepped away from Jack and his partner and used Mark and John as a buffer. I suspected that he must have had an unpleasant experience with Officer Ryan in the past.

John began to tee up a ball. He hated to stand around and wait.

"Watch this swing," Jack said to Officer Ryan as John addressed the ball and waggled a couple of times.

John took a big swing and the there was the usual thud as his club made impact with the hollowed out clear plastic ball. The fluorescent green tracer streaked upward through the sky and down the middle of the fairway. He hit it so far that we couldn't see it come down.

"Nice Shot," said Officer Ryan

"Thanks," said John. "Now why don't we see what the boys in blue can do?"

Timothy McHugh

"I want to see one more professional first," said Jack.

"All right, if you insist," replied Nate as he stepped onto the tee.

"I guess law enforcement would consider you a professional," suggested Mark.

"Funny," answered Nate. "Five bucks says mine will be longer than yours."

"You're on," replied Mark.

"How do you tell the balls apart?" asked Officer Ryan. "We put our initials on them with a marker," I answered.

"In Nate's case, it's a dollar sign of course," said Mark.

"Of course," said Jack. "He's a professional."

Nate snuck up to the ball and took an aggressive swing. The ball flew low and straight with the glowing tracer bouncing down the middle of the fairway. It was nowhere near as far as John's because we could see the ball faintly glowing near the crest in the fairway before it begins to slope downhill.

"Nice try," said Mark as he stepped onto the tee. "Yeah, pretty weak," added John.

"Let's see what you got golf pro," Nate said to Mark who was teeing up his glow ball.

Mark calmly addressed the ball and waggled the club a couple of times. He took a smooth and simple swing obviously not trying to kill the ball. The green tracer was a beautiful sight as it rose straight over the fairway. The ball appeared to bounce very close to where Nate's ball had come to rest. They took two very different paths, but the balls seemed to be in about the same spot.

"That's going to be a close one," said Jack.

"Yep, it all depends on the bounce it took," added Roger.

18 Holes of Green

"I've got five on Mark," said Willie.

"No faith in me my brother?" asked Nate.

"Just going with the odds," said Willie. "In fact, another five says I'm past both of you."

Mark and Nate both agreed as Willie teed up his ball and made his confident and almost cocky address. He swung and hit a powerful shot with a trajectory somewhere between Nate's low ball and Mark's arching shot. The ball appeared to bounce close to the other two balls and then rolled over the crest and out of sight.

"I'll just put that on your tabs," said Willie as he walked off the tee.

Roger quickly jumped on the tee and made it clear that he was not wagering on hitting his ball past anyone. He aimed a little left and took his usual hard swing. The green tracer highlighted his pronounced slice and the ball ended up in the right rough well short of the other balls. I hopped onto the tee and announced that I also was not attempting to out drive anyone. I hunkered down over the ball and tried to clear my head of the fat asshole that had attacked me just a little earlier. I finally got the angry thoughts out of my head and took a nice easy swing. I caught the ball a little thin, but it looked like it was going to turn out all right. The ball flew low and straight rolling to almost where Mark and Nate's balls rested.

"I'll take it," I said as I walked off the tee box.

"Good miss," commented Mark.

"Time for the boys in blue," suggested John.

"Yeah, which one of you is going first?" asked Mark.

Officer Ryan of course wanted Jack to go first since he was the better golfer of the two. Jack unbuckled his belt and handed it along with his gun and other tools of the trade to his partner. He borrowed John's driver and stepped onto the tee.

"Does it matter which way glow stick is pointing?" asked Jack.

"Oh, here we go again," I said preparing for another vigorous debate.

"Vertical is best," said Mark.

"Better make it parallel to the ground if you want it to fly straight," said Nate.

"I say parallel," added Roger.

"I like it vertical," commented Willie, who was still keeping his distance from the men with badges.

Jack adjusted his ball to make the glow stick parallel to the ground and then took his stance.

"You're going to regret it," said Mark.

"It only really matters when you're putting," commented John.

Jack addressed the ball. He swung and hit a low fade into the right rough near Roger's ball.

"Boy, that felt weird," commented Jack.

"And I've been getting tips from you?" asked Officer Ryan. Feeling some newfound confidence after his partner's difficulty, officer Ryan trotted onto the tee and quickly teed up his ball. "I'm going with vertical," he said with a smile. Then he took a big swing and hit a high arching slice that started out heading way left, but ended up in the fairway.

"Not bad," said John.

"I'll take it," said Officer Ryan.

We tried to convince Jack and Officer Ryan to join us and play out the hole, but they were a little too professional to do that on the clock. They promised to join us on an off night and we bid farewell to the boys in blue. They walked back to their patrol car and we saddled up in our three golf

18 Holes of Green

carts and headed down the first fairway. I was riding with Mark as we headed to pick up Officer Ryan's ball. Roger and Willie headed toward Jack's ball since it was near Roger's. John and Nate drove directly to my ball which was just short of the two glowing balls that appeared to be Mark and Nate. Before Mark and I could get there, Nate was inspecting the two balls.

"Hands off 'em!" shouted Mark as we approached.

"Relax," said Nate. "You got me by a couple of inches."

"And my ball is farther than yours too," commented Mark.

"Funny," said Nate. "It won't happen again.

Meanwhile on the right side of the fairway, Roger was about to swing. He hurriedly addressed the ball as if trying not to hold the rest of us up. It's an unfortunate reality of golf that when you hit a bad shot, you are the first to hit again. Additionally, in the age of ready golf, the others in your group who hit better shots are generally moving ahead of you. So, you're left with the feeling that you're holding up the group and you rush through your next shot. However, the fact that you just hit a bad shot could be a reson to regroup and take your time. Granted sometimes rushing keeps the bad swing thoughts at bay, but that's not a long term strategy. There are the few brave souls out there that can block out such social pressures of uneasiness and take their time on this critical next shot. But for all too many of us, we yield to the pressure of our own self-consciousness and we hurry more than is necessary. That is exactly what Roger Merchant did on his next shot.

We were all standing precariously in the middle of the fairway looking back at Roger as he swung. Unlike a real golf ball in the daylight that you can't see coming at you until it's too late, we all saw Roger's bright yellow ball coming at us. Within a moment, Mark, Nate and I were all face down on our bellies.

John remained standing in the fairway stoically as Roger's low screamer whizzed by and rolled up the fairway about 50 yards past us. Its yellow tracer seemed to hang in the air.

"You caught it a little thin Roger," shouted John.

We could hear Willie laughing out loud at us as Roger sheepishly acknowledged with a wave of his hand.

I was away at that point and was lining up my shot. I took my time and addressed the ball cautiously. I was still pretty pumped up from the incident with the crazy father so I was a little more aggressive than I should have been. With night golf, your depth perception is severely impaired. I moved my body in the middle of my swing as I struggled to focus on the ball. I ended up catching it thin, but luckily the ball made it all the way to just in front of the green.

"Not too bad," said John as Willie and Roger pulled up in their cart.

"It was awfully ugly," commented Nate. "I'll take it," I replied.

"Looks like you made it past me and Nate," Mark said to Willie.

"I'm just glad those cops are gone," said Willie.

"Yeah, I saw a little uneasiness there," said John. "What's the story?"

"That Officer Ryan pulled me over for a DUI," answered Willie.

"Did it stick?" asked Mark.

"No, he was blessed to have a star defense attorney for a brother," proclaimed Nate.

"Oh shit," said Mark.

18 Holes of Green

"I had that judge eating out of my hands," said Nate.

"I'm surprised you weren't found in contempt," I said.

"Oh, he threatened us with it," said Willie.

"That judge loved me," said Nate as he addressed his glow ball with his seven-iron in hand. As usual, he slowly snuck up to the ball and swung aggressively. He hit a low knock-down shot that hit the green and appeared to stay on.

"How do you like that," Nate proclaimed. "I stuck a glow-ball."

"I'll tell you what you can stick," replied John.

"Five more says I get inside you," said Mark.

"Gambling is illegal at Bushwood," I commented.

"And I never slice," added Mark.

"You're on," said Nate.

Mark took his usual methodical swing and hit a nice high arching shot. The glow ball's yellow tracer seemed to hang in the air. The ball hit the green and rolled to the back.

"We're back to even," said Nate.

Willie walked up to his ball with his cocky stride. He stood over the ball with confidence holding his wedge and took a strong swing. The ball flew high and landed on the green a few feet inside of Nate's ball. John and Nate immediately hopped in their cart and headed up to John's ball as the rest of us popped open some more beers and began to follow them.

By the time we arrived, John was addressing his ball. He waggled his club a few times and took a nice smooth swing with his wedge. The ball flew extremely high and appeared to stick very close to the pin. We all immediately gave him a hard time for not getting it closer to the hole. John may have been the best golfer, but that didn't mean he was going to get off easy. He'd be waiting a long time for compliments from his friends, but he didn't really expect any.

Timothy McHugh

Roger quickly hit his approach shot onto the fringe and soon we were all encircling the dark green. The night shadows played with our eyes and hid the undulations of the green. They all stood and watched as I lined up my shot. I knew the green well, but the shadows were showing me a slope I had never seen before. It took a very conscious effort to ignore what my eyes were telling me and to trust my memory. There should have been a slight break to the left and uphill to the hole near the center of the green. I decided to limit the room for error by running the ball to the hole. I closed my pitching wedge a little with my hands pressed forward. Using just an easy back and forth motion with my shoulders, I popped the ball onto the green. It rolled steadily right up to just a few inches short of the hole.

"Nice chip!" proclaimed Mark.

"Good one Bri," commented Nate.

Willie, Roger and John all acknowledged as well with the standard, "good shot."

I walked up and tapped my ball into the hole and was happy with a par. I left my glow ball in the hole to help light up the target for the others. The "hole-ball" as we had come to call it was an essential part of night golf. Roger was on the fringe so he hit next. As he did, the others were busy lining their shots up as well. We were very serious about "ready golf."

From the left fringe, Roger hit his putt hard. It broke twice while racing to the hole and went two feet past. Mark immediately tapped his putt softly from the back of the green on a downhill path to the hole. While it was still rolling very slowly to the hole, Nate smacked his ball from about 15 feet away on the right side of the green. The two glow balls streaking across the dark green looked like shooting stars in

18 Holes of Green

the night sky. Mark's ball trickled into the cup just a split second before Nate's ball followed it in.

"The old hootchie coochie," shouted Nate.

"Great putts," said Roger as he knocked his ball in on top of the others for his bogie.

Two Birdies so far and there were now four balls in the cup. Roger's was sitting mostly out of the hole resting on top of the others. Willie was away, but demanded that at least two of the balls be removed from the hole so it didn't affect his chances. We all harassed him as Nate picked up his ball and Roger's. Willie knocked in his ball from seven feet and John quickly tapped his in making it four birdies. It was unheard of, especially in night golf.

"That's a push," said Nate.

"Big push," added Willie.

"It's a waste of four birdies," I commented.

You might say the round of night golf was all downhill after the first hole. I began dinking more and more to forget about the asshole that attacked me. The rest of the guys of course had to keep up with me beer for beer. Needless to say, there weren't any more birdies, but John did play well as usual. It got to the point where Roger and I began playing as a two-man scramble team to compete against the others. It actually worked out fairly well because it gave one of us more time to drink while we waited for the other to hit.

We finished the first nine and retired to the clubhouse patio to have a few more drinks and play some cards. Nate and Willie were determined to get their money back from John, but I was content to watch. I was also very grateful that I did not have the opening shift the next day. Opening the golf course on weekends was best left to retirees. They were the only ones who could be trusted to show up.

Timothy McHugh

We carried on until two in the morning trading stories and insults. By the end of the night, the story of my assault by a crazed golfer had grown somewhat. I may not have been in mortal danger, but I was attacked and therefore entitled to get a good story out of the ordeal.

Emergency on Eleven

The next morning, after the assault and night golf extravaganza, I was scheduled to close the golf course. I slept-in until almost 11:00 after our late night and was making my way in about 1:00 in the afternoon. It was 97 degrees with a heat index of 103. I was looking forward to a slow afternoon in the air conditioning watching golf on TV. It was a miserable time of day to be playing golf. As I was making my way down the long and curving driveway to the golf course, I couldn't imagine many golfers braving the heat.

As I passed the driving range and turned the corner to the golf course parking lot, I was shocked to see two police cars out front with their lights flashing and a satellite truck from Channel Seven News. My stomach began to tighten as I tried to recall the events of the night before. Memories went flying through my mind as I attempted to remember if I did anything that bad. I was attacked by a crazed golfer. I played night golf and drank a lot of beer.

Suddenly it hit me. The poker tournaments. The county had caught-on to our Texas holdem tournaments and we were in big trouble I thought to myself. This would be all over the news. A countywide scandal and my future would be ruined. My parents would be pissed.

I parked my car under one of the few trees near the parking lot to protect it from the unrelenting sun. I then sat in my car for a few moments as I tried to come up with a good story. I didn't know it was illegal. I was just following orders.

Timothy McHugh

I'm just a college kid. As I sat there brainstorming, I heard more sirens approaching. My head sunk even lower as I sat in desperation thinking things were just getting worse and worse. As the sirens came closer, I started to think about just leaving and never coming back.

`Just as I was almost totally freaked out and sweating, an ambulance appeared around the corner and drove right up to the clubhouse. Never was I so happy to see a life squad. Someone's apparent misfortune only meant one thing to me. I was safe. I hopped out of my car and ran to the backdoor of the clubhouse as the paramedics began wheeling a stretcher to the front door. As I entered the clubhouse it was much quieter than I expected considering the scene out front. Rounding the corner inside the grill I could see that the emergency was not in the clubhouse, but rather outside on the patio. The clubhouse was entirely empty except for Nate who for some reason was behind the snack bar with a glass pitcher in his hand.

"What's going on out there?" I asked him.

"Old Ralph collapsed on the course from the heat," he replied.

"So, what are you doing, getting him some water?" I asked naively.

"No man, he's unconscious," answered Nate. I'm getting a free pitcher of beer while Lisa is outside with the others."

"That's cold," I commented.

"Hell, there's nothing I can do to help the poor old guy," responded Nate. "I'm just making the best of the situation."

I walked to the window and peered out to see the paramedics lifting Ralph onto the collapsed stretcher. He had an oxygen mask on and looked white as a ghost. Lisa, Mark

18 Holes of Green

and Andy Pader were standing next to him. Paul, Hank and Al Harper were there as well. The camera crew from Channel Seven was standing off at a distance, but no doubt zooming in on the ordeal. News Junkie Fred was there bending the ear of the female reporter. There were police officers talking to Charlie Pendyke and a couple of other guys from the Birdie Hunters.

The phone was ringing off the hook in the pro shop so I stepped behind the counter to field some calls. The first one was some irate guy bitching about no one answering the phone. I just stared out the window as saying uh huh to the caller as the life squad rolled Ralph past the window and out toward the ambulance. I fielded a few more calls from golfers wanting to know how hot it was, and then I saw the somber look on Andy as he walked back into the clubhouse.

I turned the ringer down on the phone and asked him what happened as Mark and Paul entered the clubhouse as well.

"Ralph collapsed from heat stroke," Andy answered.

"Is he ok?" I asked.

"No, it doesn't look like he's gonna make it," said Andy.

"How do you know?" I asked.

"They couldn't resuscitate him," Andy replied.

"You can tell when someone has passed, Brian," added Paul. "I don't think he's coming back."

"Where was he when it happened?" I asked.

"He was on eleven," said Mark. "Luckily, Hank wasn't far away in the ranger cart. I was in front of the TV and suddenly I hear Hank screaming over the radio, "emergency on eleven, call an ambulance." So, I called 911 and Hank was able to drive him in to the clubhouse."

"Well, he died doing what he loved," said Mark.

"Sneaking on the golf course?" I asked.

"That's cold," responded Nate who was now standing between Paul and Mark.

I nodded to him to as if to say touché and the others chuckled a little uncomfortably.

"He died because of the greedy son of a bitch downtown," said Paul angrily. "And I'm going to let those news people know."

Paul turned and stormed out of the clubhouse with a determined look. We all knew that Paul wasn't messing around.

"Something tells me this is going to be trouble," commented Andy.

"Trouble for Hugh Cunningham," said Mark.

"He better take it easy, or he'll be the next victim of heat stroke," I said.

"Yeah, new rule," said Andy. "No one over 55 goes out there during peak sun hours."

"You won't be able to stop them," said Mark.

"You will if you eliminate the senior rate," I commented.

"Then we'd need a lot more cops here," said Andy.

"I was scared to death when I pulled up and saw all the police cars," I said. "I thought they were here about last night."

"You didn't do anything wrong," said Nate. "Hell, you ought to sue that fat ass who attacked you. We can say that you're too afraid to work anymore."

Yeah, I heard you had some excitement last night," replied Andy. "Now, I have two things to call downtown to Cunningham about."

"Make that three," said Mark as he pointed out the window.

18 Holes of Green

We all gazed out the window to see that not only was Paul talking to the news crew, he was being interviewed on camera. His face was bright with color the way it gets when he's very passionate about something.

"Oh, this ought to be interesting," said Andy.

"I hope he tells them everything about Cunningham," I said.

"I hope he makes some things up," said Nate.

"Yeah, you've got nothing to lose," said Andy.

"Hey, it's not your fault what happened to old Ralph," said Mark.

"Yeah, but I'm going to have a lot of shit to deal with," said Andy.

"It's not going to help business any either," I added.

"More good news," sighed Andy as he walked back into the office.

After about 30 minutes, the police had finished taking statements from everyone who was within 10 square miles of Ralph when he collapsed and the media had left. For an unbearably hot day, there sure were a lot of folks milling around the clubhouse. Lisa was behind the snack bar selling beer and food. News junkie Fred was back in his seat in front of the television and a few unsuspecting younger golfers came in, paid and headed out to play. We didn't even bother with a starter since business was so slow.

The few golfers who had gone out to play were visibly excited at the how wide open the course was at the time. I couldn't blame them. I sure took advantage of any opportunity to play an open course no matter what the temperature. I did feel a little funny taking people's money considering what had just happened, but the course had to stay open. The average golfer doesn't get many opportunities to play. Whether his wife is out with friends or the kids are at a friend's house; opportunities to play golf ought not to be wasted.

Harley was sitting at a table with Hank and Nate sharing his thoughts. As I approached, he was opining that he hoped that he would die doing something physical.

"Harley, you damn near died the time a ball slipped though the cage on the jeep and caught you in temple," said Nate.

"Yeah, that old Jeep just kept moving once you passed out," I added. "It would have run over a few people on the grass tees if the ball picker hadn't gotten stuck on the rope tee markers."

"I'd still rather die doing something physical than in my bed," replied Harley.

"I'd like to die doing something physical in my bed," responded Nate.

"There are more than a few people who have gone that way," said Hank. "Sure, leaves the woman a little messed up,"

"I don't think that would be a problem for Nate," I added as Paul walked inside.

He came over to our table and took a seat looking pretty exhausted.

"Did you get on TV?" asked Hank.

"I sure gave them plenty of material," replied Paul. "I told them the reason that poor Ralph collapsed was because Hugh Cunningham had removed all of the drinking fountains. And I told them all about Cunningham's wife and that damn bottled water."

"You did not," replied Hank in doubt.

"I did too," argued Paul. "And it just so happened that there was a reporter from the Daily Times out there as well and he was very interested in what I had to say."

18 Holes of Green

"Sounds like you got the ball rolling," I said.

"I sure hope so," Paul replied.

It was then that Andy came walking over from the pro shop with a serious look on his face. We all knew what he had come to say. He had gotten the word that Ralph had died on his way to the hospital. We were all quiet for a moment and then Nate broke the silence.

"Talk about a lawsuit," he said.

"It's criminal is what it is," said Paul.

The phone was ringing so I went back to the pro shop. It was the first of many calls from the local media. It wasn't long before the death of old Ralph on the golf course was all over the local TV and radio news. By late afternoon though, things were getting back to normal. It had cooled down to the low 90s and more golfers were coming out to play. Some seemed to know what had happened, but most did not. That was ok with me. I wasn't in the mood for a lot of questions.

Andy had left for the day. Mark and Harley had gone down to the driving range. Paul and Hank sat by the window sipping Maker's Mark and staring out the window. Ralph wasn't the most loved person at the golf course, but no one wanted this. You couldn't help but be affected by seeing someone die right in front of you.

Shortly after six o'clock, news junkie Fred began shouting. We all looked over at the TV and there was Paul being interviewed on the evening news. I ran from behind the counter to get closer to the TV as I yelled to Fred to turn it up.

Paul and Hank got up from their seats and we all gathered in front of the big screen listening to Paul being interviewed. It lasted for several minutes and they got him saying some pretty harsh stuff about the Cunninghams and the water fountains.

But the big surprise was after the interview when the news anchor announced that the County Prosecutor and the Park Board were both launching investigations. There may be "charges filed and or disciplinary action taken."

"Charges filed?" I asked out loud. "That would sure be something."

"They should file charges against that damn Director of Golf," said Paul.

"Of course, Cunningham was unavailable for comment," added Fred.

"Nice work, Paul," I said. "You may have brought us Christmas in July if they get rid of Cunningham."

Fred began flipping through the other local channels to see if they were covering the story. Sure enough, they each mentioned the incident and the impending investigation. However, the other channels didn't have an exclusive interview with old Paul.

The excitement of the day had eventually worn off and things were winding down. I had successfully shutdown the golf course without being attacked by anyone this time. After locking up the clubhouse, I stopped in at the driving range to see Alice and hit some balls. I generally always stopped in before heading home. I liked to check on Alice because Fred would rather head home and continue watching the news than wait for his wife to finish up at the driving range. The late evenings were the best time to practice anyway. The sun was down so you got a break from the heat and you didn't have to squint to see the flight of the ball. Of course, I spent more of my time that night gossiping with Alice than I did hitting balls. After all, there was big news to discuss between Ralph, Paul and the investigations.

The next day I was scheduled early at the golf course. I got to the clubhouse just before 7:00 am and Hank

18 Holes of Green

already had the place opened up. As usual, the carts were pulled out and lined-up, the tee sheet was printed out and the coffee was brewing. There were also two guys in suits looking around behind the pro shop counter. Hank introduced me to them as county auditors.

One was looking through files on the tee time computer and the other was rummaging through the cabinets. I walked behind the counter and started working as if they weren't there, but it was a little challenging. I was a little nervous about what types of questions they might ask. They were obviously there to investigate the bottled water scandal, but I couldn't get over the fear that somehow night golf and gambling would come up. As I answered my first phone call of the day, the guy rummaging through the cabinets pulled out one of the large cardboard boxes containing bags of tees. He began sifting through the box and held one of the bags of tees up to his eyes to examine it as I hung up the phone.

"You put golf balls on them," I said sarcastically.

Unfazed by my hostility, the auditor seized upon the moment to engage in some questioning. "What do you do for water during the day?" he asked.

"There's a water fountain right over there," I said as I pointed to the drinking fountain around the corner from the grill.

"Where do you get the cups?" he asked.

"I've got my own," I said as I pointed to my empty plastic Taco Bell cup that my last large Mountain Dew came in. The auditor went back to rummaging through the cabinets of the pro shop.

A couple of customers came in to pay for golf so I greeted them and began to ring them up. The auditor who was busy looking through the computer we use for tee times stopped and watched my every move on the cash register. When I finished with the twosome, he asked me what else we use the tee time computer for.

"Porn," I responded.

He just glared at me for a few seconds so I went on to explain to him that we make signs for the pro shop, track tournament scores, handicaps and such. He seemed satisfied for the moment with that answer and returned to examining the computer.

That's pretty much how the morning went. The two auditors poked and prodded at every inch of the clubhouse. They found things that had been missing for a while. They even found our stash of liquor, but they didn't seem too interested in it. They stayed at White Lake through my entire shift. It was such agony that I left early to go play. It was Hank's turn to entertain the two Bobs. We named them after the two consultants from the movie Office Space. Hank would talk them silly, which seemed appropriate.

The two Bobs returned every couple of days to look at something different. A couple of times they went out on the golf course with workers from the Water Works. Each day there was an article in the paper about some aspect of the investigation. This all went on for almost two weeks. It really started to wear us all out. Between questions from the auditors, the media and the customers, most of us employees were growing very frustrated.

On the third Friday after old Ralph died, I was working the morning shift at the driving range pro shop when Andy called down from the clubhouse and asked me to come up there. I coaxed Harley in from the back room where he was running balls through the large washer and asked him to cover the counter. Although Harley didn't much care for dealing with customers, he kindly obliged.

18 Holes of Green

I walked out back and hopped in one of the maintenance golf carts. I drove down past the open stalls where golfers were practicing and then up the path to the clubhouse. When I walked inside, I was surprised to see the two auditors standing behind the counter with Andy, Mark and John. My heart started pounding as I grew more and more nervous.

"These guys just want to talk to us all together for a few minutes," said Andy.

"No problem," I replied.

Mark, John and I followed Andy and the two auditors back into the meeting room where the birdie hunters and other leagues would hold their meetings. I glanced at Mark as we walked and he just shrugged his shoulders. Then, I looked at John and he rolled his eyes and smirked as if to say it was no big deal.

When we got in the meeting room, we all sat on one side of the long table and one of the auditors closed the door. Then they both took seats across from us and pulled out notebooks. They introduced themselves as they had done in the past, but as far as I was concerned, they were still the two Bobs.

Bob One began by asking who was working the morning that Ralph died. Mark began recounting the day's events saying that he was working at the clubhouse with Hank while John and Andy were at the driving range giving lessons.

"It was 97 degrees with a heat index of 103," said Mark. Ralph had come in with Al Harper and Charlie Pendyke to walk 18 holes with their pull carts as usual. I remember that Ralph took a drink from the water fountain inside the clubhouse. As they stood at the counter, he registered his usual complaint about the price of the bottled water."

"Did Al or Charlie get any water?" asked Bob Two.

Andy chuckled as Mark replied, "no, they each had a thermos, but they didn't put water in them. They preferred bourbon."

"And you permitted them to take liquor onto the golf course?" asked Bob One.

"Hey, it's not my job to search people before they play," responded Mark.

"We have a policy of respecting our customer's right to privacy," responded Andy. "Don't want to get sued you know."

After Mark had finished recounting the events of that morning, the Bob's turned to me. They asked me a few questions about the night golf events and I told them how well they were going over. Then it got interesting.

"Tell us Brian, who was responsible for arranging the exotic dancers?" asked Bob One.

"Exotic dancers?" asked Andy in shock.

"We know from our surveillance that you were always the one handling the bank for the poker tournaments, so someone else must have lined up the entertainment."

My heart sunk as I could feel the pressure mounting. I was speechless and Mark just gulped. Andy expressed his dismay and denied knowing anything about any of it. I thought for sure that we were all fired or going to be arrested and then finally John spoke.

"Well, we're all pretty hesitant to rat people out, but I guess it's time to come clean," said John as I grew tenser.

"Hugh Cunningham and his brother-in-law had arranged everything," John continued. "He was the one who pushed the night golf tournament and we were just following his orders. He used the façade of a benefit for junior golf as a cover."

18 Holes of Green

There was silence for a moment as I hoped for something miraculous to happen. And within a few seconds, it did.

"That was our suspicion," said Bob Two. "He already failed the polygraph test downtown, but we had to confirm everything."

"Yes, we didn't believe there was any way that all that madness could be happening every weekend without the Director of Golf's support," said Bob One.

A great feeling of relief quickly came over me as it appeared we had gotten away with it. Hell, Cunningham was already going down so what was the harm with piling it on? He was an asshole anyway.

"Well, I think we have gotten all the information that we needed," said Bob Two. They both thanked us for our honesty and cooperation and asked us to keep what we knew to ourselves until the investigation was over.

Andy walked them out bullshitting with them all the way. He was the master schmoozer. The rest of us all hoped that would be the last we would ever see of the two Bobs. With Andy out of the room, our attention turned to our newest predicament.

"We may have gotten off the hook with the auditors, but Andy isn't going to be happy," said Mark.

"Yeah, who's taking the blame for this one?" I asked.
"Mark and I are responsible for it," said John.

"Maybe, he won't care," I said.

But when Andy returned to the meeting room, we could tell that he was angry. I wondered if any of us would still have jobs. I felt worse for Mark and John. After all, this was their career. I was just biding my time as a college student. I was never going to make a career out of golf. I was too bad at it.

Timothy McHugh

Andy sat down at the table and just stared us down. His eyes were piercing through us as if he could see what we were thinking. It was as if he suddenly knew everything we had hidden from him all this time. I had worked for him so long; it was as if I just disappointed my own father. There was a brief silence and then he finally spoke.

"The next time you assholes hire strippers for night golf, you better invite me," he said.

"That's a deal," said Mark as the three of us smiled in relief.

For the second time in the course of an hour, I had gone from shear fright and anxiety to complete relief. I was ready to unwind and Andy was eager to hear all about the real night golf in a more appropriate setting. "How about we head down to Hangar for some beers," he suggested.

By this time, Alice had arrived at the driving range to relieve Harley and the golf course was under control, so there was nothing holding us back. It was still early afternoon, but we set out on a mission to get crazy.

"It's five o'clock somewhere," said John.

"Amen," I replied.

And with that we all piled in Andy's minivan and headed to the Hangar to recount all that had happened in the past week. Between Ralph dying, Cunningham being investigated and the truth coming out about night golf; we had a lot to cover. For a couple of hours, the three of us carried on and scared off the blue hair 4:00 dinner crowd. By 5:15, Nate Boylan had joined us and Willie was on his way. Mark's uncle Wesley who owned the place presented us with four orders of chicken wings "on the house."

He was likely just trying to keep us quiet for a while. As long as we were busy eating, we couldn't scare off his best dinner customers. We had the opening round of the

18 Holes of Green

British Open on the TV behind the bar so we were quite content with our beer, wings and golf. By the time Willie joined us we were in rare form. Tiger was off to a rough start and Sergio looked promising. It was the first round though, and nobody believed Tiger was out of it. At least nobody at the bar thought Tiger was out of it.

Indictments and Alligators

"Tiger is out of it!" shouted Charlie Pendyke.

"You're full of shit," replied Al Harper. "I've got twenty dollars that says he's in the final pairing on Sunday."

"You're on'" responded Charlie.

"It will be Tiger and Els," suggested Paul as he returned to their table with his fresh cup of coffee.

Their arguing lasted most of the morning with news junkie Fred chiming in from time to time as I worked behind the counter of the pro shop. I was still feeling the effects from the night before at the Hangar and their shouting wasn't helping. As I continued working, I heard their discussion move from the British Open to something more thought provoking.

Al put forth the theory that the guy who invented soft-spikes was a partner in one of the largest golf course management corporations in the country. He believed that this mystery executive by day and inventor by night was able to start the trend of outlawing metal spikes in order to sell more of his product.

"It's the truth," Al continued. "I read it on the internet."

"Well, I read that soft spikes were invented by a greens keeper who was tired of repairing spike marks," countered Charlie.

"You don't get enough traction with those damn plastic spikes," commented Al.

18 Holes of Green

"Well, you're not supposed to spin in your shoes," replied Charlie.

Paul took a much more romantic approach to the advances in golf footwear accessories. "I miss the sound that metal spikes made," he stated. "All the good sounds in golf are gone. No longer do we hear the tapping of metal spikes in the clubhouse or on a pathway. No more do we hear the clicking of the old sprinklers. They've been replaced with modern smooth and silent sprinklers. Instead of the crack of hitting a persimmon wood on the screws, we get the metallic ting of duffers with oversized watermelons. And worst of all, 'nice shot,' has been replaced with 'you the man.'"

"My favorite golf sound is the opening of a fresh can of beer," added Charlie.

"They haven't taken that from us yet," I shouted over to the guys from the pro shop.

"They're trying to with those plastic bottles," shouted back Paul. "Who ever heard of bottles of beer on a golf course?" he asked.

Plastic bottles did take up too much room in a cooler. Paul had a point I thought to myself as I worked. I did like the sound of the old sprinklers and metal spikes. But soft spikes were much more comfortable to wear.

By the time it was noon, things were starting to slow down. Paul had gone home to feed his cat and I was on the computer in the pro-shop.

That was when I heard Fred's breaking news alert.

"They've indicted Hugh Cunningham," he shouted.

"Hot damn!" exclaimed Al Harper.

"Turn it up," added Charlie as we all rushed to gather around the TV.

Lisa darted from behind the grill and Harley came running from the back room. There before all our eyes was a

County Prosecutor speaking into a cluster of microphones reading the indictment. It was the biggest news the county had seen in years.

"The wicked witch is dead," I proclaimed.

"Ding Dong," replied Harley.

The indictment read like the story of our lives. It highlighted the frustrating hell we had all put up with for years. "Numerous malfeasance in public office, improper awarding of government contracts, misuse of public property and funds, as well as bribery." There were details of Cunningham using kickbacks from the bottled water contract to bribe the health commissioner into declaring the White Lake drinking fountains unsafe.

The phone was ringing in the pro shop, but I just ignored it as I listened to the prosecutor continue. He detailed Cunningham giving sweetheart contracts to his wife and brother-in-law. He also presented charges that we were unaware of. Apparently, Cunningham had the greens crew from Heather Valley, the nicest county owned course, maintain his own yard and landscaping. Then of course the prosecutor mentioned several tawdry night golf tournaments with details too lurid to convey on television.

The news conference eventually came to an end, but the talk of Cunningham's indictment had just begun. Andy, Mark and John all stopped down in-between lessons to hear about the media coverage and news junkie Fred was eager to recount every second of it. Even old Paul had called from home to make sure we had seen the announcement. He was on his way down to the golf course. He said he was coming to help answer the phone, but I had a feeling he was looking for some more airtime on the news.

Paul arrived in a change of clothes and dressed a bit more dapper than normal. He had on one of his best Polo

18 Holes of Green

golf shirts and neatly pressed pants. His silver hair was slicked back and he even smelled of cologne. As soon he walked in the clubhouse he greeted everyone and then quickly began surveying the outside through the windows.

"There's no one from the media here," I said to him. "Oh, I'm just looking to see how crowded the course is," he replied. "I'd like to get out for a round of golf before they shut the whole place down."

"That's not a bad idea," I said. "I haven't played in a while myself."

"It's only supposed to get up to 87 degrees today," announced Fred.

It had been a while since the high was below 90 degrees I thought to myself. While I was certain they would never close White Lake, there were sure to be some changes coming. It would be nice to get in a few rounds of golf while we still had it so good.

Paul finally sat down with Al and Charlie while I went back to work for a while. It hadn't been too busy, but I didn't tell that to anyone who called. I wanted to keep it that way so the course would be wide open for us to play.

Paul and I weren't the only ones with the idea to play that day. Nate Boylan soon showed up with his golf bag over his shoulder. He was likely trying to get in some golf before any changes might occur that would preclude him from playing for free in the future. He did have several complaints registered against him as a starter on file with the County. If any of us would get cut, he would no doubt be the first to go.

"They finally nailed good old Hugh Cunningham, eh boys?" he asked.

"Yeah, it's been a long time coming," I replied.

"And Pauly, I hear we have you to thank," said Nate.

"Just doing my due diligence as a concerned citizen," Paul replied.

"Don't be modest," said Nate. "You're a TV star now. If you need representation, I'm available."

"I'm sure you are," answered Paul.

Nate asked if I wanted to play when I got off and I told him that Paul and I both did. He challenged Paul to a little putting match on the practice green to get ready and they both headed outside. Even Al and Charlie followed them out to provide commentary. Of course, Fred stayed right in front of the television. After all, he only had an hour or so of news watching left before the golf tournament came on and we made him change the channel.

By the time Hank relieved me in the pro shop, the crowd had grown outside at the practice green. I walked outside with a beer and a hot dog that Lisa gave me to see what was going on. Mark, John and Harley had joined Paul and Nate on the green and there were about ten one dollar bills lying by one of the cups. The competition had apparently gotten fierce.

I took a seat on the patio with Al and Charlie and joined in watching the spectacle. It appeared that Paul was winning and Nate was complaining a lot. Harley appeared very focused. He took his short game very seriously. Mark and John were bickering between themselves. I think Paul had psyched out the two professionals.

"Hurry up and finish your lunch, Brian," shouted Mark. "The six of us are going to play."

"Yeah OK," I replied. We were all eager to get out and play to take our minds off all the bullshit at the golf course. There'd been so much attention on us lately that we couldn't have any fun.

"A sixsome?" asked Charlie.

18 Holes of Green

"Well, we'll play as fast as a foursome," I replied.

Indeed, we could play pretty quickly when we all got together. We had taken "ready golf" to the next level. There were times when we pushed twosomes playing as an eightsome. However, there had also been a few incidents over the years when our "ready golf" became a little dangerous. I personally had to dive out of the way of an errant shot more than once.

After I finished my lunch, I grabbed a cart and drove to the parking lot to get my clubs. I was amazed at how beautiful a day it a turned out to be and how empty the parking lot was. Perhaps the news stories had frightened golfers away or maybe the heat wave had lasted so long that they had gotten used to doing other things. Whatever the reason, we had a beautiful day and a wide-open golf course. It didn't get much better than that.

I drove my cart back around behind the clubhouse and found everyone leaving the practice green. Nate and John had already put their clubs on a cart together and Paul had latched on to Mark's cart. That left me riding with Harley and his famous golf ball.

Harley methodically strapped his bag on my cart. Not only did he use the normal cart strap, but he kept a bungee cord on his bag for added security. You'd never see his bag fall off the back of a cart.

John didn't like to wait around and was standing on the first tee taking some practice swings. Nate quickly pulled his cart up next to the tee and began shouting back at the rest of us. Harley was busy washing his ball so I pulled our cart up behind Nate's. Mark and Paul followed us.

"Two dollar skins, two-tie all-tie with carry-overs," proclaimed Nate.

"Of course," replied Mark.

Timothy McHugh

"I'll gladly take more money from you young whipper snappers," said Paul.

"You may be a putting machine, but you still gotta get to the green," responded John as he teed up his ball.

John took his usual long and graceful swing hitting the ball well over the crest of the hill and down the middle.

"You wuss," I said. "Whatever," replied John.

"You young guys still think length is what it's all about," said Paul.

"That's what the girls keep telling me," said Nate.

"Too damn social," proclaimed Harley. We were used to his colorful interjections.

Mark stepped onto the tee and went through his usual routine. He hit a high arching shot that just made it over the crest in the fairway.

"Age before beauty," I said to Paul.

"I'm old and beautiful," replied Paul as he walked onto the tee.

Paul was in his glory. He was dressed as dapper as ever and his silver mane was slicked back. He pulled his homemade 460cc Golfsmith driver out of his bag and smiled as he teed up his ball.

"Watch the old man kids," said Paul.

He took his short but precise swing and knocked the ball right down the middle just short of the crest in the fairway.

"Where'd it go?" he asked sincerely. "It felt good."

"It's just short of the ladies' tees," answered Nate.

"It's down the middle about 225," said Mark.

Paul always seemed to lose sight of the ball when he hit it well. Every time he hit a good shot, he would say "where'd it go?" Sometimes I would think he did it on purpose in order to call attention to his good shots, but I couldn't be certain.

18 Holes of Green

"It's actually more like 230," suggested Harley. "The crest is 235."

Harley was a stickler for accuracy. He also knew the course as well as anyone. He had finished polishing his ball and walked onto the tee with his driver. Going through his typical routine, he looked like a baseball player. He swung his driver back and forth even with his shoulders. He also stepped into his practice swings like a baseball player.

Harley finally lowered his club to the ball. He took a couple of actual waggles and then he swung aggressively. The ball flew low and straight but then kicked a little to the right of the crest in the fairway.

"Could have been worse," stated Harley. He was the eternal optimist. I guess after cleaning out nuclear reactors, anything else seemed great. Nate practically shoved me out of the way to be the next one on the tee. However, when he got to the tee markers, he didn't seem to have a tee.

"Anyone got a long tee I can borrow?" he asked.

"I don't think so," replied John. "Borrowing equipment from someone else is a violation of the rules."

"Rule four-dash-4a," announced Paul.

"You guys suck," replied Nate as he continued to search for a long tee.

"Nice to see you were prepared to hit since you were so eager to go ahead of me," I said.

"Relax, I'm ready," responded Nate as he teed up his ball on a broken tee. We all laughed as he struggled to get as much length out of the broken tee as possible. He was trying to just barely stick the end in the ground so that he would have as long a tee as possible, but the ball kept falling over. Finally, he balanced the ball on top of the tee and quickly addressed the ball with his cigar hanging from his lips.

Timothy McHugh

It was a funny sight to see his ball teed up so low with such a big club head behind it. I was sure he was going to miss it. Then, he made his typical aggressive flat swing with the cigar still hanging from his mouth. The ball flew low and straight landing in front of the crest and bouncing over it.

John stepped toward Paul and me and whispered, "four-dash-four only applies to clubs, not balls and tees."

"I know," responded Paul.

I couldn't help but laugh as I walked onto the tee with my Ping Driver and went through my routine. I stood behind the ball and lined it up with a target. Then I addressed the ball and took one last look at the target. The last time I had played I was cutting across and pulling the ball so I concentrated on correcting that. I focused on loosening up my grip with my right hand and keeping my right elbow loose so I could swing out.

Well, as is typical with amateur self-analysis I over corrected and pushed the ball right. It flew on a nice trajectory and straight as an arrow, but it started right and stayed right. My ball ended up just short of the crest and in the right rough not too far from the second green.

"Whoa Brian," said Nate. "You gotta finish the first hole before you go for the second green."

"Yeah, yeah," I replied.

"At least you're playing good cart golf," commented Paul.

"Yeah, it is convenient," I said trying to learn a little optimism from Harley.

We all saddled up in our carts and headed out on the war path. It felt good to get out with guys again after all the shit that had been going on around the golf course. If I had one more person ask about the scandal I was going to kill them.

18 Holes of Green

Harley and I broke formation as we neared our balls. I parked our cart halfway between his ball and mine. Then, I succumbed to the temptation to rush to my ball and hit it quickly. I always felt self-conscious when I hit a bad shot and was the farthest away. It was as though I had to hurry and hit my ball quickly before I was left behind; when in reality I had plenty of time.

I hurriedly addressed my ball without going through my full routine and swung. The ball flew straight and landed just in front of the green bouncing to the edge of the apron. My five-iron still had a clump of mud and turf stuck to the clubface, but I slid it into my bag without wiping it off. I sat down in the cart and took a sip of my Bud Light.

"Nice shot," yelled Mark from farther up in the fairway.

"Good recovery," added Harley as he addressed his ball.

Perhaps the instinct to hurry actually had helped me on that shot. I didn't give myself time to think and over analyze before I swung. As I thought about that to myself, Harley swung aggressively and knocked his ball onto the front of the green. I complimented him on his shot and pulled the cart up even with him. Harley diligently wiped off his six-iron, placed it into the appropriate slot in his bag and hopped in the cart.

By the time we were approaching the others; Paul was addressing his ball, and preparing to swing. I let my foot off of the gas pedal to stop the cart engine from running while he swung. Paul made his usual short swing with his five-wood and the ball rolled onto the center of the green.

"Nice shot, old man," said Nate as Harley and I pulled even with the other two carts.

"It may take me more club these days, but I can still get the ball to the green," replied Paul.

Nate jogged up to his ball and quickly lined up his shot. Anytime he was out driven by Mark, he would run to his ball to try to hit it before Mark could make any comments. He had time on his side, because Mark had to wait for Paul to get back in the cart before he could drive up to Nate's ball. John sat in his cart back with us while Nate hurriedly addressed his ball.

"He's going to push it right," said John.

"It does look like he's aimed right," I replied.

"Yeah, he usually does aim right, but most times he's able to pull across and still hit the ball straight," added John. "But he's in such a hurry; it looks like he's going to "chicken wing" his right elbow and that means it's going right."

Sure enough, Nate's ball flew right of the green and kicked even more right toward the second tee box. The five of us rode up to join Nate as he walked to Mark's tee shot.

"You have to putt out before you tee off on number two," Mark said to him.

Paul and John laughed. I was just glad they were picking on someone besides me for a change. Harley smiled as he lit a cigarette and wiped off his clubs with a towel.

Mark and John each hit their second shots onto the green without much fanfare. We just expected them to do so. After all, they were professionals. They each finished the hole with a birdie and the rest of us all managed to make pars. Even Nate was able to get up and down from over by the second tee.

The second hole was a short par three. It ran back toward the clubhouse and had a large oak tree on the left side of the green. The wind was slightly against us now having been helping us on the first hole. The sun was shining

18 Holes of Green

bright, but it wasn't too hot for a change. It was a beautiful day on the golf course. The kind of day that really made me appreciate how good we had it there. At least we did for the time being.

"Savor the moment boys," said John as we stood on the tee. "We all may be looking for jobs when they bring in some corporation to run these courses."

"Corporate golf, that doesn't sound like fun," said Harley.

"These fun days may be coming to an end," replied Mark.

"You guys are too young to be so depressing," said Paul.

"No shit," said Nate. "Closest to the pin for a buck a man."

We all agreed and began assessing the situation. Harley paced off the yardage from the concrete marker at the side of the tee box to where the blue tee markers were.

"One fifty-four," he declared.

John grabbed his wedge and Mark his nine iron. The wind was still just straight against us with no side breeze. The pin was in the right center of the green, a pretty easy set up. John confidently made a nice and easy swing. His ball flew on lower than normal trajectory and landed softly a few feet past the hole and then sucked back.

"Don't come back too far," he shouted.

"Roll off the green," shouted Nate.

The ball stopped about two feet in front of the pin. John turned and smiled at Nate. Then, Mark teed his ball up. He appeared to be concentrating over the ball a little more than normal. I sensed a bit of uncertainty as he stood over the ball thinking. When he swung, something seemed off. The ball flew on a nice high trajectory for an eight iron, but it appeared to be a bit of a pull. He just caught the left side of the green about pin high. For anyone else in the group it would have been a great shot, but it had to be a little disappointing for Mark.

"Good distance," commented Paul as he walked onto the tee. He made a few sweeping practice swings with his seven-wood. His practice swings were longer than his normal swing, but still relatively short. I think Paul's swing shortened over time with his loss of flexibility due to age and girth. He teed up his ball and made his address. Then, he took his short swing and hit the ball low and straight. It landed just in front of the green and rolled onto the center.

"Not bad for an old man," said Nate.

"You sure know how to play your game," said Mark.

"You've got to know yourself," he replied.

"I know myself extremely well," said Nate as he stepped forward to tee up his ball.

"I'll bet you do," I commented.

Mark and John both broke into laughter. We never missed a chance to rip on Nate and I was proud to have seized that moment.

"Screw you guys," replied Nate as he lined up his shot.

"It's ok, we won't tell anyone how well you know yourself," said Paul.

"That's sick," added Harley.

"Can I get some fucking quiet please," Nate asked as he addressed his ball.

We all shut up out of courtesy and Nate made his usual aggressive swing. This time it was a little too aggressive. He nearly jumped out of his shoes as he swung through the ball.

18 Holes of Green

Naturally, he caught the ball thin, but he also put some wicked spin on it. The ball flew low and sliced hard right well short of the green. He was practically in the first fairway.

"Hey, we already played that hole," said John.

"Go to hell," answered Nate as he walked off the tee.

I almost felt bad for him, but then I realized it was Nate I was dealing with. Within moments he would be back on top of his game and putting the rest of us down. It was the cycle of life played out in a few quick holes of golf. One moment your up, and the next you're down. I tried to keep that thought as I made a few practice swings and waited for Harley to hit.

He stepped onto the tee, made a few baseball swings and then addressed his ball. Then, he quickly made his strong swing with his seven-iron and the ball flew high and straight.

"You're going to like that one Harley," said Mark.

"Be the one!" shouted John.

Harley's ball stuck in the green right next to John's ball. It's didn't bounce, kick or roll. It just stuck.

"Must be embedded," I said.

"It's going to be a close one, Harley," said John. "Hope you're not inside me."

"Don't worry, I'll break the tie," I said as I walked to the tee markers with my seven iron. I teed up my ball and stood behind it for a moment to line up my shot. Then, I took my stance and waggled the club a couple of times. Trying to think of nothing but the pin, I slowly began my back swing. As I took the club head back I tried to keep it low to the ground. I thought of the toe of the seven iron and tried point it straight up as I took the club back. I made an effort to try to stop at about the three-quarter mark to keep from going past parallel. Pausing at the top, I concentrated on keeping my swing smooth.

I started my down swing and struck the ball cleanly following through with poise. The swing felt great and the ball flew high and straight at the flag. I held my follow through pose in an effort to will the ball to the hole.

"The distance looks good," said John.

"This could be really good," added Mark.

"Hit the pin!" shouted Nate.

Sure enough, my ball smacked the pin about halfway up the pole. It took a hard kick and shot backwards, bounced on the fringe and ended up twenty yards short of the green.

"That's a shame," said Paul.

"Rub of the green," added Harley.

I just stood there motionless for a few seconds. I couldn't believe it. I hit the ball so well that it hits the pin and I wasn't even on the green. Just as when I hit the weather vane earlier in the summer, a perfectly hit golf ball can easily go awry.

"Oh well," I sighed as I turned to join the others as they walked back to the carts.

Nate ran to his cart. Obviously, he was in a hurry to get to his mishap and try to save par. John obliged Nate's eagerness and walked quickly to their cart. As the rest of us made our way to our carts, John and Nate were headed down the path in a hurry. Nate hung out of the cart and screamed "bonsai" as they went by. Paul just shook his head as he and Mark got in their cart. As I sat down in my cart next to Harley he chuckled.

"That Nate sure is peculiar," he commented.

It was interesting to hear Harley call someone else peculiar. Coming from someone who kept his golf ball

18 Holes of Green

cleaner than he kept himself, it was significant. Harley loved sports and the camaraderie of playing golf with friends, but at the same time he was socially inept. Obviously, it had a lot to do with his nervous breakdown while working at nuclear plants.

Harley and I tailed Mark and Paul in their cart up the path and parked on the left side of the green. As I was searching for my sand wedge and putter, Harley raced onto the green to see if he had gotten inside of John.

As I pulled my clubs out of my bag and began to jog back to my ball some 20 yards short of the green, Harley proclaimed John victorious. Paul walked up onto the green to see and Mark slipped behind the oak tree to relieve himself.

"He got me by two inches," Harley said. "I better leave the balls there for John to see."

"I think he'll trust you saying he won," I replied still hustling to my ball.

"I'm a witness," said Paul. "You can mark your ball."

"I guess you have to trust an ex-cop," I shouted as I reached my ball.

Harley was very relieved that he could mark his ball, pick it up and begin to clean it. It would have killed him to wait for John before he cleaned his ball. It was an obsession of his.

Nate had reached his ball and just finished a few practice swings with his pitching wedge. He quickly addressed his ball and made a smooth but strong swing sending the ball soaring high into the air. I lost perspective on its trajectory as it peaked over my head. Then, his ball dropped a few feet from the flag striking John's ball. John's ball went scooting across the green stopping just short of the fringe. Nate's ball rolled back about five feet short of the hole.

"Looks like I'm closest to the pin now," stated Harley.

Timothy McHugh

"What happened?" I could hear Mark ask from behind the oak tree.

"I think John gets to replace his ball," I said as I lined up my pitch shot.

I heard Paul quoting rules to Harley as I addressed my ball. I closed the face of my sand wedge slightly and made a nice easy swing. My ball landed just past Nate's, rolled a few feet toward the hole, and stopped about an inch short of the hole.

"Nice shot," commented Harley as he scooped up my ball with his putter.

"I thought it was in," added Paul.

"Me too," I responded walking toward the green. "I'll take par though." It felt pretty good after getting screwed on my tee shot.

Harley tossed my ball to me, and Nate and John pulled up behind the other two carts. When Nate and John walked onto the green, they seemed a bit confused.

"Where'd my ball go?" asked Nate.

"It hit John's ball and kicked back to the front of the green," I explained.

"Is that my ball by the fringe?" asked John.

"Yeah," replied Harley. "You had closest to the pin by an inch."

"Had closest to the pin," replied Nate. "He doesn't have it anymore."

"Bullshit," responded John. "I get to replace my ball where it was."

"Whatever," answered Nate.

"Rule nineteen dash five," announced Paul.

"Yeah, nineteen dash five," added John.

"They're right," added Mark.

"Nineteen dash five sucks," said Nate.

18 Holes of Green

"You must be a hell of a lawyer," I commented.

John picked his ball up and walked it back toward the hole. Harley began repairing the ball mark that was made when Nate's ball hit the green. It wasn't difficult to see where John's ball was, but eagle eye Paul made sure they placed it precisely in the correct spot. Either way, John had won closest to the pin, and was now twenty-five dollars richer. The danger of having six balls going at the hole was there were bound to be collisions.

Nate putted first nearly saving par, but he ended up tapping in for bogie. Mark went next leaving his first putt a few inches short and easily making par. Paul, Harley and John each made birdie. We expected it from John, but it was a great hole for Paul and Harley. Paul was known for scoring well on par threes. He may have lost his distance over the years, but he still had a hell of a short game. Harley generally plugged along consistently with very few birdies, but even fewer blow up holes.

Having made par myself, the beautiful day had become even more enjoyable for me. We were all soaking in the pleasant sunny afternoon and a break from the heat wave. We played the next two holes pretty quickly. John and Mark both birdied number three, the par four soft dog- leg to the left. The rest of us made pars. Everyone made par on number four, a par four sharp dogleg right.

By the time we got to the fifth tee, we all had a couple more beers in us and were having a good time. We were all playing decently and had a wide-open golf course. Mark and John had a good game going between the two of them and Nate was trying to get a piece of the action every chance he got. He had John giving him a stroke on numbers three and five and Mark giving him a half a stroke on five. Harley, Paul and I were smart enough not to get involved in a hole by hole struggle. Playing total skins was enough for us.

The fifth hole was a par four slight dog leg right. The jungle bordered the left side of the hole and a wooded area guarded the right side. Vader's creek ran along the left edge of the hole for about twenty yards right about where most drives landed. It was in play, but you really had to pull it.

John walked onto the tee with his driver in hand, while Nate scavenged the area in front of the tee markers for forgotten whole tees. The afternoon sun lit up the fifth hole like a portrait. The bright glare kept us from seeing all of the unrepaired divots that dotted the fairway. John lined up his shot and addressed the ball. After a few waggles he made his usual strong and smooth swing. The ball flew on a medium trajectory and faded around the bend a little.

"Nice job cutting the corner," commented Paul.

"Thanks old man," replied John.

Mark walked onto the tee next and was addressing his ball when a buzzing sound came from his cart.

"Oh Mark, I think the wicked witch is calling," said Nate.

He ran from the tee to the cart faster than I had ever seen him move.

"Cell phones on the golf course," commented Harley with disgust. "That's social bullshit. Those damn women just want to yak yak yak."

Mark picked up his phone and walked away from us for some privacy, but we could hear that he was using his cutesy voice. Nate walked onto the tee box and announced that he was going over the trees on the corner.

"Good luck with a broken tee," I said to him.

18 Holes of Green

"I think I'll manage," he replied as he pulled a pencil from his pocket. He stuck the pointed end of the pencil into the ground and attempted to balance his ball on the flat end.

"This ought to be good," commented Paul.

Nate struggled for what felt like several minutes but was probably less than one. Finally, he somehow got the ball to rest on the end of a pencil, which ended up being a pretty long tee. He quickly set up to the ball and swung. His quick aggressive swing came in handy in such situations. The ball went soaring toward the tree line guarding the right corner and kept climbing as it cleared the trees.

"Hoochie coochie," proclaimed Nate.

"Nice shot," I said as I walked onto the tee.

"Yeah, I'm back in the game baby," responded Nate.

The banter went back and forth as everyone both poked fun at and complimented Nate's shot at the same time. I tried to concentrate as I went through my routine. As they all carried on, I stood behind my ball and attempted to block out their voices. Then, I walked around the ball, setting up with my feet together. Moving my right foot back in my stance I took care to ensure my feet and body were both lined up.

As I took the club back, numerous thoughts quickly ran through my head. Keep your right elbow bent and your right hand loose. Keep the club head square. Did I pick up my sand wedge off of the last green? Don't swing too hard.

Then, I commenced my down swing. I pulled down and across my body with my left arm too much and the ball flew low and left. It was headed toward Vader's creek.

"Kick right," shouted John. "Sit baby," commanded Paul.

"Hit something," I begged out loud.

Luckily, I didn't catch the ball cleanly and it died well before the creek. It was one time that I was happy to have missed the ball. It wasn't a long hole, so I wasn't in terrible shape.

"Better short than in the creek," said John.

"I hope not to follow my cart partner," said Harley as he walked onto the tee. He had spent the last five minutes washing and drying his ball. He was like Barney Fife with his bullet. He kept it shiny and clean and always knew where it was. It really was amazing that he had played with the same ball all year. I think he was able to do it because White Lake is the only golf course he ever played. He knew every inch of the golf course and he had unlimited time to find his ball. Only once could I remember Harley having a problem finding his ball. He ended up letting his group play on and proceeded to let the next two foursomes play through him as he searched.

Harley teed up his ball and began making his usual baseball warm up swings. He swung his driver back and forth at chest level as he stepped up to the ball. Then, he bent over and waggled the driver lower to the ground settling in behind the ball. He made his aggressive swing but pulled the ball dead left.

"Oh shit," said John.

"Sit ball!" I shouted, but it was to no avail. Harley's ball was headed straight for Vader's creek. His ball just continued on through the dogleg and toward the point where the creek bends in toward the rough.

"It could have made it over, but it looked like it went in," said John.

"I think it's in the creek," said Paul.

"I thought you weren't going to follow Brian?" asked Nate.

"I'm sure we'll find it," I suggested.

"Oh, we'll find it," answered Harley.

"I don't know," said Nate. "It could be plugged."

18 Holes of Green

"You're such an optimist," said Paul as he stepped onto the tee with his driver in hand. He had an extra-long tee ready to go. There would be no pencil for Paul, although I have seen him hit his ball off of a pile of sand like in the old days.

Mark had finished kissing Ashley's ass on the phone and now returned to a chorus of kissing sounds and other ridicule.

"Never talk to a woman right before you get ready to tee off," stated Paul. "They'll get you thinking about other things and their goes your swing."

"Yeah, you'll be too busy thinking about all the chores she's got for you," added Nate.

"Uh huh," acknowledged Mark.

"Oh, you have a honey-do list," said Paul with a laugh as he addressed his ball. He took is usual short swing, but knocked the ball high and just over the first few trees guarding the corner on the right of the hole. His ball managed to clear them and came down in the center of the fairway. It wasn't a long hit, but he took the shortcut ended up in great position.

"Nice shot," I commented.

Everyone else joined in with praise including Nate who for all his bullshit, never failed to sing the praises of a well hit golf shot.

"Damn, you're a tough act to follow," proclaimed Mark as he grabbed his driver out of his bag.

"Let's go while we're young," complained John.

"I'm ready, I'm ready," replied Mark. He hurriedly made his way on to the tee and looked for a spot to tee his ball up. He settled on the far-left side of the tee giving him as much room to cut the corner as possible. He actually had his feet outside of the tee marker, but his ball was just inside it.

Timothy McHugh

Mark made a couple of waggles and took his normal fluid swing sending the ball on a rather high trajectory. The ball had plenty of height to carry the trees guarding the corner, but he seemed to have pulled it a little. He didn't end up needing all that height as the ball flew straight down the middle of the fairway rather than cutting off the corner.

"It better sit," said John.

"Kick right!" Mark shouted at his ball hoping it would listen.

"Kick right into the creek," said Nate with a laugh.

"I think you'll be ok," suggested Paul.

Indeed, Mark's ball did seem to settle pretty quickly. It must have been the high trajectory, because the ground was hard as a rock from the heat wave. The ball rolled through the fairway, but stopped just barely into the left rough. He was well past my ball and where Harley's went into the creek, so he wasn't in too bad of shape.

"Let's saddle up," proclaimed Nate loudly as we all walked to our carts.

The sound of beers popping open one after another filled the air.

"Music to my ears," commented John.

He and Nate headed down the right sided of the fairway as the rest of us went down the left side. Mark and Paul split off to head to Paul's ball in the middle of the fairway as Harley and I continued on toward Vader's creek. We stopped at my ball which was well short of the creek and got out. I began determining what club to hit and Harley jogged up to the creek. He was on a mission to find his ball. It was definitely going to get ugly if we couldn't find it. I settled on a six iron and glanced back at Paul who was still lining up his shot.

18 Holes of Green

Harley walked down to the edge of the creek with his seven-iron in hand. He stepped onto some rocks out in the creek and began searching for his beloved ball. He prodded at the dark spots in the water feeling for his ball. He stared holes through the water hoping to see a white sphere somewhere.

I walked past my ball now that I knew where it was in an effort to aide Harley's search. I knew how important his ball was to him and it's proper etiquette to assist your fellow golfers anyway. I walked along the grass ridge looking down into the creek for anything white. I heard Paul hit his second shot and turned around to see it. His ball went sailing toward the green and stuck in the front right.

"Nice shot!" I yelled across the fairway.

Harley and I walked together further down the creek and farther from the fairway. He hopped from stone to stone in the middle of the creek and I paced along the ridge on the bank of the creek bed. It was one of those situations where you start to think that your search is hopeless. There were so many places for his ball to hide or even plug in the creek bed. Our search continued as Mark hit his second shot, but I didn't bother looking over at it.

It was getting to the point that we really had to consider giving up. If it were anyone other than Harley, I would have told them to take a drop several minutes earlier, but these were uncharted waters. Harley's ball had never been lost in such a dangerous location before. Searching in a field of tall grass is one thing. The ball has to be there somewhere, but a creek is a whole other matter. I was starting to think we were going to have to leave him behind when we both stopped at the same time as a white spot caught our eyes about 20 yards further down the creek.

"That could be a ball," I suggested.

"Hot damn," said Harley in excitement. "I hope that's it," I replied.

Harley walked toward the object and I followed. The closer we moved, the more obvious it appeared to be a golf ball. It was spherical and definitely shiny enough to be Harley's ball.

"Did you find it?" shouted Mark from across the fairway.

"I think so," I replied assuming that it was Harley's ball.

Harley had to straddle the water on two small stones in order to get close to the spot where the ball had come to rest. He reached forward with his seven-iron and attempted to scoop the ball toward himself, but he wasn't quite close enough.

I had gotten to within ten yards and across from the ball as Harley stepped precariously forward onto another less stable stone. The stone wobbled a little as Harley steadied himself.

"Don't fall in," I said.

He stretched his seven-iron out toward the ball and almost had it when a splash of water shot into the air and the golf ball disappeared into a fuzzy dark green emptiness.

Harley stood motionless for a moment. As the splash subsided, the large head of an adult alligator stuck out of the water. Its nostrils pointed directly at Harley and then it snapped its head to the side as it swallowed Harley's beloved Titleist.

"Holy shit, it's Vader," I whispered loudly to Harley trying to be heard, but not to startle the alligator.

Harley's motionless state of shock quickly turned to panic and he jumped back several steps. I turned and started running toward our cart which was back by my ball.

18 Holes of Green

Paul and Mark were headed toward me in their cart to help search for Harley's ball.

"Run away! Run away!" I shouted instinctively quoting Monty Python as I sprinted. I reached our cart and jumped in.

"What's going on? Where's Harley going?" asked Mark as they pulled up.

"What do you mean?" I asked as I turned to look back.

I had thought Harley was right behind me the entire time, but apparently, he was going after his beloved golf ball. I could see him on the other side of the creek running toward the jungle.

"He's chasing the gator," I replied plainly.

"He's chasing an alligator?" asked Mark.

"Apparently," I replied out of breath and a bit shaken.

"He's chasing Vader?" asked Paul. "What the hell for?"

"The bastard ate his ball," I answered as I stepped on the accelerator of the golf cart and spun around.

"He's nuts," said Mark.

"Yeah, something like that," I replied as I stomped on the accelerator again and headed after Harley.

"I'll call Hank in the clubhouse and tell him to call someone," I heard Mark say as I drove off. I could also hear Paul shouting across the fairway to Nate and John. As I approached the creek, I had to turn south and head to the maintenance bridge. It took me about 50 yards out of the way, but I wasn't getting out of the cart to cross the creek on foot. The cart probably didn't provide much protection, but I did feel safer in it than standing on the ground. I sped across the bridge and then turned back north and toward where I last saw Harley disappear into the jungle.

Timothy McHugh

I couldn't see or hear Harley and there really wasn't a trail or path to follow. I drove in the general direction that I last saw him running knocking down tall grass as the cart moved forward. After driving through the tall grass for about 30 yards, I came to the start of the tall brush. I stopped the cart and stood up on the back of it for a better view.

"Harley!" I shouted.

There was no reply. Just the sound of golf carts behind me. The jungle as we called it was a vast expanse of tall grass, honeysuckles and locust trees densely inter-woven and all living off the marsh. It was so thick that you couldn't see more than 20 or 30 yards into it. I shouted for Harley a few more times, but there was still no response. I had visions of him walking out of the jungle with his golf ball in one hand and alligator skin in the other just like Michael Douglas in Romancing the Stone. However, that was a movie, a crocodile and an emerald worth much more than Harley's golf ball.

It was then that Paul and Mark pulled up in their cart. I could hear John and Nate not far behind them.

"Where is he?" asked Paul.

"He's out there somewhere," I replied. "Should we help him?" I asked.

"Help him do what?" asked Mark. "Chase a fucking alligator through the brush to find a golf ball. I don't think so."

"Shouldn't we see if he's ok?" I replied.

Nate and John arrived in a skidding stop in front of Mark and Paul. We told them what we knew. John was genuinely concerned for Harley, but Nate began carrying on about it and laughing out loud.

"Old Vader exists after all," said Nate. "Well, I'll be damned. Did you all see him?"

18 Holes of Green

"I did," I answered. "He was big and a lot faster than I would have thought. It scared the shit out of me. That golf ball was gone in a flash and we never saw him lying in the creek."

"He got Harley's ball eh," continued Nate laughing while he spoke. "Must have thought the thing was an egg."

"He's chasing after it," I said.

"What the hell does he think he's going to do when he catches it?" asked Paul.

Nate's face was turning red as he tried to keep talking, but he was laughing too hard. His eyes were watering up as he tried to spit out a joke.

"He doesn't need to chase the thing," said Nate still barely controlling his laughter. "He just needs to start checking all the gator shit starting tomorrow. It will pass right through him."

We all laughed at that one. Mark's cell phone rang. Hank called to let us know that the cops were on their way and animal control should be coming as well. John wanted to go in the jungle and look for Harley, but we were able to talk him out of it. He had his driver in one hand and towel in the other.

"That towel will come in handy when he rips your leg off," said Paul. "You can make a tourniquet."

Nate had me laughing about the situation now.

"What the hell were you going to do with the towel anyway?" I asked.

"Play matador?" asked Mark.

"I could throw it over his head and blind him," answered John.

"You'd be better off throwing a full can of beer at him," suggested Paul.

"Now that would be a sin," said Nate as he opened the cooler in his cart.

We all followed his lead and began popping open fresh beers while we waited.

"A full swing with my driver might work if I could get the ball to hit him," suggested John as he sipped on his beer.

"No, that would just piss him off," I replied. "This guy was large."

It was then that we began to hear a rustling in the brush. We all stopped talking and looked at each other. I slowly climbed back on top of the back of my cart and Mark did the same on his. Paul slid onto the seat of his cart and raised his legs up resting his feet on the console. John and Nate got back into their cart and they both had worried looks on their faces. Nate had gone from pure lunacy to pure fear.

The rustling was definitely getting closer and louder. As we heard twigs snap and leaves rustle, there were two thoughts running through my head. It was either Harley or Vader the gator.

Suddenly there was a loud crack followed by several quick footsteps just behind the tall weed trees. I looked over at Mark and he looked back with a glare of concern. I was prepared to hop on top of the roof of my golf cart at any moment.

"Shit! Damn tree," said Harley has he stepped into view through the brush.

We all relaxed for a moment and then played off our fear as if it never happened.

"What the hell happened out there?" asked John. "That bastard can move," said Harley breathing heavily. "I lost sight of him after only about 20 yards. After that, I was trying to follow the sounds of his movements, but he must have crawled down into a hole or into a den somewhere."

18 Holes of Green

"You could have been killed out there," said John.

"He ate my golf ball," replied Harley as if that obviously justified risking his life.

"You know that ball will come out of him eventually," said Nate who was now making the same point in a more constructive way than earlier.

"Yeah, but how do you find gator shit?" asked Harley.

"Just follow your nose. It always knows," I couldn't help but suggest.

"Maybe there's a dog that's trained to follow the scent," added Paul.

As our conversation about alligator excrement continued, the sounds of sirens were heard coming closer.

"You guys called the cops?" asked Harley.

"Hey, your best golf ball was stolen," replied Mark.

Harley smiled at the fact that someone was finally recognizing his loss, even if it was in jest. The sirens stopped at the clubhouse, but a few moments later we could see flashing lights on two police cruisers coming down the left rough of hole number one. The two cruisers were following a ranger cart which was leading them out to us. As the caravan passed the first green, it proceeded up the left rough of number five. As it came closer, we could see that it was old Leo driving the ranger cart.

"Man, now you know it's a big deal," said Nate. "Leo woke up."

"It must have been the sirens," replied John.

Leo looked as proud as ever sitting up straight with a big smile on his face. He was enjoying the feeling of being useful and important for the first time in a long while. He held his walkie-talkie in one hand while he steered the cart with the other. His radio hadn't worked in years, but that didn't matter. He was having a moment of glory. The batteries in his radio hadn't been replaced in 3 years. He never heard the thing, so it would have been a waste to replace the batteries.

"I hope he doesn't try to lead them through the creek," said John.

"I hope that he sees the creek," replied Mark.

Thankfully Leo stopped just before the creek. The two police cars stopped as well. To our delight, Jack Kelly and Officer Ryan stepped out of the first car. The other two officers looked familiar. They must have played golf once in a while.

"So those stories about Vader the gator were true after all," said Jack from the other side of the creek.

"Apparently so," replied John.

The other two officers followed Jack and Officer Ryan as they walked toward the creek. There were enough big rocks in the area for them to easily make their way across. Leo, however wasn't about to get out of his cart. He slowly turned and started heading back along the creek looking for a place to cross.

The four police officers traversed the creek by stepping from stone to stone. One by one they hopped from the last stone and onto the grassy plateau between the creek and the jungle.

"You guys going to hunt it down?" I asked.

"Hell no," said Jack. "Only an idiot goes running into the brush and marsh chasing an alligator."

We all smiled at each other and Harley's face began to turn red. However, the moment quickly passed as Jack introduced us all to the other two officers as Officers Blake and Walters. They acknowledged that they played at White Lake occasionally and thanked us for the free golf we always gave them.

18 Holes of Green

"What do you know about their biological functions?" asked Harley.

"I think they're both pretty regular," replied Jack with a funny look on his face.

"No, I meant the Alligator," said Harley.

The rest of us couldn't help but break out into laughter. Nate practically fell to the ground as he bent over clutching his stomach. I spit beer out I was laughing so hard.

"Why do you ask?" inquired Officer Ryan.

"The bastard swallowed my golf ball and I'm hoping to get it back," answered Harley.

"It's just a golf ball," said Officer Blake.

We all cringed when he said that hoping it didn't spark an outburst from Harley, but Harley just turned and stared into the jungle like a concerned parent.

"He's very attached to that ball," replied Mark.

"You can ask the Animal Control Officers when they arrive," suggested Jack.

"Yeah, they can probably tell you all about gator crap," added Nate.

"Did you guys hear that Cunningham was indicted?" asked Jack.

"Yeah, great news," replied John.

"The rumor is that his wife caught a flight to Mexico," replied Officer Ryan.

"That sounds like her," I replied.

"Not the type to stand by her man in times of trouble," added Nate.

It was then that old Leo finally made his way to us. It had taken him a while to find a way across the creek. However, as soon as he arrived, John asked him to go back to the clubhouse and guide Animal Control out to us. He dutifully turned around and headed back toward the clubhouse with a smile on his face.

"Old Leo hasn't had this much to do in years," I proclaimed.

"Yeah, and he's loving every minute of it," said Mark.

We hung out talking about the Cunninghams long enough for an Animal Control squad to show up. There were 2 guys with a caged truck and a supervisor in a Jeep. They reminded me a little of Larry, Darrel and Darrel from the Newhart show. The questions we were asking them didn't help things either.

"How often do they shit?" asked Harley.

"Does the male get on top of the female?" asked Nate.

The Darrels were too busy adjusting their extension poles with wire loops on the ends to even think about responding. Larry, the supervisor deferred answering our questions and got right to some questions for us.

"Where did you see it last?" he asked. "How big was it?"

"It was sitting down in the creek and it was just a standard 1.68 inches in diameter," answered Harley. He immediately began giving a very detailed description of his poor golf ball. "It's a Titleist Pro V1, number 3 with a blue Capital "H" written on it with a Sharpie."

"I was asking about the alligator," replied Larry the animal control guy.

The Animal Control guys didn't seem as interested in the golf ball description as Harley thought that they should.

"Do they generally eat things like golf balls?" I asked.

"Alligators are nocturnal and feed primarily at night," responded Larry. "He was likely sleeping and disturbed by your movement. Younger alligators eat bugs, rodents, small fish, tadpoles and frogs. Adult gators eat fish, birds, turtles, reptiles, and sometimes small dogs."

"I guess a golf ball wouldn't stand a chance against its big teeth?" asked Nate.

"They swallow their prey whole. Their teeth are used for catching their food, not chewing."

"Even if you have to kill him, I'll get my ball back, right?" asked Harley. "I mean, you'll cut him open for me, won't you?"

"We're not going to kill him sir," replied the Supervisor. "Well then, you have to save me all of his crap," replied Harley.

Nate turned toward the rest of us with disgust. "This alligator crap discussion is all very interesting, but gentleman, we're burning daylight," he stated.

"The man has a point," agreed John.

"It could take them hours to find that gator," I added.

"Maybe days," said Mark.

Paul was enthralled by the excitement and didn't seem to want to continue playing. The rest of us weren't about to waste any more time when there was golf to be played. It was shaping up to be one crazy summer at White Lake. We were finally rid of Hugh Cunningham and his BS.

I was just glad to be playing golf with no one in front of us. It didn't matter how the opportunity presented itself, but a chance to play golf couldn't be wasted. After all, that's why we were all there. An alligator may eat your golf ball today, but you never know what might happen on the golf course tomorrow.

"You try too hard and you think too much."

-Shivas Irons

"Gunga galunga"

-Carl Spackler

About the Author

Timothy McHugh studied English and Jornalism at the University of Cincinnati. He worked at Cincinnati Municipal Golf Courses throughout High School and College. He resides in Northern Kentucky and works in Finance.

For more great books vist:

www.brunswickpublishing.com

www.ingramcontent.com/pod-product-compliance
Lightning Source LLC
Chambersburg PA
CBHW020847090426
42736CB00008B/267